D0821335

# Rwanda's Genocide

# RWANDA'S GENOCIDE

## THE POLITICS OF GLOBAL JUSTICE

*Kingsley Chiedu Moghalu*

The views expressed in this book are those of the author alone. They do not necessarily represent the official positions of the United Nations, the International Criminal Tribunal for Rwanda, or any other organ or specialized agency of the United Nations.

First published in 2005 by
PALGRAVE MACMILLAN™
175 Fifth Avenue, New York, N.Y. 10010 and
Houndmills, Basingstoke, Hampshire, England RG21 6XS
Companies and representatives throughout the world.

PALGRAVE MACMILLAN is the global academic imprint of the Palgrave Macmillan division of St. Martin's Press, LLC and of Palgrave Macmillan Ltd. Macmillan® is a registered trademark in the United States, United Kingdom and other countries. Palgrave is a registered trademark in the European Union and other countries.

ISBN 1–4039–7081–5

Library of Congress Cataloging-in-Publication Data is available from the Library of Congress.

A catalogue record for this book is available from the British Library.

Design by Newgen Imaging Systems (P) Ltd., Chennai, India.

First edition: November 2005

10  9  8  7  6  5  4  3

Printed in the United States of America.

*For Maryanne, and our children Tobenna,*
*Sọchi, Yagazie, and Chidera*

# Contents

# LIST OF FIGURES

# ACKNOWLEDGMENTS

Authors are debtors to the people who help them in various ways in the process of creative work. I am no exception, and owe much to a number of people. I would like to thank a number of key actors in the life and work of the International Criminal Tribunal for Rwanda over the past several years, who granted me research interviews for this book. I am grateful to Pierre-Richard Prosper, Carla Del Ponte, Agwu Ukiwe Okali, Bernard Muna, Martin Ngoga, and Catherine Cisse for taking the time to talk with me at length in various capitals, on the telephone, and by email correspondence.

To Angeline Djampou, the chief librarian of the International Criminal Tribunal for Rwanda, who provided me with excellent research assistance, much of it long distance and online, I am grateful. Viola Rugege-Kamara assisted me in compiling, several years ago with ease and expertise, many of the official public documents and other materials I was to draw upon later for this book. Beatrix Heward-Mills played the crucial part of typing and preparing the manuscript. Bocar Sy, senior public affairs officer at the International Criminal Tribunal for Rwanda, kindly provided most of the photographs. My thanks to them.

By far my greatest debt is to my wife Maryanne and our children. I am grateful for their understanding and support as I worked at odd hours to write this book. Without their love and support it would not be in your hands.

# INTRODUCTION: POLITICAL JUSTICE

In 2004, exactly 10 years after the Rwanda genocide, the conflict in the Sudanese province of Darfur focused minds yet again on the question of genocide even as the ghosts of Rwanda continue to haunt world politics and the international society. An estimated 200,000 black Africans have been killed in Darfur by Arab militias known as *janjaweed*, using civil war as a pretext. In Rwanda, 800,000 victims, mostly Tutsis and some politically moderate Hutus, were massacred in what was unquestionably genocide—although not without some obfuscation around the "G-word" and attempts to clothe the slaughter as collateral damage in a civil war.

The United Nations (UN) Security Council established an international war crimes tribunal,[1] the International Criminal Tribunal for Rwanda (ICTR, or "Arusha tribunal") at Arusha, Tanzania, to prosecute persons responsible for the genocide and other serious violations of international humanitarian law. This book is about the political and strategic factors that surround and influence the quest for international justice for Rwanda—the accomplishments, hopes, and frustrations of that process in a world of politics and contending moralities. That story has three important dimensions. First, the ICTR has made an enormous impact on the development of international humanitarian law. It has the distinction of being the first international court in history to judge and punish the crime of genocide. This normative impact is part of the tribunal's political dimensions.

The creation of norms by war crimes tribunals is something that ultimately has—or is expected to have—a political impact on how nations and individuals behave. This impact, qualified though it is, exists because the norms that are created by such institutions often progressively displace those that existed in previous eras. For example, genocide has surely always been considered evil, and, to the amazement of commentators like David Scheffer, "has become a growth industry."[2] But "international judicial intervention"[3] to punish it—still a rarity, lest we forget—is largely a product of the international society's evolution in the twentieth century. The concept entered the lexicon of world politics in the 1990s when the UN Security Council created the International Criminal Tribunal for the Former Yugoslavia (ICTY, or "the Hague Tribunal") in 1993 in response to ethnic cleansing in the Balkans and established the Arusha tribunal in late 1994.

This process has been called "norm entrepreneurship,"[4] and like much of international law it is a political phenomenon. The task of international war crimes tribunals is "political justice"[5]—the use of law and legalism to construct new political orders. This is what the Security Council was doing when it stated, in its resolution creating the ICTR, the hope that the tribunal would deter future genocides and contribute to reconciliation and the maintenance of peace. Norm creation too has another political dimension, one in which it is seen from a realist interpretation of world politics as "façade legitimation,"[6] or "the kinder, gentler face of naked power considerations in pursuit of state interests."[7]

The second important dimension of the story is the actual political and societal impact the Arusha tribunal has had, or is likely to have in the longer term, in Rwanda, in Africa's Great Lakes Region, and in the continent as a whole. This is a basic point since, as noted a moment ago, the tribunal was created not just to achieve technical judicial outcomes, fundamental as punishing genocide undoubtedly is, but also to contribute to a hoped-for emergence of a new political order. In this light, it is necessary to look at whether the means chosen (retributive justice by an international tribunal located in a foreign country) match the desired ends of wider political and social outcomes. Thus the question of how relevant the international tribunal is to the Rwandan society and to African politics is an important one. Of course, this is a question that is validly raised about international criminal justice in other regions of the world as well.

The third dimension, the most important from this book's standpoint, is the latent tension between the Arusha tribunal and the Rwandan government, and the ebb and flow of relations between the two entities—the tribunal seeking to preserve its independence as a court of law and justice (even as it depends on Rwanda's cooperation and the political and financial muscle of the great powers such as the United States and Britain), and Rwanda pursuing its own strategic interests, the tribunal being one path toward achieving those interests.

Two core components of those strategic interests are (1) the use of the judicial process of the international tribunal to put the country's former genocidal leaders permanently out of commission and the destruction of the ideology of genocide, and, at the same time, (2) the prevention of its own forces from getting prosecuted for war crimes by the Arusha tribunal.

The tribunal's defendants have so far been the Hutu extremists accused of perpetrating genocide. It is no coincidence that they also happen to be the side that was defeated in the civil war. No Tutsis, members of the victorious Rwanda Patriotic Army (RPA), the erstwhile military wing of the Rwandan Patriotic Front (RPF) that now governs Rwanda, have been publicly indicted by the tribunal, much less arrested and put on trial. Is this victor's justice? And if it is, who is to blame—the Arusha tribunal, or the externally imposed political framework within which it must function? In this sense, the phrase "the independence of the tribunal" is one that needs proper contextualization. I will come to this point in a moment.

The underlying point of this book, then, is that the ICTR has notched up momentous normative achievements but is hemmed in by international politics that exists at the level of grand strategy, and the facts that its possibilities are limited by these factors, and that this situation is not unique to the tribunal. It has much to do with the fundamental nature of these institutions, a topic I explore at a wider conceptual level in *Justice and High Politics*.[8] As such, it is often not just the defendants who are on trial at the tribunals set up to advance political justice, but the very concept of justice itself as understood by the average person—that the scales will weigh the crimes and the evidence, and the chips fall where they may.

International war crimes tribunals are created by politics. They are therefore surrounded and affected by that hardy constant of international life. We see this in the problem-prone trial of Slobodan Milosevic, former president of the Federal Republic of Yugoslavia, at the ICTY at The Hague. It is evident in the controversial circumstances of the U.S.-led invasion of Iraq and the capture and imminent trial of Saddam Hussein, and in the politics of the permanent International Criminal Court. The wheels of justice nonetheless continue to turn. The Arusha tribunal is no different. Like the Hague tribunal for war crimes in the Former Yugoslavia, it was created by a political body, the Security Council, and, in UN parlance, is a "subsidiary organ" of the Council. Like other war crimes tribunals, its work proceeds apace in the midst of swirling political currents in the domestic society for which it has been established, and also in the

wider international society. Consider the challenge that Serb national-
ism has posed to justice in the Balkans, and the widespread belief
amongst Serbs that they are the victims of the Hague tribunal, rather
than understanding its work as an opportunity to see without blinkers,
and repudiate, the crimes that were committed in their name.

In a recent book about the Hague tribunal, Rachel Kerr has
captured its nature with a characterization that is just as relevant to the
Arusha tribunal:

> The question of politicization is not a straightforward one. The
> decision to establish the [Hague] tribunal was political, and it was
> established for a political purpose, but its internal mandate was to
> deliver justice. Thus, while politics permeated every aspect of the
> tribunal's operations, including its establishment, proceedings had to
> be conducted in a political vacuum. On a conceptual level, while this
> form of justice is inherently political, the judicial process is not neces-
> sarily "politicized." On a practical level, the interaction of politics and
> law was central to the tribunal's ability to perform its judicial function,
> it did so independently of politics, which was crucial for its success as a
> tool for the restoration and maintenance of peace and security.[9]

I had earlier made a reference to this symbiotic relationship between
politics, law, and diplomacy in administering international justice for
war crimes, adopting the phrase "political justice" to reflect its
essence. Kerr has attempted a fine but perhaps ultimately academic
distinction between this situation and what she calls "politicization":
" 'Politicization' is the manipulation of the judicial process by politics,
not the manipulation of politics to serve the judicial process, or the
apolitical administration of justice to serve a political goal . . . Whilst
they are intertwined, law and politics are not merged: The boundary
exists at the doorway of the courtroom."[10]

All of this is largely true. The best example is probably that of the
indictment of Slobodan Milosevic after Western powers had negotiated
a peace agreement with him in Dayton. But the distinction between
law and politics is not quite as clear cut as the finality with which the
"boundary" has been asserted. In adopting law for expressly political
ends, a fusion takes place not necessarily in the courtroom proceedings of war crimes tribunals, which are certainly generally fair, but in
the very definition of the targets of that judicial process (and those
*excluded* from it) in a manner that becomes inherently political. Some
observers of the Hague tribunal's controversial attempt to investigate
accusations of war crimes allegedly committed by NATO forces
during the alliance's bombing campaign in Kosovo in 1999 would

have a decidedly different view from Kerr's distinction. The tribunal's chief prosecutor ultimately decided that adequate grounds did not exist to pursue an investigation,[11] but even the very fact of an *attempt* to investigate elicited a furious response from NATO capitals, and a backpedaling in the rhetoric of chief prosecutor Carla Del Ponte. The political reality is that international law, especially as it concerns the use of force including international humanitarian law, is partly a function of power relations in the international system. This is why the enforcement of this aspect of international law is selective and arbitrary.

Put simply, indicting NATO personnel for alleged war crimes in an area within the Hague tribunal's jurisdiction would have amounted to institutional suicide by the tribunal. Is it surprising, then, that some commentators have made an elegant distinction between the Hague tribunal's (legal) "jurisdiction," which covers the territory of the former Yugoslavia and violations of international humanitarian law committed therein, and its (political) "mandate," which, from this perspective, was focused on the states of that region, not on the great powers that launched a humanitarian military intervention to restore international order.[12]

Similar skepticism was generated in the case of Rwanda when the Arusha tribunal's appeals court reversed itself in a controversial case in which it had ordered the release of an alleged genocide mastermind on technical grounds (see chapter 5). In a sharp allegation of what would be politicization, British journalist Tim Sebastian charged that "[judicial] decisions are taken in order to keep Rwanda sweet."[13] Whether these cases represent "political" or "politicized" justice is not so much the point here. The point, from this book's perspective, is that these cases demonstrate the dilemmas of political justice. The final judgment of how this dilemma is resolved in each particular case is in the eye of the beholder. When it comes to war crimes justice, perception and reality are frequently intertwined. Navanethem Pillay, then president of the ICTR, noted in a 2002 media interview that: "Yes, justice can be selective, it can be political. But if you ask me whether I think justice is done here, I can say yes."[14]

All of these explain why war crimes justice—and war crimes tribunals—simply cannot be understood from a strictly legal or judicial standpoint, which is divorced from an understanding of international relations and world politics. "International judicial intervention," David Scheffer has noted, "can never be completely isolated from politics."[15] And Pierre-Richard Prosper, the former trial lawyer who prosecuted the Arusha tribunal's historic first genocide trial, the

*Akayesu* case, and went on to succeed Scheffer as U.S. ambassador at large for war crimes issues, confirms without equivocation that "war crimes justice is political."[16] Prosper has been a gladiator in the courtrooms of justice, which he then believed to be "pure," and subsequently in the conference rooms of diplomacy from where he directs the high politics of war crimes justice for one of the great powers. The important role that American war crimes diplomacy has played in molding the political framework of the Arusha tribunal and supporting its work, as with other ad hoc international war crimes courts, will become apparent in chapters 6 and 7.

It is in this wider context, which points up the nature of war crimes tribunals, their strengths and limits, that I undertake this review of the politics of accountability for the genocide, crimes against humanity, and war crimes in Rwanda by the Arusha tribunal. This book sets out to demonstrate how these overarching political factors have impacted on the search for justice for one of the most horrific crimes of the twentieth century. In Rwanda's case, one fact more than others is politically pertinent as a point of departure: there was no external intervention to stop the genocidal slaughter as it unfolded in 1994, although a UN peacekeeping force was stationed in the country to monitor and mediate the civil war. The RPF, which today forms the government, stopped the killings with its military victory in 1994. In Yugoslavia and Sierra Leone, there were external military interventions—in the former by NATO, albeit late and initially reluctant, and in the latter by Nigerian and regional forces of the Economic Community of West African States (ECOWAS). The problems that devolved to the Arusha tribunal as a result of it being the *sole* form of international intervention in Rwanda are significant. No one can argue that perpetrators of genocide should not be punished, but the lopsided nature of the tribunal's judicial process, which has so far been unable to enforce accountability for war crimes committed by the RPF, raises the troubling specter of the tribunal as an agency for victor's justice.

There is no book I know of that is dedicated to the political context of the ICTR, either as a work of scholarship or serious nonfiction. More narrowly focused legal tomes have been written of the tribunal's work, and there is a treasure trove of articles about it in scholarly journals. This book has been written to fill the gap. It is an analytical and interpretative narrative work. It examines important moments in the process of international justice for Rwanda, beginning with the genocide, and in that context attempts to throw some light on the three dimensions of the story that I noted at the beginning of this introduction—the tribunal's normative value, its contextual relevance, and the political/strategic factors inherent in its relationship with Rwanda and the great powers.

Chapter 1 examines the historical prelude to the 1994 genocide, showing how the expansion of the European-dominated international system through colonialism exacerbated ethnic intolerance in Rwanda. It explains the failure of the "international community" to intervene in Rwanda as merely reflective of an international *society* dominated by the divergent self-interests of its component states, and how this moral and political failure has conditioned the framework in which the quest for international justice is taking place—with important consequences for the Arusha tribunal.

Chapter 2 charts the diplomatic and political process that culminated in the creation of an international tribunal to prosecute the genocide and other violations of international humanitarian law. It then analyzes the framework of the tribunal—the attributes that have given it its peculiar character, such as the noninclusion of the death penalty in its statute, the superiority of its fiat over that of national jurisdictions, and its location outside Rwanda, and the political and strategic maneuvering that lay behind these decisions.

Chapter 3 describes the establishment of the tribunal as an institution, its principals, and how their legal and policy actions and perspectives have linked into the three-dimensional paradigm from which I review the tribunal. In chapter 4, I examine, in nontechnical language, some of the international tribunal's historic judgments and trials, as well as the political dimensions of such related processes as the defense of alleged *genocidaires* and the question of where those convicted by the tribunal go to jail.

The political tensions referred to in the third prong of the analytical paradigm burst into play in chapter 5, in what was nothing short of a political and judicial baptism of fire—the circumstances in which a high-ranking defendant was ordered to be released on technical grounds of human rights violations, and the decision later reversed. In chapter 6, the tension over fundamental strategic questions comes to a head as international war crimes chief prosecutor Carla Del Ponte is removed from the Arusha tribunal. Chapter 7 examines the politics, law, and diplomacy involved in the hot pursuit of accused war criminals across several countries. Chapter 8 analyzes the image of the Arusha tribunal, globally and in Rwanda, followed by the conclusion, which includes a discussion of the political impact of the tribunal and an attempt at a forward look at how history might judge the international court.

This book incorporates more nuanced views of international war crimes justice than I had some years ago. Its purpose, as I have noted earlier, is to contribute to a greater understanding of the work of one of only two ad hoc international war crimes tribunals created by the UN Security Council in the 1990s, which was a major building block in the establishment of a permanent International Criminal Court.

Finally, the analysis and the views expressed in the book are mine alone in my personal capacity. They should not be interpreted as necessarily representing the official positions of the UN or the ICTR.

# CHAPTER 1

# THE "FINAL SOLUTION" TO THE "TUTSI PROBLEM"

Turning and turning in the widening gyre
The falcon cannot hear the falconer;
Things fall apart; the centre cannot hold;
Mere anarchy is loosed upon the world.
—Y.B. Yeats, *The Second Coming*

The Rwandan genocide of 1994 was the indirect result of the expansion of the European-dominated international system of the late nineteenth century. That expansion occurred mostly through colonization. Rwanda is made up of three ethnic groups—the Twas (historically pigmy hunters believed to have been the area's first inhabitants), the Hutus of Bantu origin (believed to have come from Cameroon), and the Tutsis (who reportedly came from Ethiopia in the thirteenth and fourteenth centuries). The Hutus, who constitute 85 percent of Rwanda's population, were mainly farmers, while the Tutsis, who comprised 14 percent prior to the genocide, were mainly pastoral keepers of cattle. "This was the original inequality: cattle are a more valuable asset than produce," writes Philip Gourevitch.[1]

## THE ROOTS OF HATE

There are nonetheless contending historical accounts of the nature of the relations between Hutus and Tutsis—conflicted or harmonious, hierarchical or egalitarian.[2] What is clear is that the Tutsis eventually established a kingdom around the fifteenth century in the east of today's Rwanda, and had expanded westward and southward by the sixteenth century. This expansion engendered a corresponding loss of autonomy for the mainly agricultural Hutu.[3] The Tutsi and Hutu groups lived in a mutual arrangement of symbiotic and organic integration for the next three centuries. Certain cultural practices of Hutu origin and Hutu participation in the advisory councils to the Tutsi monarchy were, significantly, part of this relationship. The dividing line between the two groups was not as rigid as is commonly presumed by non-Rwandans—they both spoke (and still speak) a common language, Kinyarwanda; intermarriage was not infrequent, and, with the performance of certain sociocultural rites, a successful Hutu could "become" a Tutsi.[4]

But tensions between the two groups emerged even in the pre-colonial period in the nineteenth century. The appropriation of private pasture land by the Tutsi monarchy and the institution of payment of dues—in commodities or service—by the Hutus and socially lower ranked Tutsis in exchange for access to land was a major contributor to this changed texture of relations. This institution was known as *ibikingi*.[5]

Europe's "scramble for Africa" in the late nineteenth century made Rwanda a German protectorate as a result of the Anglo-German treaty of 1880 by which much of East Africa became German colonies. Germany was to lose these territories after World War I, and Rwanda was transferred to a Belgian mandate under the League of Nations in 1919. Belgium asserted its political authority in Rwanda far more actively than Germany had. To sustain and strengthen its hold over the country, the Belgian colonizers used a classic divide-and-conquer method, first among the Tutsis to select those who would most willingly advance Belgium's agenda, and then between Tutsis and Hutus. A struggle ensued within rival camps in the Tutsi ruling class for the colonial administration's patronage. A group opposed to the Rwandan king *Mwami* Musinga (whose independent streak had earned him Belgium's displeasure) emerged victorious. The Belgians dethroned Musinga and banished him to neighboring Burundi in 1925. It is noteworthy that in the neighboring Belgian Congo (today's Democratic Republic of Congo), the Belgian king Leopold had presided over grotesque massacres of Congolese natives in order to enforce rubber production quotas that supplied his personal wealth. King Leopold is estimated by historians to have ordered the killings of some 10 million victims between 1880 and 1920.[6]

Over the next several decades in Rwanda, Belgium supported the Tutsi ruling class in expanding the colonial power's delegated hegemony to other parts of the country. It introduced several radical reforms in Rwandan society, which widened ethnic divisions. The education of children of Tutsi notables in European-style schools was encouraged. This in turn gave the Tutsis great advantages over the Hutus in recruitments for administrative positions in the colonial administration as well as in business. During 1933–1934, Belgium introduced identity cards that divided Rwandans along ethnic lines between Tutsi and Hutu.

These policies were based on Belgian perceptions of Tutsi racial superiority over the Hutu. The Tutsis were taller, lankier, and thin-lipped and had aquiline noses; so Belgian colonialists judged them closer to Europeans in their physical traits than the generally shorter and thick-lipped Hutus. The pseudoscience fostered by the Belgian colonialists coincided with Hitler's theory of the Aryan "master race" that led inexorably to the Jewish Holocaust by the Nazis in the 1930s and World War II. In an interesting demonstration of the parallel that exists between the roots of the Rwandan genocide and the Holocaust, Amy Chua has argued that genocides that target economically domi-nant minorities such as Rwanda's Tutsis and Europe's Jews are the backlash of economic globalization and liberal democracies.[7]

Regarding Rwanda, Philip Gourevitch describes how Belgian colonialists fostered myths of racial superiority through dubious "science":

> In addition to military and administrative chiefs, and a veritable army of churchmen, the Belgians dispatched scientists to Rwanda. The scientists brought scales and measuring tapes and calipers and they went about weighing Rwandans, measuring Rwandans cranial capacities, and conducting comparative analysis of the relative protuberances of Rwandan noses. Sure enough, the scientists found what they believed all along. Tutsis had "nobler," more "naturally" aristocratic dimensions than the "coarse" and "bestial" Hutus. On the "nasal index," for instance, the median Tutsi nose was found to be about two and a half millimetres longer and nearly five millimetres narrower than the median Hutu nose.[8]

Tutsis warmed to these pseudoscientific myths in order to perpetuate their political, economic, and social dominance in Rwanda. As Bill Berkeley puts it, "elitism evolved into racism, and a myth of historic Tutsi domination—and cunning—came to be broadly accepted by Hutus and Tutsis alike."[9] This situation fostered progressively increasing resentment on the part of the Hutu population.

Three factors created the immediate conditions for the first major wave of violence in colonial Rwanda. The first factor was the increasing agitation by Tutsis for independence from Belgium in the mid-1950s.[10] The second (and most important) was the arrival of mostly Flemish Belgians as missionaries in Rwanda in the 1940s, in contrast to the predominantly French Belgians who preceded their compatriots at the turn of the century.[11] The Flemish Belgians transposed Belgium's domestic politics into the combustible mix that was Rwanda's, for they—the majority of Belgium's population—were engaged in a struggle against the political dominance of the franco-phone political leadership class. Not surprisingly, they empathized with Rwanda's Hutu and began to provide them with political sup-port. This led to an alliance between the Belgian missionaries and the Rwandan Hutu within the religiously dominant Roman Catholic Church. Here the Hutus, largely shut out from the alternative profes-sional educational system and having gone instead to religious semi-naries, were dominant as clergy. The church was thus to play a strategic role in the political mobilization of the Hutus. Ultimately several clergymen and women were active perpetrators of genocide. The third factor that triggered violence during the colonial era was the Belgian colonizers' resistance to the scenario of an independent Rwanda led by Tutsi, who by now enjoyed the support of elements of the international communist movement.[12]

A group of nine Hutu intellectuals published the *Hutu Manifesto* in March 1957, demanding "democracy."[13] The manifesto embodied the rising degree of intolerance and xenophobia that had become typical among the Hutus. It branded the Tutsis "foreign invaders" and asserted that "Rwanda was by rights a nation of the Hutu major-ity."[14] In November 1959, these tensions and a series of events (most immediately that of an attack on a Hutu politician by Tutsis) triggered a "social revolution" in Rwanda. This new movement of extremist Hutu politicians and peasants announced that it had cast off the yoke of centuries of domination by the Tutsi minority. The movement was led by Grégoire Kayibanda, who later became the president of the new republic in 1962. Kayibanda's Parmehutu party utilized ethnic differences as a wedge to consolidate power. Its primary agenda was not governance, but to establish a tyranny of the majority. A referen-dum organized in 1961 consolidated the 1959 revolution and facili-tated full independence in 1962. That process was accompanied by mass killings of Tutsis and the flight of tens of thousands more to the neighboring countries of Burundi, Tanzania, Uganda, and Belgian Congo.

The events of 1959–1962 arguably amounted to the first genocide in Rwanda, even if the number of victims was nowhere near the death toll in 1994. Certainly the killings were crimes against humanity. At any event, they were the first of cyclical waves of mass atrocities that would continue, with impunity, for the next 35 years. From 1961, a group of Tutsi refugees in the diaspora organized themselves into a military force and launched repeated stealth attacks on Rwanda from bases in Uganda and Burundi.[15] These attempts by Tutsi rebels to reenter Rwanda by force of arms during the 1960s led to revenge massacres of Tutsis inside Rwanda.

In 1973, Kayibanda was ousted in a military coup by Juvénal Habyarimana, a Hutu army officer from the northwestern part of the country. The coup was the direct result of tensions between southern Hutus, on the one hand, and northern Hutus who felt marginalized by their southern brethren, on the other. Although Habyarimana pledged to end mass killings of Tutsis, he was just as steeped in nepotism as his predecessor in office. He concentrated power and access to wealth in the hands of a small group of Hutus from his home region, especially a core group of relations of his wife, Agathe. This group was known as the *Akazu* (small hut), borrowing a term used for the courtiers of a king,[16] and it played a major role in the genocide of 1994.

## WAR AND GENOCIDE

Habyarimana's policies toward the Tutsis were contradictory. He severely restricted opportunities for the Tutsis in education and in government, while maintaining financially beneficial relationships with Tutsi businessmen.[17] Most important, he firmly denied Tutsi exiles and refugees the right of return to their country, to which they were entitled according to international law, claiming that pressures on land made refugees' return impracticable.[18] This policy led to the revival of the armed struggle by Tutsis outside Rwanda and the civil war that served as an immediate context for the genocide.

A combination of factors, namely an economic downturn as a result of the fall in export commodity prices and the end of the Cold War, led to donor pressure on Habyarimana to embark on political reforms away from a one-party state to multiparty democracy. He was reluctant reformer, but was faced with little choice. For the Tutsi rebels, all of this was too little and too late. On October 1, 1990, the Rwandan Patriotic Front (RPF) Army attacked Rwanda from their base in Uganda. A full-scale war had begun.

The RPF was commanded by Paul Kagame and comprised mostly Tutsi soldiers who had fought alongside Yoweri Museveni in the civil war that brought the latter to power in Uganda in 1986. Kagame had risen to become deputy director of military intelligence in the Ugandan army under Museveni. But he and his fellow Rwandan Tutsis in that army were not Ugandan citizens by birth, although they acquired Ugandan nationality as Rwandan exiles—Kagame was in fact an infant survivor of the massacres of Rwandan Tutsis in 1959 who had been taken into exile in Uganda by refugee parents. Kagame and his fellow travelers thus felt a strong psychological pressure to return to Rwanda, by force of arms if necessary. Museveni, while not ungrateful for their support, was relieved to see them return to Rwanda, for ethnic tensions had developed between the "Rwandan–Ugandans" and some indigenous Ugandan ethnic groups.

Predictably the RPF invasion triggered a new wave of massacres of Tutsis in Rwanda in the months that followed. Rwandan Government Forces (RGF) initially beat back the RPF attack with the military support mainly of France,[19] but the French government nonetheless prodded Habyarimana to open up Rwandan politics.[20] The Rwandan despot made reluctant, half-hearted gestures in that direction but had no intention of ceding real power. Meanwhile the Rwandan Patriotic Army (RPA) had regrouped following its initial military setback. In 1991 and 1992, it captured enough territory in Rwanda to bring Habyarimana to the realization that it presented a credible threat and forced him to the negotiating table.

International peace talks to end the Rwandan conflict began in the northeastern Tanzanian town of Arusha in 1992, but stalled on the sensitive questions of representation in a proposed broad based transitional government (BBTG) and the makeup of new Rwandan armed forces. Habyarimana and his acolytes feared that granting the Tutsi rebels and the internal Rwandan opposition a dominant role in the transition would be tantamount to a "negotiated coup."[21]

The pressure of circumstances however—military, economic, and domestic political pressure—left him with few alternatives. In August 1993, he buckled and signed the Arusha peace accords. The agreement included protocols on refugee returns, as well as political power sharing and shared membership and command of the armed forces. Habyarimana's nightmares were happening in real time—the Arusha Accords awarded the RPF and domestic opposition parties a majority of seats in the interim cabinet and the parliament, and the RPF 50 percent of officer-level positions in a reintegrated national army, including 40 percent of the army rank and file.

The combination of the Arusha Accords and the RPF's progressive military victories radicalized and polarized the Rwandan polity even further. Hutu extremists felt betrayed by Habyarimana and were extremely apprehensive about the inevitable loss of power and privilege that would flow from the implementation of the Arusha agreements. From their perspective, the accords amounted to political class suicide. The peace deal could not be allowed to stand.

Following the Arusha Accords, the United Nations (UN) Security Council established a peacekeeping operation, the UN Assistance Mission for Rwanda (UNAMIR), in 1993. The UNAMIR absorbed an earlier, smaller UN military observer force, the UN Observer Mission Uganda–Rwanda (UNOMUR), along the Uganda–Rwanda border. The new peacekeeping mission's mandate included securing Kigali, the Rwandan capital, monitoring observance of the ceasefire between the warring parties, monitoring the security situation in the lead-up to elections for a longer term government that would replace the transitional government, investigating breaches of the Protocol of Agreement on the Integration of the Armed Forces of the two parties and reporting to the Secretary General, monitoring the return of refugees, and supporting humanitarian assistance activities. Lt. Gen. Romeo Dallaire, the Canadian soldier who had commanded UNOMUR, was appointed force commander of UNAMIR. With a force strength of 2,548 troops, which included two infantry battalions—only one of which was eventually deployed on the ground in Rwanda—UNAMIR was a small force in comparison with other UN peacekeeping missions in the early 1990s. Dallaire recalls his distinct impression at the time that compared to UN peacekeeping operations in Bosnia-Herzegovina, Somalia, and Mozambique, Rwanda was a sideshow—a "tiny central African country that most people would be hard-pressed to locate on a map."[22] This foreboding was to be proved right by the international response to subsequent events in Rwanda.

Meanwhile Habyarimana was busy attempting to derail or delay the implementation of the Arusha Accords. He bribed, coerced, and rallied Hutu politicians, including his more moderate political opponents, by casting all Tutsis as the common enemy. The opposition parties split into factions in mid-1993 between extremist "Hutu Power" factions and more moderate ones as a result of these machinations. Jean Kambanda, who was later to become the country's prime minister, was the favorite candidate of the Hutu Power factions of the Democratic Republican Movement (MDR) party for the post of prime minister, while signatories to the Arusha Accords stuck to their choice of the more moderate Faustin Twagiramungu. With each of the opposition parties presenting conflicting candidates for posts in the BBTG, the government could not be established, essentially rendering the peace accords inoperable.

These ominous events were fuelled by the influence of anti-Tutsi hate propaganda spewed by the *Radio Television Libre des Milles Collines* (RTLM) and *Kangura* newspaper, and the militarization and transformation of youth wings of the main Hutu political parties into militias. In its broadcasts, RTLM claimed that the RPF's agenda was to restore Tutsi hegemony and wipe out the benefits of the 1959 social revolution. It called for attacks against all Tutsis in Rwanda, who were branded accomplices of the invading RPF. The RPF, sensing an imminent breakdown of the Arusha Accords, prepared for a decisive military push against Habyarimana's government. Hutu extremists, on the other hand, were planning an equally decisive "final solution" to the "Tutsi problem"—genocide. This plan included the preparation of lists of individuals to be targeted, large-scale importation and distribution of machetes to the extremist Hutu militias. Events in neighboring Burundi, which has a similar Hutu–Tutsi population ratio as Rwanda, were grist for the mill. There Melchiore Ndadaye, a popularly elected Hutu president, was assassinated in October 1993 by extremist Tutsi soldiers in the Burundian army, stoking the diabolical rage of the Rwandan Hutu extremists.

On April 6, 1994, a regional summit of heads of state was convened in Dar es Salaam, the Tanzanian capital where, it is believed, Habyarimana finally agreed to implement Arusha.[23] President Ali Hassan Mwinyi of Tanzania hosted the meeting. Others present in addition to Habyarimana were Vice President George Saitoti of Kenya, President Yoweri Museveni of Uganda, and President Cyprien Ntayamira of Burundi. Traveling back to Kigali the same day in the company of Ntayamira, the Rwandan president's jet was hit by two missiles as it circled for landing in Kigali, killing him and his Burundian counterpart instantly. RTLM immediately blamed the assassination on the RPF, although other schools of thought believe that Hutu extremists disappointed at Habyarimana's "betrayal" were the culprits. At any rate, within an hour of the plane crash Hutu militias and the Presidential Guard established roadblocks around Kigali and commenced massacres of the Tutsis.

One of the first targets early the next morning was the Rwandan prime minister Agathe Uwilingiyimana, a moderate Hutu politician who advocated peaceful coexistence with Tutsis. She was killed by members of the Presidential Guard believed to have acted on orders from Col. Theoneste Bagosora, chief of staff at the Rwandan Ministry of Defense. Bagosora is widely believed in Rwanda to have been the mastermind of the genocide and is on trial at the International Criminal Tribunal for Rwanda (ICTR) at Arusha.[24] Ten Belgian

UNAMIR peacekeeping soldiers assigned to protect Uwilingiyimana were also murdered along with her. This prompted the withdrawal of the Belgian UNAMIR contingent from Rwanda—an outcome that was evidently planned, or at least desired, by Bagosora and his associates on the so-called crisis committee he established immediately after Habyarimana's death.[25]

Over the next 100 days, an estimated eight hundred thousand Tutsis and moderate Hutus, roughly 10 percent of Rwanda's population of seven million, were massacred in all regions of Rwanda—the fastest genocide in history, occurring thrice as fast as the gas chambers of the Holocaust of the Jews in World War II Europe. The victims of Rwanda's slaughter were killed at a rate that has been calculated as three hundred and thirty three murders an hour—or five-and-a-half lives per minute.[26] Over half of the victims were killed within the first four weeks of a "low-tech" genocide, which was nevertheless executed with stunning administrative efficiency.[27] Machetes (*pangas*) worked hand in hand with hoes, guns, and hand grenades to wreak destruction. Rwanda in 1994 was a country overpowered by the stench of death. As a witness famously told *Time* magazine, as the killings unfolded, "there are no more devils left in hell; they are all in Rwanda."

On April 8, extremist Hutus in the RGF, led by Bagosora, installed an interim government headed by Jean Kambanda as prime minister. It was precisely in order to execute this plan that Agathe Uwilingiyimana had to be assassinated—to create a vacuum of power and engineer an unconstitutional succession. Kambanda and his government then presided over the genocide of Tutsis and moderate Hutus, reviewing the progress of the massacres at cabinet meetings.[28]

Despite Dallaire's best efforts, UNAMIR was too thin on the ground to affect the course of the genocide. The world failed Rwanda in its hour of need as Rwandans hacked other Rwandans to death. This was not, as some Western analysts are wont to characterize it, "a tribal slaughter." Rather, it was a coldly calculated genocide motivated by a desire to maintain political power, capitalizing on ethnic cleavages. Genocide occurred in Europe in the twentieth century, claiming six million victims. A million Armenians were massacred in the Ottoman Empire during World War I. Two million Cambodians were victims of genocide at the hands of the notorious Khmer Rouge in the 1970s— a crime inspired by a warped political ideology. And more than 200,000 Bosnians were killed during the wars that followed the disintegration of the former Yugoslavia, some of them victims of genocide. In Sudan in 2004, no less than 100,000 Sudanese were slaughtered and raped by militias loyal to the government of Sudan in acts of ethnic cleansing. In short, the genocide project has been a consistent aspect of world history.

## AND THE WORLD WATCHED

The world did not respond to stop the Rwandan slaughter while it happened, rather, it was occupied with debates about military intervention and nonintervention in the Balkan wars—a response undoubtedly inspired by the occurrence of the Rwandan genocide in a country of little strategic significance, which was located in a historically disadvantaged continent. But the society of states intervened afterward to seek justice for the perpetrations of the genocide, crimes against humanity, and war crimes in Rwanda in 1994. It is to why and how this was so that we shall now turn.

The world's failure to launch a military intervention to stop the genocide has been copiously analyzed in several books and reports.[29] However it is not the main focus of this work. Rather judicial intervention, the use of international legal institutions to intervene in the Rwandan conflict—after the fact of the genocide though it certainly was—and the political and strategic context of that intervention are what this chapter is about. Events and processes in international affairs, however, are rarely coincidences. It is in that context that the world's nonresponse in a military–humanitarian sense will be discussed here, in order to demonstrate how the nature of the international society affected the likelihood of humanitarian intervention in Rwanda. As well, the purpose of this discussion is to link that nonintervention to the judicial interventions that followed in its wake and to point out how the former has impacted the latter.

The idea that a close-knit international *community* exists was tested during the Rwandan genocide and found wanting. There is a combination of factors that accounted for the nonmilitary/humanitarian intervention to prevent or halt the genocide. But the most important factor, at a conceptual level, was that of a *society*, not a community of states. At a practical level that factor is demonstrated by the actions or inactions of states and the limitations of the UN as the institution where states collaborate in the pursuit of sometimes common but at other times divergent interests.

The three states whose foreign policies and actions had the greatest impact on the course of the genocide in Rwanda were the United States, Belgium, and France. Of these, America was by far the most influential. Its positioning will therefore be considered first.

Humanitarian intervention, despite the phrase, is frequently guided by strategic interest. The U.S. administration under President Clinton judged that it had little strategic interest in Rwanda. Thus not only did it not act, but worse, it blocked actions or initiatives that might have affected outcomes on the ground even if not prevented the genocide. As Samantha Power has noted, "the United States has never in its history intervened to stop genocide and had in fact rarely even made a point of condemning it as it occurred."[30] America's characterization of the massacres in Darfur, Sudan, as genocide while other nations dither and differ is a recent exception that has placed the shoe on the other foot. In this context, the interventions in Bosnia in 1995 and in Kosovo in 1999 were also exceptions to this characteristic of American foreign policy. These interventions can be credited largely to sustained pressure by Madeleine Albright, ambassador to the UN and later secretary of state in the Clinton administration, and other interests in the United States. This insularity has a long history, going back to the late eighteenth century when Thomas Paine signed the American Declaration of Independence because Europe was "too thickly planted with kingdoms to be long at peace" and George Washington warned his country against "entangling alliances."

Not only did Rwanda offer no strategic interest to warrant American intervention, but it was doomed, even before the genocide erupted, by the shadow of Somalia. In 1993, 18 American soldiers participating in a UN peacekeeping operation under U.S. command were killed by Somali militias, and their bodies dragged through the streets. This setback so traumatized American public opinion that the Clinton administration enacted a new restrictive peacekeeping policy known as Presidential Decision Directive (PDD) 25. The policy laid out 16 factors that would influence U.S. decisions on whether to support or participate in peacekeeping operations. U.S. participation required that such participation advance American interests, be deemed essential for the operation's success, and have domestic and legislative support in Congress. The likelihood of casualties had to be low, and a clear exit strategy had to be articulated.[31] The American experience in Somalia was unquestionably the most powerful influence on U.S. policy toward the Rwandan genocide.[32]

Unwilling to intervene in Rwanda, the U.S. government took a number of far-reaching policy positions. First it studiously avoided calling the massacres in Rwanda genocide. Using the "G-word," as Power termed it, would have raised the stakes for the international society and put further pressure on America and other nations to take action to halt the genocide as required by the Genocide Convention. In other words, legalism would have kicked in, and that scenario was out of kilter with political and strategic considerations in some other capitals. From late April—by which time the genocide was well advanced in its progress—and for the next several weeks this policy continued. The U.S. administration, with support from Britain and China, blocked the use of the word "genocide" in a statement by the president of the UN Security Council on April 30. The original draft of the statement clearly specified genocide: "The Security Council reaffirms that the systematic killings of any ethnic group, with intent to destroy it in whole or in part constitutes an act of genocide . . . The Council further points out that an important body of international law exists that deals with perpetrators of genocide."[33] But the final statement was to read: "The Security Council condemns all these breaches of international humanitarian law in Rwanda, particularly those perpetrated against the civilian population, and recalls that persons who instigate or participate in such acts are individually responsible. In this context, the Security Council recalls that the killing of members of an ethnic group with the intention of destroying such a group in whole or in part constitutes a crime punishable under international law."[34]

Meanwhile on April 13, the RPF representative at the UN Claude Dusaidi had written to the president of the Security Council, stating that "a crime of genocide" had been committed against Rwandans in the presence of a UN peacekeeping force. Dusaidi called on the Council to establish a UN war crime tribunals and apprehend persons responsible for the atrocities.[35] This appears to have been the first time the issue of war crimes trials by a UN tribunal was brought before the Security Council. In an irony reflective of sovereignty as the hallmark of the international society, Rwanda held a rotating seat on the Security Council in 1994 and was represented by Ambassador Jean-Damascene Bizimana, permanent representative of the extremist Hutu government, which was perpetrating the genocide. This situation, however, while a personal embarrassment for most of the other ambassadors on the Security Council, was not a weighty factor for decision making by the Council on the genocide.[36]

Second the United States rejected proposals from the UN to jam the RTLM and so stop its broadcasts, which were inciting the genocidal massacres. The UN did not have the capacity to do so. While a State Department adviser for the region supported this position, the U.S. Department of Defense recommended a rejection of the proposal on the grounds that it would cost $8,500 an hour to position a jamming aircraft over Rwanda, and that jamming a national radio station would violate Rwanda's sovereignty.[37] Dallaire commented: "The Pentagon judged that the lives of the estimated 8,000–10,000 Rwandans being killed each day in the genocide were not worth the cost of the fuel or the violation of Rwandan airwaves."[38]

Here one disagrees with Kuperman who, in arguing that the genocide could not have been prevented or halted after it had gotten underway, asserts that the radio broadcasts were not an essential driver of the massacres.[39] The evidence, anecdotal and judicial, establishes exactly the opposite. The judgment of the ICTR in the "media trial" has established once and for all the crucial role hate media, including RTLM, played in fanning the genocide, beginning several months before and continuing during the massacres.[40] Kuperman recalls the curious legal opinion of a Pentagon lawyer that silencing a hate radio that was broadcasting explicit instructions for genocide would have violated the American principle of freedom of speech.[41] The noted American First Amendment lawyer Floyd Abrams has rebuffed this argument, asserting that inciting genocide does not rise to a standard that could be protected by the First Amendment.[42]

Third American policy during the genocide was perceived as sympathetic to the RPF.[43] This raises the question of whether there was a grand strategic design to replace French influence in the African Great Lakes Region. If such a design can be identified at all, it can only be one that evolved in response to events. Those events were not driven by any Anglo-Saxon master plan, but rather by the excesses of Rwanda's francophone, Hutu-dominated governments. As for France and Belgium, their main diplomatic roles during the genocide lay in the former's decision not to reinforce UNAMIR and instead, obtaining Security Council authorization to establish a controversial, parallel humanitarian intervention force in the waning days of the Rwandan conflict. The force, named Operation Turquoise, was blessed with the robust mandate under Chapter 7 of the UN Charter that UNAMIR never had. The Security Council authorized Operation Turquoise[44] on the strict condition that it would last for no longer than 60 days. It was also operationally restricted to western Rwanda. Despite its misgivings about the French, the RPF was consulted by the French government on the humanitarian operation and, for its own strategic reasons, it agreed.[45] Belgium pulled its troops from Rwanda the week of April 14, 1994 after the troops were targeted in early April as part of the genocide plan. This development broke the back of UNAMIR and removed any viable threat to the armed forces and militia that carried out the slaughter. It has been observed that Belgium also played a major role in the practical disintegration of the UNAMIR, not only by withdrawing its troops, but also by persuading other countries involved in Rwanda at the time to leave the country in order to justify its own response to the Belgian public.[46]

The UN Secretariat, meanwhile, like most players in the crisis (with the exception of one or two governments) interpreted the information it received from UNAMIR in early 1994 in the context of the ongoing political and ethnic violence, rather than as portends of genocide. Kofi Annan, then under-secretary general for peacekeeping operations, instructed Dallaire to discuss information the latter had received about weapons caches in Kigali with President Habyarimana. The UN Secretariat has been criticized for not doing enough to prevent the genocide. And Kofi Annan, who has been personally targeted by Rwanda on this score, has expressed regret for not having done more than he did to stop the massacres.[47] But, as Kuperman explains, this criticism needs to be placed in context.[48] Member states of the UN *decided* by their actions and inactions not to intervene in Rwanda.

The UN's response is more indicative of the role of international institutions as epiphenomenal, relying on the power and political will of the states; a will to act was not forthcoming in the case of the Rwandan genocide. Thus the real issue was the mandate of UNAMIR, inspired by the reluctance of states to intervene. Framed as it was within the traditional concept of peacekeeping—effective neutrality—in Chapter VI of the UN Charter, the mandate constrained aggressive military action to halt the slaughter.

Meanwhile another group of states in the UN Security Council in 1994 favored intervention to stop or contain the genocide, or at least were not in favor of a reduction of the force strength of UNAMIR at the time it was desperately needed and thus sending a signal of lack of resolve to the *genocidaires*. Czech Republic, New Zealand, and Nigeria were active members of this group. On April 13, 1994, Ibrahim Gambari, Nigeria's ambassador to the UN, presented a draft resolution on behalf of the Non-Aligned Movement (NAM) calling for an expansion of UNAMIR's size and mandate. Nigeria was concerned that the Security Council was far more preoccupied with the security of UN personnel and foreigners than the fate of Rwanda's innocent civilians.[49] Again, on April 28, Gambari called the Security Council's attention to its focus on a cease-fire but not on civilian massacres.[50] But Nigeria had voted for Security Council resolution 912, which reduced the UNAMIR strength—largely due to institutional pressures to reach a consensus—a vote that Gambari, in retrospect, regrets.[51]

It was New Zealand's ambassador Colin Keating, supported by Czech ambassador Karel Kovanda, who proposed that the Security Council issue a statement calling the killings in Rwanda a genocide. Keating it was, as well, who proposed a draft resolution on May 6 that would beef up UNAMIR and change its mandate to peace enforcement after the political embarrassment that followed resolution 912. But his proposal was watered down into a compromise, based on a report to the Council by Secretary General Boutros Boutros Ghali that recommended a force of 5,500 troops. The Council adopted resolution 918 a few days later, but without Chapter VII enforcement powers. When resolution 929 authorizing Operation Turquoise was tabled and adopted by the Security Council on June 22, New Zealand and Nigeria, together with Pakistan, Brazil, and China abstained.

Returning to the nature of the international society, the question must be asked, in light of Rwanda: would the society of states take robust action to prevent or halt another genocide? If the answer is yes, then the society of states has made progress and ethics have become stronger forces in international affairs. If the answer is no, then the "international community" as I have posited, remains more of an aspiration than a reality.

There exists a widespread global sentiment that another Rwanda-like genocide should not be allowed to happen.[52] But the gap between the recognition of moral values and state action remains wide. And the massacres and deportations in Darfur in 2004 have made the point. One simple reason is that intervention is not cost-free. It involves putting soldiers in harm's way and few states, especially democracies, are willing to take that risk with little to justify it to their public other than moral concern. As Nicholas Wheeler has argued persuasively, there is a certain moral bankruptcy to this position. But it happens to be the prevailing reality, though one that is without question under assault by the solidarist worldview of international politics.[53] Even in the context of a restricted solidarist interpretation that does not go the full length of cosmopolitan universalism, genocides such as Rwanda and Darfur merit military intervention.

Kofi Annan has stated: "I long for the day when we can say that confronted with a new Rwanda or a new Srebrenica, the world would respond effectively, and in good time. But let us not delude ourselves. That day has not yet come. We must all do more to bring it closer."[54] Annan has created a new position of special adviser on the prevention of genocide and appointed the respected human rights expert Juan Mendez to the post. In Rwanda, the conspicuous absence of intervention to halt the genocide colored the subsequent international judicial intervention that took place in a number of significant ways.

First, the failure to intervene meant that the RPF ended the genocide in July 1994 and established a new government in Rwanda. The RPF government thus believes it is on moral high ground vis-à-vis the international community. The question is whether this has left the Security Council with limited practical leverage to ensure Rwanda's cooperation with the international tribunal and other attempts to investigate human rights abuses by its own troops, during and after the genocide.

Second, the international society's failure to stop the genocide has left Rwanda believing that only it can guarantee its own security in the face of continuing threats from the remnants of the *genocidaires* scattered in its neighboring countries, especially the Democratic Republic of Congo (DRC). This has practical implications for order in the Great Lakes Region. Third, nonintervention has left a sense of guilt over policy toward Rwanda in some Western countries, leading to strategic alliances with the RPF government in Kigali.

Fourth, nonintervention has affected the overall dynamic of Rwanda's relations with the UN, and thus with the ICTR. Rwanda has tended to view the international judicial intervention that the tribunal represents as a fig leaf, even if an important one that also serves Rwanda's strategic interests. Rwanda has tended to assess even the tribunal's officials from the perspective of the politics of intervention and nonintervention in the genocide. Officials of the tribunal from non-francophone countries are generally viewed with less suspicion than those from France or francophone African countries close to France, who have to prove their bona fides. This factor is not decisive in the scheme of things, as Rwanda must deal with the tribunal as an institution, regardless of who represents it. Nevertheless, in combination with others, it has affected the dynamics of Rwanda's cooperation with the international tribunal in significant ways.

These then are some of the issues that formed the backdrop to the all-important debates in the Security Council, which has shaped the framework of the international tribunal, and affect the international tribunal to this day.

# Chapter 2

# Send in the Lawyers:
# The Political Architecture
# of Justice

We believe that the independence of the International Tribunal is its most important attribute: independence vis-à-vis Governments, independence vis-à-vis national tribunals and even independence vis-à-vis the United Nations itself.

—Yáñez-Barnuevo, permanent representative
of Spain to the United Nations (1994)

The society of states, whether through the United Nations (UN) or alternative arrangements, did not send troops to halt the slaughter in Rwanda. But within the Security Council, a clear dynamic evolved toward international judicial intervention—the establishment of an international war crimes tribunal to hold individuals accountable for the genocide and other violations of international humanitarian law. The road to the international tribunal began in April 1994—the first month of the mass killings. Although, as we have seen, the United States and Britain were reluctant to put the label "genocide" on the killings in Rwanda at that time, the statement issued by the president of the Security Council on April 30, 1994 condemned all breaches of international humanitarian law in Rwanda and noted that the persons who instigated or participated in such acts where individually responsible. The statement referred to the killing of members of an ethnic group with the intention of destroying the group, wholly or partially, as a crime according to international law.

The Security Council later called for an investigation of violations of international humanitarian law in Rwanda. In its resolution 925 of

June 8, 1994, following a report by the secretary general on the situation in Rwanda dated May 31, 1994 in which he concluded that the killings constituted genocide, the Security Council noted that "acts of genocide" had occurred in Rwanda and that genocide was a crime punishable under international law.

## INVESTIGATING GENOCIDE

Against this backdrop, the Security Council adopted resolution 935 on July 1, 1994, instructing the secretary general to establish urgently an impartial Commission of Experts to investigate the atrocities and provide conclusions on the evidence of grave violations of international humanitarian law in Rwanda, including genocide.[1] The Commission was also to obtain information through the work of other bodies, notably that of the UN special rapporteur for Rwanda Mr. Réne Dégni-Ségui, who had a similar mandate from the UN Commission on Human Rights in Geneva.[2]

On July 26, 1994, the secretary general established the Commission of Experts. The Commission had three members: Mr. Atsu-Koffi Amega of Togo (chairman), Ms. Habi Dieng of Guinea, and Mr. Salifou Fumba of Mali. The Commission, whose members served in their individual capacities, began its work on August 15, 1994 in Geneva. Information on the details of the genocide and other atrocities poured in to the Commission of Experts from nongovernmental organizations (NGOs), private individuals, churches, and the governments of Spain, United States, France, and Ireland. The submissions from the United States included those from the Foreign Affairs Committee of the Senate and the Department of State. All the submissions pointed to a well-planned and executed massacre of Tutsis and Hutus who were political opponents of the Habyarimana regime. They cited the particular responsibility of specific high-ranking officials of the regime and the journalists of the *Radio Television Libre des Milles Collines* (RTLM) for instigating the slaughter. Most of the reports (especially those from the NGOs) recommended the establishment of an international tribunal to try the perpetrators of the killings in Rwanda.

Dégni-Ségui, the special rapporteur, submitted two reports to the Commission on Human Rights, made available as well to the Commission of Experts. His first report confirmed the responsibility of the Hutu *interhamwe* ("those who work together") and *impuzamugambi* militias and the "interim government" of Rwanda that was established on April 9, 1994. Dégni-Ségui recommended that an ad hoc war crimes tribunal be established, or else the remit of the International

Criminal Tribunal for the Former Yugoslavia (ICTY) at The Hague be expanded to cover the Rwanda crimes.[3] His second report condemned RTLM's role in the genocide and that of the former interim government that had by then fled Rwanda to Zaire and was actively preventing the return of Rwandan refugees to the country.[4] Significantly both Dégni-Ségui and the secretary general's Commission of Experts found that the Rwandan Patriotic Front (RPF) troops had also undertaken revenge killings and persecution of Hutus on a systematic scale. These included the murder of the archbishop of Kigali, the bishop of Kabgayi, and 11 other priests—all Hutus—on June 3, 1994 at the historic Catholic Centre in Kabgayi, which had recently been captured by the RPF in the course of the conflict. Given the influential role of the Catholic Church in Rwanda, this massacre caused quite a stir, but even this paled in comparison to the slaughter of hundreds of thousands of Tutsis during the genocide. Dégni Ségui also reported the massacres of 63 other individuals by the RPF. The RPF itself, which by July 1994 had established a new government in the country, acknowledged these killings by Rwandan Patriotic Army (RPA) soldiers, although it described them as "isolated incidents." The victims had been summarily executed and their floating bodies, with hands and feet bound, were recovered from the Kagera River (the same River where Hutu extremists had dumped the bodies of Tutsi victims months earlier) in late August and early September 1994.[5]

The work of the Commission of Experts became a statistical battleground between the genocidal Hutu-dominated former government, now exiled in Zaire, and the RPF government, with both sides submitting lists of alleged perpetrations and victims. As reported by the Commission, the RPF gave it a list of Hutu individuals who instigated and organized the genocide. The leaders of the *ancien* regime provided the Commission with (1) the names of several persons it claimed were massacred by the RPF, (2) the specific sites of 15 mass graves that held the victims of RPF atrocities, and (3) written testimonies of some Hutus who had escaped from RPF-occupied zones during the war.[6] The politics of justice had begun in earnest. These facts were important because they were to frame the mandate of the international judicial intervention that followed. And, especially regarding the admittedly lesser crimes by the RPA that could nevertheless not be swept under the carpet, they were central to the battle for what the future historical record of that international intervention would say.

The Commission of Experts concluded that individuals from both sides of the war in Rwanda had committed serious breaches of international humanitarian law—genocide, crimes against humanity,

and war crimes. It found that acts of genocide were perpetrated by
Hutu elements against Tutsis in "a concerted, planned, systematic and
methodical way."[7] These acts, the Commission reported, constituted
genocide within the meaning of the Genocide Convention of 1948—
chiefly the commission of the massacres with the intent to destroy,
wholly or partially, the Tutsi group. The Commission also concluded
that some Tutsi soldiers had carried out mass assassinations, summary
executions, and crimes against humanity against Hutu individuals and
that these acts deserved further investigation. However it did not
uncover any evidence that RPA forces acted with genocidal intent.

The Commission had to rule on whether the conflict that formed
the immediate context of the crimes in Rwanda was an *armed* conflict
and, if so, whether it was an *international* or *non-international* armed
conflict. These determinations would in turn point to which rules of
international humanitarian law would apply. Rwanda became a party
to the Geneva Conventions on May 5, 1964 and acceded to the
Convention's Additional Protocols on November 19, 1984. The
Commission found that an armed conflict undoubtedly existed in
Rwanda between April 6 and July 15, 1994, and that the conflict was
of a non-international character because it was confined to Rwandan
territory and did not involve the active military engagement of any
other state.[8]

In reaching this legal assessment, the Commission observed in its
report that ascribing the status of a non-international armed conflict
did not mean the Rwandan civil war did not have serious consequences
on its neighboring states, which had to absorb a massive influx of
refugees from Rwanda, and on the wider international community.
The threat that the Rwandan war presented to international peace and
security in the context of the Charter of the UN was obvious. But the
essential character of the conflict was non-international. Thus the
provisions of common Article 3 to the four Geneva Conventions and
Additional Protocol II thereto were applicable.[9]

Common Article 3 of the Geneva Conventions bind parties to a
non-international conflict to the humane treatment of persons not
actively involved in the fighting, including soldiers who have laid
down their arms and those removed from combat by sickness,
wounds, detention, or other causes. It prohibits "at any time and in
any in place whatsoever": (1) violence to life and person, in particular
murder of all kinds, mutilation, cruel treatment, and torture; (2) taking of hostages; (3) outrages upon personal dignity, in particular
humiliating and degrading treatment; and (4) the passing of sentences
and the carrying out of executions without previous judgment

pronounced by a regularly constituted court, affording all the judicial guarantees that are recognized as indispensable by civilized peoples.

Next the Commission examined the question of individual responsibility in international law, and that of the merits and demerits of international prosecution by an international tribunal versus the prosecution of international crimes in domestic courts. Under the circumstances, this was a no-brainer, if for no other reason than Rwanda's total lack of judicial capacity in 1994 to undertake such a task. But there were other reasons why the Commission supported an international approach to prosecutions for the Rwandan crimes. Valid as those reasons were, the Commission's analysis that led to their adoption pointed to the roots of the tensions that were later to develop between Rwanda and the international society over the very concept of an international tribunal that would pursue justice for the crimes of 1994.

The Commission of Experts recognized that prosecutions in a municipal tribunal would be more sensitive to the expectations of a local community. Such trials would be near to where the crimes occurred. They would have less difficulty gathering evidence. And the judgments of such courts would have an impact multiplied several times by the local ownership of the process by the affected community. Conversely an international tribunal may be perceived as being too remote from the communities they were meant to serve.[10] The Commission reasoned that an international jurisdiction and the local relevance of such a jurisdiction were not mutually exclusive, and the two could be reconciled if such a tribunal were to be in Rwanda.

However recognizing the high possibility that, in the emotionally charged atmosphere prevailing in post-genocide Rwanda, municipal trials for violations of international humanitarian law could fall victim to perceptions of bias, the Commission came down in favor of an international tribunal sitting outside Rwanda. In its view, the need for independence, objectivity, and impartiality of such a court trumped other factors. Another significant argument was that the tribunal would have better familiarity with the "technique and substance of international law" than a municipal court.[11]

For these reasons, the Commission of Experts recommended the establishment of an international criminal tribunal to adjudicate the Rwandan atrocities. As noted above, no surprise there. The somewhat baffling recommendation by the Commission, bucking its earlier reasoning, was that the jurisdiction of the ICTY should be expanded to cover the crimes perpetrated in Rwanda, rather than creating a separate ad hoc international tribunal. In other words, the perpetrators of genocide and related crimes in a central African country should be tried not in an international tribunal situated on Rwandan territory or in the African continent, but in an ad hoc tribunal originally dedicated to war crimes in the Balkans and situated in a European capital.

This recommendation was baffling. Was it a desire to hasten the expansion of such a tribunal into a permanent international criminal court? To be sure, the International Criminal Court (ICC) later came into being and now has its seat at The Hague, but it is institutionally separate from the ad hoc Yugoslavia tribunal. And the logic of its location is a somewhat different matter, for the ICC is permanent and not limited to any particular geographical region in its jurisdiction, and so The Hague—just as any other major city—might as well have been the successful candidate to host the ICC. An ad hoc prosecution of Rwandan war criminals is, however, another matter.

The interim report of the Commission of Experts provided the formal basis for the establishment of an international tribunal by the Security Council. It was followed by a formal request from Rwanda to the Security Council to establish a tribunal.[12] The Rwandan request was a marked difference from the situation in the former Yugoslavia, where the Security Council established the ICTY without invitation from any of the warring parties. Thus, at least at the formal level, international judicial intervention in Rwanda proceeded at the invitation of the affected state, whereas in the former Yugoslavia it did not.

The United States now took the lead in creating an international tribunal. It largely drafted and negotiated with other members of the Security Council in late 1994 a draft resolution setting up such a mechanism. These negotiations, especially with Rwanda, whose rotating seat in the Security Council had by then been taken by the victorious RPF government, were difficult. Serious political tensions had developed between Rwanda and the Western states in the Security Council over several issues of policy and strategy in the emerging international framework of judicial accountability. Rwanda wanted a tribunal in its own image, with the selection of the judges and the appointment of the chief prosecutor under its control and the text of the statute largely inspired by its own government.[13] In fact, what it wanted was a hybrid court in which international lawyers would work with Rwandans and cooperate directly with its judicial system, with some oversight by the government.[14] The Western powers wanted a court that would be independent of Rwanda. Diplomatic/political wrangling over these issues wasted much time. Rwanda's requests for more time for these difficulties to be ironed out were essentially rejected by the Western powers in the Council, which had already made significant compromises in a final draft resolution based on Rwandan objections.

**Figure 2.1** The United Nations Security Council Votes to Adopt the Statute of the International Criminal Tribunal for Rwanda, November 8, 1994.

On November 8, 1994, at the 3453rd meeting of the Security Council, held under the rotating presidency of the United States, Argentina, France, New Zealand, Russian Federation, Spain, Britain and the United States sponsored a draft resolution to create a tribunal. When the draft resolution was put to a vote, 13 of the council's 15 member states voted in favor, one (China) abstained, and one voted against. The negative vote was cast by Rwanda. Thus did the Security Council, acting under the peace enforcement powers conferred on it by Chapter VII of the UN Charter, adopt a resolution establishing an international tribunal (Figure 2.1).[15]

As noted a moment ago, several political and strategic issues loomed large in the voting patterns for the tribunal's creation and the diplomatic horse trading that led up to the vote. For convenience, I will divide these issues into two broad categories. The first, which I call "framework" issues, includes those such as which crimes, committed over what period of time would be covered by the international tribunal's jurisdiction, the "primacy" of that jurisdiction, the death penalty debate, and the location of the tribunal. Many of these issues are related to the question of the independence of the international tribunal. That core requirement of judicial independence, which proceeded from an assumption that it could only be guaranteed in an international tribunal located outside Rwanda, was to come into direct opposition with the contextual relevance of the international society's judicial intervention. The second broad category of political/ strategic issues is that of the constitutional legitimacy of the Security Council creating an international war crimes tribunal in the exercise of its peace enforcement powers, in other words the legitimacy of international judicial intervention.

## THE FRAMEWORK OF INTERNATIONAL JUSTICE

In its statement after the vote on Security Council resolution 955, Rwanda cited its disagreement with the timeframe of crimes that the international tribunal would adjudicate.[16] Rwanda had proposed that the remit of the ICTR extend backward to the massacres of Tutsis from October 1, 1990, when the civil war began, up to July 17, 1994, when the RPF took Kigali, established a new government, and brought the war to an end. That this proposed time frame was calculated to maximize the delegitimization of the previous Rwandan government through the comprehensive judicial/historical record the tribunal would establish is not in question. Conversely in the pre-vote negotiations, the new Rwandan government strenuously objected to the extension of the tribunal's mandate to crimes committed after July 17, 1994, for that framework would inevitably focus on revenge killings committed by its own forces. The Security Council's compromise decision was to establish the international tribunal's temporal jurisdiction from January 1, 1994 to December 31, 1994 in order to capture within the judicial framework part of the preparations to wipe out Tutsis and the Hutu political opponents of the *ancien* regime.

The statement by Jean-Bernard Mérimée, the French ambassador to the UN, captures this tension. Mérimée, noting the significance of taking into account offences committed as of January 1, also highlighted the importance of the tribunal's remit extending to post-July offenses in Rwanda and neighboring states, especially in the refugee camps in Zaire.[17] He pointed to the possibility of further violations of international humanitarian law beyond December 1994, and asserted the Security Council's competence to further extend the tribunal's temporal remit in that event. But this was not to be, for massacres of Hutus in a refugee camp in Kibeho near Zaire in 1995 by the now Tutsi-dominated Rwanda army in response to the use of that camp by the extremists who carried out the genocide, went unpunished for lack of any effective international jurisdiction.

The RPF, having won the war in Rwanda, and with Tutsis the victims of a genocide, did not intend that an international tribunal judge its own crimes and thus introduce any "moral equivalency" in the historical record it would doubtless establish. As will become clear when we examine Rwanda's subsequent relations with the international tribunal, this was really the heart of the matter. This tension was also foreshadowed in the statement by Rwanda's ambassador Bakuramutsa after the vote on the ICTR, when he expressed concern that the statute of the international tribunal would lead it to "dispense its energy by prosecuting crimes that come under the jurisdiction of an internal tribunal" (a reference to war crimes, to which the RPF had admitted in the report of the Commission of Experts), "instead of devoting its meagre human resources, and probably equally meagre financial ones, to trying the crime of crimes, genocide . . ."[18]

## Primacy

The statute of the ICTR provided that both the international tribunal and national courts would have concurrent jurisdiction to prosecute violations of international humanitarian law in Rwanda and neighboring states during the calendar year of 1994. But, in what was to establish the normative supremacy of the international court, the statute provided as well as that: "The International Tribunal for Rwanda shall have primacy over the national courts of all States. At any stage of the procedure, the International Tribunal for Rwanda may formally request national courts to defer to its competence . . ."[19] What this means is that although Rwandan and other national courts (the latter in the exercise of universal jurisdiction) could try the culprits of the crimes of 1994, the international tribunal had the first call. As such, even if proceedings against an accused person had begun in such national courts, the international tribunal could request that such proceedings be discontinued and the persons on trial handed over to it—and be backed up by international law.

This is the essential quality of international judicial intervention, under the auspices of the Security Council, in Rwanda and the former Yugoslavia. In the case of Rwanda, the international tribunal's primacy has not been asserted through a takeover of cases in the Rwandan courts, for such a scenario would have been truly absurd except a national judicial proceeding could be manifestly shown to be a kangaroo court,[20] but by ensuring that the Arusha tribunal had the upper hand in obtaining custody of the "big fish" accused of responsibility for the genocide. Thus in the early years of the tribunal, efforts by the Rwandan government to apprehend major accused persons hiding in foreign countries were unsuccessful, as several countries preferred to surrender fugitives from justice to the international tribunal. As for other national courts, initial judicial proceedings against some Rwandan accused persons in Belgium and Switzerland, for example, were terminated and the accused handed over to the international tribunal at the latter's request.[21]

Legally speaking, the primacy provision had the *formal* effect of rendering the international tribunal independent of Rwanda and its authorities. This presaged major tensions between the two entities, for it also meant that not only did Rwanda have minimal input into the judicial work of the international tribunal in respect of the prosecution of the *genocidaires*, but also, as we shall see later, from a legal standpoint it was on weak ground in terms of influencing how and by whom RPF forces might be prosecuted for war crimes and crimes against humanity.

New Zealand, which together with the United States was an original sponsor of resolution 955 and had led the Security Council's pre-vote negotiations with Rwanda over six weeks, was quick to assert the need to prevent the international tribunal from coming under Rwanda's thumb. "New Zealand could not support any proposals that would change the international character of the tribunal or introduce any suggestion that the tribunal could be subordinated to Rwandan political intervention," Ambassador Keating stated.[22] Pointing to the future tensions between Rwanda and the international tribunal (but almost certainly not intending that his words would become a self-fulfilling prophecy), Keating urged Rwanda, although having voted against the tribunal's creation, to cooperate with it in light of the efforts made by the Security Council to accommodate Rwandan concerns about the court's framework.[23]

Spain, in a similar vein, emphasized the importance of the tribunal's independence: "Just as in the case of the tribunal for the former Yugoslavia, we believe that the independence of the international tribunal for Rwanda is its most important attribute: independence vis-à-vis Governments, independence vis-à-vis national tribunals and even independence vis-à-vis the United Nations itself."[24] Britain's ambassador, Sir David Hannay made clear that the "international character" of the tribunal had to be maintained, and some changes proposed by Rwanda could not be made without sacrificing that character.[25]

If, as we have seen, other states in the Security Council were prepared to—and did—ultimately override Rwanda's objections to the framework of the international tribunal, China was not. Despite its reservations on the very concept of international judicial intervention (which will be discussed shortly), China had been prepared, based on Rwanda's initial request for an international tribunal, to support the draft resolution on the establishment of such a tribunal. From China's standpoint, however, the eventual absence of Rwandan support for the resolution had changed the picture in a fundamental manner. Rwanda's full cooperation was essential if the international tribunal was to be effective, China argued. The Security Council's efforts to address Rwandan objections did not go far enough, and Rwanda's request for further consultations should have been acceded to Li Zhaoxing, China's ambassador, thus concluded that, "it is therefore an incautious act to vote in a hurry on a draft resolution that the Rwanda Government still finds difficult to accept, *and it is also hard to tell what impact this may have on relevant efforts in future.* Therefore, the Chinese delegation cannot but express its regret and has abstained from the vote"[26] (emphasis added).

The actual effect of international judicial intervention's primacy, then, is to suspend the sovereignty of state actors in the judicial sphere and to vest it in the Security Council, in the case of international criminal tribunals such as The Hague and Arusha. Nigeria's ambassador Ibrahim Gambari alluded to this normative anomaly in his post-vote statement in the Security Council: "It is our understanding that the international tribunal for Rwanda is designed not to replace, but to complement, the sovereignty of Rwanda . . ."[27] In fact, legally speaking, what Gambari warned against had already happened. (Politically, however, the reality turned out somewhat differently, as we will see later.)

Rwanda was not the only country affected by this normative scenario. Resolution 955 conferred jurisdiction on the ICTR for genocide, crimes against humanity, and war crimes committed, first within Rwanda in 1994 (no matter what the nationality of the perpetrator was), but also in respect of such crimes committed by Rwandan citizens in "neighboring states" during the same period. There was no indication of just who those neighbors were, but the provision is understood to refer to the countries with which Rwanda shares a border—Democratic Republic of Congo (DRC) (then Zaire), Uganda, Burundi, and Tanzania.

In just one illustration of the tension between sovereignty and international judicial intervention, Odyek Agona, charge d'affaires ad interim of Uganda's Permanent Mission to the UN, addressed a letter to the president of the Security Council one week before the vote on the draft resolution.[28] Uganda pronounced itself opposed to the language of the draft statute of the international tribunal, which conferred the latter with primacy over national jurisdictions. The East African state asserted that it "considers that its judicial system has primacy and supreme jurisdiction and competence over any crimes committed on Uganda territory by its citizens or noncitizens, at any particular time."[29] Uganda said it would agree to language that circumscribed the jurisdiction and competence of the proposed tribunal to "Rwandan territory and the territory of those member states which expressly declare acceptance of such jurisdiction." It pointed to the ongoing debates in the UN General Assembly on a standing international criminal court as a forum to which it would refer its full view on the surrender of its national jurisdiction over violations of international humanitarian law.

## Independence = Distance

Closely interwoven in the primacy of the international tribunal was that of its eventual location. While it was not until February 1995 that the Security Council was to decide on the seat of the tribunal, it was already apparent in early November 1994 (when the tribunal was formally created) that it would not be located in Rwanda. Rwanda read this as a slap on its face. How could an international tribunal "for Rwanda"—especially given the country's unique need to *see* and *feel* justice for the genocide—be situated outside Rwanda?

The answer is to be found, again, in the emphasis on the international tribunal's primacy and its independence from Rwanda. The ICTY had already been situated at The Hague, far away from the Balkans and setting the precedent. Indeed as we have seen, the ICTR avoided being consigned to The Hague by a whisker. In that context, it is not surprising that it was not located in Rwanda itself. One reason for this is that, as Yale University law professor Jose Alvarez has noted in a study of the logic and limitations of the primacy of international tribunals, the prevailing wisdom at the time was to organize trials for mass atrocities away from the regions where the crimes occurred.[30] That approach reinforced the state-centric context in which international lawyers situated blame for such atrocities (although the purpose of criminal trials were to assign individual responsibility), thus necessitating top–down intervention by the "international community's most reputable enforcer, the United Nations."[31] Trials held where the crimes occurred were likely to be show trials, or selective and incompetent in applying the international norms that are the legacy of

Nuremberg.[32] This is the argument about the will and the capacity to mete out justice for the most heinous crimes. In the former Yugoslavia, it would have been inconceivable in 1993 that any national court would put senior political or military figures on trial for the crimes that accompanied the break up of that entity. In Rwanda, the infrastructure for such an effort simply did not exist. And the Rwandan government's willingness to put members of its own forces on trial for committing mass atrocities was debatable. Moreover the atmosphere in Rwanda in the aftermath of the genocide was one of an eerie, pent-up tension. Kigali had the definite feel of a ghost town. In these circumstances, it was not surprising that several, especially Western members of the Security Council concluded that an environment in which impartial justice could be handed down was absent.

For Rwanda, China, Nigeria, and Pakistan, however, Kigali was the best place to establish the international tribunal provided necessary arrangements could be made for its efficient operation.[33] While these countries appeared focused on the tribunal's potential positive impact on Rwandan society, the group of states that opposed locating the tribunal in Rwanda were more concerned about the independence of the tribunal from Rwanda, and focused on it as a post-Nuremberg instrument to advance international law for a global audience. As of the vote on resolution 955 in November 1994, Pakistan argued that the Security Council should consider alternative locations only in the event it was clear that citing the tribunal in Kigali would undermine its efficiency and impartiality—an indication of which way the wind was blowing. And Rwanda, citing this as one of several reasons for voting against resolution 955, expressed its "surprise to see that the authors of the draft still hesitate to indicate where the future seat of the tribunal will be."[34]

This was an admittedly difficult political tension to resolve, for while the independence of the tribunal was seen as paramount at the time, subsequent lessons from international judicial intervention have shown the limited relevance of the ad hoc tribunals to the societies whose conflicts they were established to address. The compromise that was already imminent by the time the vote was taken on resolution 955 by the Security Council was that of the imperative of establishing a major arm of the tribunal in Kigali. The statement of the United States supporting the establishment of such an office and underscoring that a large part of the international tribunal's work should be done in Rwanda was a clear indication of this compromise.[35] That office was to be that of the prosecutor who was to conduct investigations, mostly in Rwanda. The Security Council later established the seat of the tribunal in Arusha, Tanzania.[36] Still the question must be asked whether citing the judicial seat of the ICTR in Rwanda would have undermined the independence of the tribunal. In retrospect, a former senior official of the tribunal acknowledged that the answer is "yes."[37] Indeed subsequent events also indicate that "independence" and "impartiality" are relative terms. This is so not in the context of trials and judgments in individual cases before the tribunal (these were unquestionably fair), but rather in that of carrying out of the mandate of the tribunal to investigate and adjudicate atrocities by both the genocidal, extremist Hutu government and the RPF forces that formed the post-genocide government.

At any rate, the safe distance between Arusha and Kigali created space in which the judges of the international tribunal could consider evidence and adjudicate in a dispassionate manner. The obvious disadvantage of this situation was that the tribunal's judges were somewhat divorced from the reality of the enormity of the genocide. Thus in the early years of the tribunal, they bent over backward so as not to be seen as a victor's court—a situation the defendants manipulated with great success to slow down or disrupt the trials. Moreover in its early years, the cases moved at a plodding pace, a situation that has been progressively reversed to one of brisk courtroom hearings. Indeed for several years after the tribunal was established, its judges resisted pressure to visit Rwanda and see the mass graves of genocide victims, believing that this would taint them emotionally and politically. It was only in 2000 that one of the tribunal's trial panels went to Rwanda on a technical visit to the scene of some of the crimes.

That the tribunal may have come under direct Rwandan political influence had its seat been in Kigali is apparent from a number of factors. The first is the effective sociopolitical organization established by the victims of the genocide through civil society associations such as *Ibuka* (meaning "remember"), the widows group AVEGA, and their close links with the Rwandan authorities—many of the latter genocide survivors as well. Second while the Rwandan authorities fully understood the high standards of impartiality the ICTR had to maintain, they included self-confident, strategic thinkers capable of playing political "hardball." Their strong public reactions to occasional judgments of the ICTR that did not accord with their perspective, coupled with the "spontaneous" protest rallies and demonstrations by citizens and victims groups, leaves open to conjecture what might have been the psychological impact of such activities on international judges sitting in Kigali. It is this anecdotal peculiarity of the Rwandan national context that makes the situation there different from, say, Sierra Leone, where a mixed national—international court adjudicating mass atrocities in that country is situated. And third were the ICTR situated in Kigali, the prospects for investigations into crimes allegedly committed by the RPF would have been even more difficult; not that the tribunal's location in another country has made it any easier, for reasons we will see later.

Bound up as well in the question of the independence of the Arusha tribunal was that of its independence from the Hague tribunal. The implications of the Security Council's decision to extend the ICTY chief prosecutor's responsibilities to cover the ICTR, as well as the rationales that have been offered for it, will be discussed in chapter 6. It suffices to say at this juncture that failure to appoint a separate chief prosecutor for the Arusha court, despite its institutional status as one separate and independent from The Hague, was an additional ground on which Rwanda cast the sole vote against resolution 955. Argentina, in its statement after the vote, noted that it would have preferred a separate prosecutor for the ICTR. In 2003, almost a decade later, this issue was to come to a head.

## The Death Penalty Debate

The death penalty was perhaps the most emotional issue for Rwanda, which led it to vote against resolution 955. The framework of the international tribunal, as contained in the resolution, ruled out capital punishment, which is part of Rwanda's penal code. The tribunal's statute provided for a maximum sentence of life imprisonment. Given that the ICTR was to try the architects of Rwanda's genocide, this situation created what Madeline Morris has called "anomalies of inversion" in which the big fish got better treatment at the international tribunal in accordance with international human rights standards, while foot soldiers tried in Rwandan national courts could presumably get the death penalty if convicted.[38]

But the death penalty issue was really a proxy battle in the global politics of international human rights. The European states in the Security Council would not support the inclusion of the death penalty in the remit of a UN tribunal. That would be viewed as antithetical to (1) the "ethical" foreign policies of several liberal European states, and (2) to UN human rights standards that have moved away from capital punishment in the past four decades. Thus the choice was between creating an international tribunal with death penalty sentencing powers (a near impossibility in the contemporary international society) and having no tribunal at all. In this context, it is not surprising that Colin Keating, who possessed much moral authority and who was a strong advocate of humanitarian intervention to halt the genocide, made clear his country's firm position on this thorny topic. Following the principle of "an eye for an eye," he stressed, was not "the path to establishing a civilized society, no matter how horrendous the crimes the individuals concerned may have committed."[39] Rwanda, which was later to execute 22 persons convicted of genocide in 1998, brushing aside appeals for clemency from Pope John Paul II and human rights groups, saw things rather differently.[40] Not surprisingly, the United States, much criticized by European states for its tradition of capital punishment, was consistent in its sympathy for Rwanda's position on this particular point.[41]

The Security Council's efforts to create an independent court notwithstanding, the novelty of its action in setting up courts of law was a revolution in international politics. It did not go unchallenged, for the Council's authority to establish the Arusha tribunal and its sister court at The Hague was to be vigorously questioned.

## A QUESTION OF LEGITIMACY

Did the Security Council exceed its powers when it created ad hoc international courts to adjudicate massive human rights violations? This question has been raised both by states in diplomatic conference rooms in New York and defendants in courtroom docks in Arusha and The Hague. Like the Hague tribunal, the UN Security Council established the Arusha tribunal as a form of intervention, after the fact though it was, flowing from its determination that the situation in Rwanda continued to pose a threat to international peace and security. That threat was obvious in the volatile situation that has persisted in the Great Lakes Region of Central Africa in the aftermath of the genocide—the massive refugee crises that resulted from the RPF's victory in the civil war (two million Rwandans, virtually all Hutus, crossed the border into Zaire within one week as the final victory of the RPF became imminent), the persistent threat to the new Rwandan government from Hutu extremist forces in DRC, which led to a subsequent war in that country that involved forces from several African countries including Rwanda.

Chapter VII of the Charter of the UN, from which the Security Council claimed legal authority to establish the tribunals, provides in pertinent part: Article 41: "The Security Council may decide what measures not involving the use of armed force are to be employed to give effect to its decisions, and it may call upon the Members of the United Nations to apply such measures. These may include complete or partial interruption of economic relations and of rail, sea, air, postal, telegraphic, radio and other means of communications, and the severance of diplomatic relations."

It is one thing to impose economic sanctions on errant states. It is quite another to establish a court of law to adjudicate mass atrocities and punish individuals in the context of peace enforcement. And it is this absence of specific mention of judicial intervention as one of the options open to the Council that opponents of that radically new interpretation of the UN Charter have latched onto to question its legitimacy.

After Nuremberg and Tokyo, the only kind of international court most international lawyers, political leaders, and the informed public expected to see judging genocide, crimes against humanity, and war crimes was a permanent international criminal court established by the mutual consent of states, which is to say, by treaty. That process was delayed by the Cold War. But the ethnic cleansing in the former Yugoslavia and the genocide in Rwanda gave the UN the chance to adapt and deploy its responsibilities and interventionist powers to the judicial arena. The Security Council's court-creating function, then, was simply an innovative application of the legislative drafting principle that a law can be interpreted to give effect to its intention.

Four factors made this re-engineering of the Council's role in international security possible. The first was the possibility of agreement across previous ideological divides that was engendered by the end of the Cold War. Second a close reading of Article 41 of the Charter reveals that establishing an international tribunal in response to threats to international peace is not ruled out. The language used is that measures to be taken by the Security Council "may include," followed by some examples of possible action. To the extent that setting up international war crimes tribunals was not ruled out, it was in effect, ruled in—with a bit of imaginative thinking by the international lawyers and diplomats of the member states.

Third the specific geographical contexts of the atrocities in Yugoslavia and Rwanda made it politically acceptable to states in the Security Council to establish ad hoc tribunals to try the perpetrators. These tribunals would prosecute crimes committed in specific geographical areas. The reaction would surely have been different had the Council—assuming that none of its permanent members cast a veto—embarked on a voyage of legislation purporting to establish a permanent court or courts for a more globalized geographical area. This is notwithstanding the fact that, in relation to the trials for these narrow geographies, the writ of the UN ad hoc tribunals is, in fact, a global one: they can compel the cooperation of *all* sovereign states with the tribunals' judicial processes.

Fourth the legal context in which the Charter gives the Security Council primary responsibility for international peace and security is an enabling one. Article 7 of the UN Charter envisages that "such subsidiary organs as may be found necessary may be established in accordance with the present Charter." The ad hoc tribunals for former Yugoslavia and Rwanda are subsidiary organs of the Security Council. Under Article 24, UN member states conferred on the Security Council "primacy responsibility for the maintenance of international peace and security. . . ." They also agreed that when the Council carries out its duties in this area, it acts on behalf of the UN's membership as a whole. And Article 25 of the Charter stipulates that decisions by the Council are binding on all member states of the world body. The Council did not invent its powers. It simply *reinvented* them. It was, then, only a short distance from having such wide powers in the first place to expanding the ambit of ways and means through which they could be deployed.

In background discussions of the legality of Security-Council–created international courts, New Zealand and Spain specifically asserted the legitimacy of the Council's action in their statement after the vote on resolution 955.[42] Spain, however, felt a need for a more permanent "universal criminal jurisdiction," although it conceded that the urgency of the situation in Rwanda justified the establishment of a tribunal by the Council. It is noteworthy that even the countries that questioned the legitimacy of international judicial intervention were nevertheless swayed by this factor of urgency. For the question was, and is: having failed to halt the massacres in Rwanda, how else could it have responded to the genocide—whatever may have been its motivations for so doing?

Argentina, Brazil, and China opposed the legitimacy of international judicial intervention, although Argentina and Brazil ultimately voted for the establishment of the ICTR on the grounds of political expedience. Argentina cosponsored draft resolution 955 because it saw the ICTR as a "*political* and legal instrument" that could impact Rwanda and the international community in a positive manner[43] (emphasis added). It nevertheless argued that a standing international tribunal could only be legitimate if created by treaty, and also that since the ICTR was an ad hoc tribunal, it could not establish new rules of international law but only apply existing law. This point appears academic, for the ICTR did not feel thus constrained when it authoritatively defined rape in international law and, furthermore, defined it as genocide if committed with genocidal intent.[44]

Brazil provided the most substantive critique to the legitimacy of the Security Council's intrusion into the judicial sphere. As in the case of Yugoslavia, Brazil was strongly skeptical of the position that establishing or operating an international criminal jurisdiction was one of the constitutional powers of the Security Council:[45]

> The authority of the Security Council is not self-constituted. It originates from the delegation of powers conferred on it by the whole membership of the Organization under Article 24 (1) of the Charter. For that very reason, the Council's powers and responsibilities under the Charter should be strictly construed, and cannot be created, recreated or reinterpreted by decisions of the Council itself . . .
>
> In particular, it should be underscored that the assertion and the exercise of criminal jurisdiction are the essential attributes of national statehood. Therefore, such jurisdiction cannot normally be presumed to exist at the international level without the participation and consent of the competent parties. . . . The Security Council's responsibilities lie not in the judicial or institution-building field, but in the maintenance of international peace and security. Therefore, the invocation of Chapter VII of the Charter for the purpose of establishing an international tribunal goes, in our view, beyond the competence of the Council as clearly defined in the Charter.
>
> The setting up of an international judicial body should be a matter for thorough discussions and negotiation by the international community, as in the case of the proposed international criminal court of justice currently under discussion in the International Law Commission and in the Sixth Committee of the General Assembly.

Confirming that it was opposed to the ad hoc approach to international criminal justice as a matter of principle because it did not have solid legal basis, Brazil stated that it was voting in support of resolution 955 simply for political expedience. It did not view the creation of the tribunal by the Security Council as establishing a precedent, and qualified its support with "serious reservations."[46]

China was the only one of the five veto-wielding states in the Security Council to debunk the legitimacy of international judicial intervention. It had stated this position during the Council's deliberations on the establishment of the ICTY, and its views had not changed.[47] China's foreign policy has remained wedded to the classic Westphalian notion of sovereignty. It has nevertheless been under pressure from the increased influence of solidarist approaches propelled by human rights and environmental issues.[48] Its response has been to recognize this pressure, simultaneously resisting it and adopting parts of it that shore up its position as a great power.[49] That propensity to question the wholesale adoption of what it regards as Western interpretations of human rights that emphasize individuals over the state explains China's abstention from the Security Council votes that created the ICTY and ICTR. Its strategy is not an aggressive one, however, and appears calculated to safeguard its own scope of action and checkmate Western attempts to criticize its human rights record. Were it otherwise, China could have gone beyond abstention and cast its veto.

China's mixed approach to human rights diplomacy is further demonstrated by its participating in various human rights treaties and its membership of the strategic UN Commission on Human Rights, where it has successfully held critical American proposals at bay. Geostrategically China has tended to stand by African states in international politics; hence its apparent willingness to support the establishment of an international tribunal for Rwanda were it not for the latter's strong objection to its eventual framework.

As Rana Mitter has noted, the stakes were raised in the strategic skirmishing between China and the Western states following the NATO bombing of Kosovo in 1999, during which the Chinese embassy in Belgrade was accidentally bombed. In the words of one Chinese scholar, an international court was necessary to ensure that the "private legal structures of the superpowers" could not exert untrammeled influence on international affairs.[50]

Against the backdrop of the preceding review, it should be no surprise that the legality and legitimacy of international judicial intervention came to be challenged in the two ad hoc tribunals. In the Arusha tribunal, the setting was *Prosecutor v Joseph Kanyabashi*.[51] The defendant, a former Rwandan mayor indicted by the tribunal for genocide and transferred from Belgium on November 8, 1996 to face trial at Arusha, filed a motion on April 17, 1997 in which he challenged the tribunal's jurisdiction on several grounds. These grounds of the motion, filed by his defense team comprising the Kenyan advocate Evans Monari and the Canadian lawyer Michel Marchand, were:

(i) that the sovereignty of states, especially that of Rwanda, was violated by the fact that the tribunal was not set up by a treaty through the General Assembly;

(ii) that the Security Council lacked competence to establish an ad hoc tribunal under Chapter VII of the UN Charter, as the establishment of an ad hoc tribunal was not a measure contemplated by Article 41 of the UN Charter, and the Security Council has no authority to deal with human rights;

(iii) that the primacy of the tribunal's jurisdiction over national courts was unjustified and violated the principle of *jus de non evocando* (the right of a person accused of certain serious charges to a trial in regular courts, not by politically inspired ad hoc tribunals, which may be unable to render impartial justice in times of emergency);

(iv) that the tribunal cannot have jurisdiction over individuals directly under international law; and

(v) that the tribunal is not and cannot be impartial and independent.[52]

Prosecuting attorney Yacob Haile-Mariam, responding to the first ground advanced by the defense counsel, rejected the argument that the tribunal was unlawfully established. The crux of his counterargument was essentially that of the urgency of the situation the Rwandan genocide presented to the Security Council, the patent need for an effective response, and the delays a treaty-based approach to creating an international tribunal would inevitably have brought about. In essence, the prosecution harked back to the political-expediency argument advanced earlier by various members of the Security Council.

The tribunal's judges ruled that the manner by which it was established, rather than by a treaty adopted by UN member states under the auspices of the General Assembly, violated neither Rwanda's sovereignty nor that of other member states. The judges noted that "membership of the United Nations entail certain limitations upon the sovereignty of the member states. This is true in particular by virtue of the fact that all member states, pursuant to Article 25 of the UN Charter, have agreed to accept and carry out the decisions of the Security Council in accordance with the Charter. For instance, the use of force under Chapter VII of the UN Charter is one clear example of limitations on sovereignty of the state in question which can be imposed by the United Nations."[53] This limitation on sovereignty, which exists to a limited degree by virtue of membership of international institutions, is what distinguishes an international society such as exists in contemporary world politics from the international system that existed before the twentieth century. In the context of Article 25 of the UN Charter, it constitutes the most important legal basis of the legitimacy of the ad hoc international tribunals for Rwanda and the former Yugoslavia.

Moreover the Arusha tribunal judges noted that Rwanda itself called for the creation of the tribunal and participated in that process—although the judges omitted mention of Rwanda's actual vote in the Security Council. This point in the judges' decision appears moot, for Rwanda's request, though politically relevant in the sense of inviting judicial intervention, was, legally speaking, not decisive for the legitimacy of a Security Council action under Chapter VII of the Charter. In any case, Rwanda voted against the establishment of the tribunal, which, again, was of no legal significance: the necessary majority of 9 out of the 15 members of the Council voted in favor of international judicial intervention and none of the 5 veto-wielding states cast a veto. The states of the former Yugoslavia did not invite the Security Council to establish the Hague tribunal. And the absence of an invitation does not detract from the legitimacy of that tribunal, which, faced with a similar, earlier legal challenge in its docket, was affirmed by its judges.[54] There a trial chamber presided by the American judge Gabrielle Kirk McDonald ruled the *jus de non evocando* principle inapplicable because UN members had surrendered sovereignty to the Security Council under the Charter. Thus in its view, the principle that tribunals be established by law permitted the creation of ad hoc war crimes tribunals by the Security Council.[55]

Regarding the defendant's argument that the establishment of an ad hoc tribunal was not contemplated by the UN Charter—the favorite argument against the legitimacy of the Hague and Arusha tribunals—the tribunal ruled that while the establishment of judicial bodies was not directly mentioned in Article 41 of the Charter, it is well within the scope of that provision. The list of actions in Article 41 was not exhaustive but simply indicative of the kinds of measures the Security Council could take in response to threats to international peace and security.[56] The ICTY Appeals Chamber had rendered a similar interpretation in the *Tadic* case.

The judges were surely on strong ground here. As I have argued earlier, the language of Article 41 left room for the contemplation of other measures. The UN Charter has proved a resilient document—as has the institution itself. The establishment of international tribunals by the Security Council—when the political will to do so existed—was an imaginative use of a latent power. It is exactly in the same manner that the concept of peacekeeping, one of the most important activities of the UN, was invented in the context of the Charter, under Chapter VI but also even as enforcement action under Chapter VII. Nowhere in the Charter is peacekeeping mentioned as a conflict resolution option for the UN.[57] One can think of no serious questioning of the legality or legitimacy of this concept of advancing international peace and security in the 50 years of its practice.

The defense argument that the primacy of the tribunal's jurisdiction over national courts violated the principle of *jus de non evocando* is, in fact, a more germane one. That principle of constitutional law in civil law jurisdictions provides that the right of persons accused of certain crimes to be tried before regular domestic criminal courts cannot be abrogated through the creation of politically inspired ad hoc criminal tribunals that may be unable to render impartial justice in times of emergency. This was a brilliant argument, one that hit at the core of the political and strategic context of the ad hoc nature of the Arusha court, forcing its judges to confront—and acknowledge—its genesis in politics, even as they reasserted its independence. This ground of challenge to the tribunal's legitimacy is similar to another brought by Kanyabashi, that the tribunal was not impartial and independent by reason of its having been established by the Security Council, a political body.

Justifying its higher purpose, the Arusha tribunal's bench, with William Sekule of Tanzania presiding, distinguished the tribunal from the *jus de non evocando* situation where, they argued, the purpose of such special criminal courts was to try the accused without guarantees of a fair trial. The tribunal ruled that the fact of its primacy, guaranteed by the tribunal's establishment under Chapter VII of the UN Charter in order to give binding effect to its legal orders, did not violate the *jus de non evocando* principle.[58]

It then went on to admit that its political context was not unique and was no bar to its judicial independence. "This Trial Chamber is of the view that criminal courts worldwide are the creation of legislatures which are eminently political bodies," the tribunal ruled. What these subtle points establish is that which is the whole point of this work, but is conveniently ignored or only reluctantly acknowledged by many supporters of international war crimes tribunals: (1) that they are created to serve ends set by politics and strategy, and (2) they are not by that reason necessarily illegitimate. Still one cannot help but note that these two particular challenges to the legitimacy of international judicial intervention resonate far more strongly in the case of ad hoc international tribunals than they would with an international criminal court established by treaty, such as the ICC.

Echoes of the International Military Tribunal at Nuremberg can also be heard here, and this is a dilemma that faces all such ad hoc tribunals: having been established, they must get the job done and will brook no challenge, valid or not, to their legitimacy. The *Kanyabashi* motion at the ICTR and a similar one in the ICTY's *Tadic*, both of which are no doubt largely unknown to all but tiny numbers of legal scholars and practitioners, raise important questions that situate the "justice" of wars crimes tribunals in the larger political arena where they also rightly belong.

The *Kanyabashi* defense motion challenged the tribunal's direct jurisdiction over individuals in international law. In response, the prosecution cited the Nuremberg trials as having firmly established the principle of individual criminal responsibility in international law, and that the attribution of such individual responsibility was necessary to give effect to the Security Council's writ. The ICTR bench recalled in its decision that the question of direct individual criminal responsibility under international law was still a matter of controversy "within and between various legal systems" and there remained differing interpretations of the Nuremberg trials. The tribunal ruled that by the establishment of the ad hoc international tribunals for former Yugoslavia and Rwanda, the Security Council explicitly imposed legal obligations on individuals for violations of international humanitarian law. This was an innovation justified by the circumstances, especially by the magnitude and gravity of the crimes committed during the Rwandan conflict.[59]

*Kanyabashi* also addressed the selectivity of international judicial intervention, one of the more endogenous characteristics of international criminal law, with the accused implying that this also undermined the legitimacy of the Arusha tribunal. In so doing, he again made the judges address the political context of international judicial intervention. Why had the Security Council not created war crimes tribunals for the DRC, Somalia, and Liberia? Why Rwanda? The Chamber responded: "The fact that the Security Council, for previously prevailing geo-strategic and international political reasons, was unable in the past to take adequate measures to bring to justice the perpetrators of crimes against international humanitarian law is not an acceptable argument against introducing measures to punish serious violations of international humanitarian law when this becomes an option under international law."[60] This brings us to the question of why the Security Council chose to intervene in Rwanda not with troops, but with an international court.

## WHY THE INTERNATIONAL TRIBUNAL WAS CREATED

There are a number of reasons why the international society intervened with a court of law for Rwanda after the genocide. First, as several other practitioners and commentators have asserted, the Arusha tribunal, as the one at The Hague, was established primarily as an act of political contrition for the failure of political will to intervene militarily to halt mass atrocities, and not because there was a *proactive*, deliberate policy to promote international justice.[61] Faced with its moral failure, the society of states did the next best thing—establishing a mechanism of juridical intervention to ensure that those responsible for the massacres were brought to justice. It was the path of least resistance, for it did not offer up the prospect of body bags that accompanied the far more risky option of sending in troops to stop the slaughter under a Chapter VII mandate. And the society of states could look itself in the face and say: "we did do something." It was largely for this reason that the United States, in light of its role in the debates on military intervention, championed the creation of the tribunal.

Other rationales were grafted on to this fundamental guilt factor. It was conceived that such a tribunal would help achieve reconciliation between Tutsis and Hutus and deter future atrocities. The latter premise should be seen in the context of the apprehension diplomats felt that the conflict, although settled in Rwanda for the time being by the RPF's military victory, could be carried into Zaire and thus a clear and present danger to international peace and security remained.[62] Thus the Arusha court became the first international criminal tribunal to be handed a remit encompassing "reconciliation" as a goal of juridical intervention. The Hague tribunal statute had no such provision, and neither did the Nuremberg Charter.

Second, reacting as it was to an event that had already happened, the Arusha tribunal, like the Hague, was then seen as a useful tool to advance the development of international criminal law—and within it a retributive model of accountability—as a post Nuremberg legacy.[63] It was clearly understood by most of the actors involved—states as well as human right advocates—that the Hague and Arusha tribunals would serve as a trial run for the creation of a permanent international criminal court.

Third, the Arusha tribunal was created because the one at The Hague had been established 19 months earlier in May 1993 and was thus a strong precedent. And there are commentators like Samantha Power who believe that the existence of the ICTY at The Hague provided a precedent that was more than merely institutional: With a UN court in place to hear charges related to the killing of some 200,000 Bosnians, it would have been politically prickly and manifestly racist to allow impunity for the planners of the Rwandan slaughter, the most clear-cut case of genocide since the Holocaust.[64]

## THE MILLION-VICTIM QUESTION: WHO KILLED THE PRESIDENT?

Like the assassination of the U.S. president John F. Kennedy in 1963, it may never be known who fired the missiles that brought down president Habyarimana's plane and killed him and his Burundian counterpart on April 6, 1994. Does it matter? From the legal standpoint of international judicial intervention, it does not. The ICTR was established to hand down justice for the genocide and other violations of international humanitarian law in Rwanda. These, by definition, are *mass* atrocities. The killings began in full force *after* the plane crash, although the conspiracy that led to the massacres was in place much earlier. Thus successive chief prosecutors of the tribunal have not considered determining who killed Habyarimana a line of inquiry worth pursuing for the tribunal's purposes.[65] The genocide, however, is an objective fact and the identity of Habyarimana's assassins is not of central relevance to the tribunal's task of adjudicating individual criminal responsibility for the massacres, although, of course, it is important for Rwandans.

Nevertheless the question of Habyarimana's assassination is an explosive political question that hangs in the background, making occasional ghost-like appearances as if to remind the tribunal and the world that the genocide and the international juridical intervention it spawned are surrounded by questions that are profoundly political.[66] Supporters of Habyarimana's regime, such as Kenya under former president Daniel Arap Moi, were quick to point out in the early days of the tribunal, ultimately to no avail, that this should have been its starting point of inquiry.[67]

The reason the assassination is so politically significant, of course, is that, if the extremist forces in the dock of Arusha are able to pin responsibility on the RPF, they would be better able to deflect their individual responsibility for the genocide at a *political*, even if not legal, level. It would thus serve as a political justification for the massacres: the Tutsis killed the president of the Republic and the Rwandan masses reacted uncontrollably. Ergo, those of us in the dock are merely scapegoats. Responsibility for the atrocities could thus be divided between the Tutsis and the Hutus, and the establishment of an international tribunal that has so far prosecuted only Hutus would be seen as victors' justice. The legitimacy of the ICTR would therefore be greatly weakened.

Hutu extremists began to allege RPF responsibility for the plane crash as soon as it happened. The French judge Jean Louis Brugiere prepared a report based on investigations he conducted on behalf of the families of four French crew members who also died in the plane crash, which blamed Rwandan president Paul Kagame and his RPF forces for the assassination of Habyarimana.[68] The report was leaked to the French newspaper *Le Monde* in the lead up to the tenth anniversary of the genocide in early April 2004. Kagame strenuously denied the report's allegations. "The RPF and myself have nothing to do with the death of Habyarimana," Kagame declared at a press conference in Brussels. "I cannot comment on what Judge Brugiere may have found or may have fabricated. The story is invented."[69]

There are several hypotheses about the identity of the persons who shot down Habyarimana's Falcon 50 jet, and Gerard Prunier ably analyses them all in his magisterial account of the genocide.[70] But it is clear that he believes—with abundant support from first hand information and commonsense deduction—that the greater likelihood is that Habyarimana was assassinated as part of a plot by the extremist *akazu* for whom he had become a political liability by virtue of his concessions to the RPF, in order to advance to the "final solution" phase of the genocide plan. There are few stronger indicators of this probability—and the connection between the two events—than the speed with which the attack on Habyarimana's plane was followed by the establishment of roadblocks in Kigali manned by death squads who began to search houses for Tutsi victims. The time lag between the two events was no more than 45 minutes.[71]

Some authoritative sources are skeptical of the Brugiere report. Bernard Muna, the former deputy chief prosecutor of the ICTR, holds the position that the Brugiere report is based largely on the theories of Filip Reyntjens, a Belgian academic who was a close adviser to Habyarimana.[72] Moreover the Brugiere report relied significantly on interviews (with the tribunal's permission) in Arusha with several accused persons on trial at the tribunal, including Hassan Ngeze, as well as a defector from the RPF who had fallen out with the regime and had gone into exile in the United States.[73]

The Brugiere report has reopened controversy—and old wounds—in relations between Rwanda and France. As noted earlier, the shooting of Habyarimana's plane appears to have merely *signaled* the start of the massacres, but put nothing new in place in terms of preparations for the genocide. From all the evidence established by the Arusha tribunal, the genocide had been meticulously prepared. Moreover the area where the plane was shot down was under the control of the Rwandan Government Forces.[74]

There are yet other angles to the question of who shot the plane, based largely on who was interested in Habyarimana's death. Contrary to the conventional wisdom that the RPF had no strategic interest in committing the act—as Prunier argues—a school of thought, speculative though it is, is that Habyarimana's death would certainly have benefited the RPF by demoralizing the Rwandan Government Forces, and the visceral slaughter of Tutsis that (predictably) followed would give the RPF an excuse to renew hostilities and push for the decisive military victory and political power that was its ultimate goal. After all, there was a state of war, and Habyarimana could be considered a legitimate target.[75]

All these theories are, in the end, speculative. Only concrete or credible eyewitness evidence can confirm who did the deed of Habyarimana's death. In the absence of either, all that Rwandans and the world have to go on is circumstantial evidence and logical deductions. And in Rwandan politics, nothing can be taken fully at face value. The real questions remain: was the genocide prepared in advance? It is clear that it was. What then could have launched it? Answer: a bold act, such as the assassination of Habyarimana that could be used as a convincing pretext. In the words of *The Economist*: "The crime was planned in advance; the machetes had already been ordered. It would have happened anyway."[76]

# CHAPTER 3

# THE ARUSHA TRIBUNAL

Neutrality does not mean passivity or lack of action.
—Agwu Ukiwe Okali, registrar, International
Criminal Tribunal for Rwanda (1997–2001)

The International Criminal Tribunal for Rwanda (ICTR) was established in the northeastern Tanzanian town of Arusha for two reasons. The first was that Kenya, whose capital Nairobi is a far more developed metropolis and the commercial hub of East Africa, did not want to host the tribunal. As noted earlier, Arap Moi's government enjoyed warm relations with Habyarimana's. The Kenyan leader's initial reactions to the Arusha tribunal's expectations of Kenya's cooperation were threats to reject summons issued by the tribunal and arrest any of its officials that set foot in his country.[1]

The second reason for the international court's location was that Tanzania was willing to host the tribunal, and Arusha had symbolic value as the town where the failed Rwandan peace process was negotiated before the genocide. It is a small, pleasant town that hosts the headquarters of the East Africa Cooperation (the regional economic community), numerous safari companies that guide tourists to the natural splendors of the Serengeti, Ngorongoro, and other world-class game parks, and prides itself as being located exactly midway between the Cape, the southernmost point of the continent, and Cairo in the North African state of Egypt. The Tanzanian government initially gave the tribunal two floors, and later a whole wing of the Arusha International Conference Centre that was built by the Chinese government in the 1970s.

Were it not for the absence in 1995 of an infrastructure network that could support the sophisticated needs of an international war crimes tribunal, it could be said that Arusha's geographical isolation—it is an eight-hour drive from the Tanzanian capital of Dar es Salaam and four hours from Nairobi—lent itself far more to the serious work of judging genocide than the bright lights of a metropolis. As it turned out, however, the problems with infrastructure had a major negative impact on the tribunal's deployment phase from late 1995 to late 1996 and created significant inefficiencies in its early functioning. It was clear that, mainly because the United Nations (UN) had no prior experience of running a war crimes tribunal—and certainly not one in an infrastructure-challenged developing country—the unsuitability of the tribunal's location had not been foreseen. This factor was compounded by that of just how complex the work of the tribunal would become.[2] The Arusha tribunal thus had to play with the hand it was dealt.

The tribunal's judges and staff were a largely dedicated lot, motivated by the concept of justice for such a huge crime. But things moved slowly at the beginning and the patience of Rwandans and outside observers eager to see quick justice was sorely tested. The Hague tribunal also faced similar delays in its early years, but more as a result of the unforeseen complexities of international justice than by reason of infrastructure problems. It, too, had inherited no purpose built facility and had to make do with the previous offices of an insurance company. As we shall see later, however, international reactions to the initially glacial progress of the two war crimes tribunals were quite dissonant. The Arusha's tribunal's facilities and the pace of its work were to be improved upon later, but not before the tribunal had undergone a management crisis and a number of corrective actions taken.

## THE JUDGES

Back in May 1995, the tribunal's first crop of six judges were elected by the UN General Assembly from candidate lists sponsored by various governments. The process of the election of the tribunal's judges, like that of most international courts such as the International Court of Justice, is a political one, for it is competitive and frequently requires a large dose of diplomatic lobbying by the national governments of interested candidates, and some candidatures inevitably fall by the wayside. The court's first judges were Lennart Aspegren of Sweden, Laity Kama of Senegal, Hossain Khan of Bangladesh, Yakov Ostrovsky of Russia, Navanethem Pillay of South Africa, and William Sekule of Tanzania.

The tribunal was divided into two panels ("trials chambers") of three judges each. The judges, whose task was to adjudicate the cases submitted to them by the chief prosecutor of the tribunal on the basis of the charges that an individual judge had to confirm, subsequently prepared the Rules of Procedure and Evidence that were to guide the court's work. The statutes of the Arusha and Hague tribunals had earlier been drafted by the UN Security Council along the lines of a predominantly Anglo-Saxon common law system. This was largely due to the influence of the United States, which led the diplomatic and political process of creating the tribunals. The implication was that the judges of both tribunals were already boxed in when it came to choosing rules to guide day-to-day and courtroom proceedings. Thus the rules adopted by the judges of the Arusha tribunal were mostly identical to those of the older tribunal at The Hague. And those rules were mainly those of the "adversarial" common law system that sought to establish guilt or innocence before neutral judges. Although seen as more protective of the rights of the defense, they result in longer trials.

This is different from the "inquisitorial" civil law system used in much of continental Europe, where the judges themselves have investigative powers to unearth the truth, criminal cases are disposed of with relative speed, but the role of defense attorneys is not as robust as in the common law system. The civil law system, for one, does not afford the defense the courtroom opportunity to "cross-examine" prosecution witnesses. One practical impact of these rules of procedure was that they put civil-law-trained defense lawyers at the Arusha tribunal at an initial disadvantage and left them struggling to catch up with their common law colleagues. On the other hand, the rules of procedure allowed hearsay evidence, a horror to common law attorneys. The dominance of common law procedure on the whole, however, has had significant implications on how Rwanda, which uses a civil-law-based criminal code, views the Arusha tribunal and its proceedings, and thus, ultimately, the international tribunal's impact in Rwanda.

Regarding appeals, the architecture of the Arusha tribunal provided that it would have the same appeals judges (a five-judge Appeals Chamber) as the Hague tribunal. The judges would, however, sit as appeals judges for each tribunal as a distinct institution, and not as a combined appeals court for the two courts. But there was a serious asymmetry here: the appeals judges—who had originally been elected as judges of the Hague tribunal—could additionally act as *trial* judges in other cases at The Hague, but not at Arusha. This situation left the

Hague tribunal with an advantage over Arusha in terms of judicial manpower available to handle Balkan war crimes trials. And the situation persisted for several years until it was abolished in a rule change in 2001. The dockets of both tribunals were nevertheless progressively overwhelmed, leading the Security Council to create a third trial chamber for both tribunals and, ultimately, the election of additional temporary or "ad litem" judges for both judicial institutions.

The Arusha tribunal's first president, or chief justice, was the late Senegalese lawyer and former prosecutor Judge Laity Kama, who was president from 1995 to 1999 and continued to serve as a judge until his death in 2001. Six feet and six inches tall, Kama had an aristocratic but genial mien and commanded respect as more than just a physical giant (figure 3.1). He was widely seen as the Arusha tribunal's founding father. Kama kept his focus despite the difficulties the tribunal faced in its early days, and went on to make history as presiding judge of the first judgment for the crime of genocide by an international criminal tribunal (see next chapter). He also displayed in all his actions

**Figure 3.1** Judge Laity Kama, President of the International Criminal Tribunal for Rwanda (1995–1999) meets UN Secretary-General Boutros Boutros-Ghali.

a keen awareness of the Arusha tribunal's place in history and its potential role as an agent of change in Africa's political evolution. As UN secretary general Kofi Annan stated in a tribute to Kama upon the great jurist's death:

> Judge Kama was an eminent jurist who played a key role in the development of the judicial work of the Rwanda Tribunal. He has made historic contributions to international humanitarian law as former presiding judge of the tribunal's first Trial Chamber that rendered judgements in the Akayesu case and the Kambanda case in 1998. It will be recalled that the Akayesu case was the first ever judgement for the crime of genocide by an international court and was also the first ever judgement to convict an accused person for rape as a crime against humanity. Judge Kama's verdict in the Kambanda case was the first ever conviction of a head of government for genocide. Beyond his judicial achievements, Judge Kama was a leader who displayed great wisdom and was a founding father to the institutional development of the Rwanda Tribunal.[3]

Kama was succeeded as president of the tribunal by Judge Navanethem Pillay in 1999. Pillay, the tribunal's first female judge, was an antiapartheid lawyer in South Africa and a civil society activist, and served briefly as an acting judge of the Constitutional Court of South Africa before her election to the bench at the Arusha tribunal. She was elected a judge of the permanent International Criminal Court (ICC) in 2003. The same year, Erik Møse, a Norwegian jurist who was elected a judge of the Arusha tribunal in 1998 and had previously served as a judge at the Court of Appeals in Oslo, succeeded Pillay as the judicial head of the international tribunal. It has fallen to him to develop and supervise the Arusha tribunal's endgame in which the tribunal, like its sister court at The Hague, is scheduled to complete its trials by 2008 and close its doors by 2010.

## J'ACCUSE

The chief prosecutor drives the judicial work of the Arusha tribunal. The statute of the tribunal makes it clear that it was established "to prosecute the persons responsible for the genocide and other serious violations of international humanitarian law" in Rwanda and its neighboring states. It is the prosecutor's job not just to prosecute those crimes, but to first investigate them. This is somewhat different from national judicial systems, where investigations are handled by the police or, in civil law countries, by investigating judges or magistrates, leaving the prosecutor with the main task of presenting courtroom arguments. But the international war crimes tribunals have no police force of their own, and the tribunals must do the investigative and forensic work necessary to build a case in court. Logically this task falls to the office of the prosecutor.

Based on the results of an investigation, the prosecutor submits an indictment to a single judge of the tribunal, where he believes a case exists on the face of things, for confirmation. And it is only on the basis of a judge-confirmed indictment that a case can go on to trial at the war crimes tribunal. To accomplish these myriad tasks, the office of the prosecutor has a prosecutions section, an investigations section, and a legal services section that provides analysis on international humanitarian law and criminal law. Until 2003, one individual served as chief prosecutor for both the International Criminal Tribunal for the Former Yugoslavia (ICTY) at The Hague, and the ICTR at Arusha, assisted by two deputies, one at The Hague and the other at Arusha. This arrangement and the political and substantive problems it created is discussed in chapter 6.

The chief prosecutor has tended to be the most public face among the principals of the Arusha tribunal. This is partly due to the post's previous responsibility for both the Arusha and Hague tribunals, with the attention devoted to the prosecutor's role at The Hague spilling over to a similar role at Arusha. But it is also because the prosecutor's role tends to be the most dramatic in most courts of law, for he or she is the one who must proclaim "j'accuse" (I accuse). Justice Richard Goldstone of the South African Constitutional Court, who was named chief prosecutor of the Hague tribunal in 1994 after a turbulent and highly political search for someone to fill the post at that tribunal,[4] automatically became the chief prosecutor of the Arusha tribunal. Goldstone's tenure was a difficult one at both tribunals because they were in their start-up phases and navigating uncharted waters. He resigned from his position in 1996 to return to South Africa's highest court, but resigned from the apex national court in 2003 to take a teaching position at New York University Law School.[5] Goldstone's high public profile in his country, where he chaired the Goldstone Commission of Inquiry into public violence that accompanied negotiations to end apartheid, invested him with much credibility in the novel and difficult task of prosecuting mass atrocities at the two international war crimes tribunals established by the UN.

The Canadian judge Louise Arbour replaced Goldstone in February 1996 as chief prosecutor of the Arusha and Hague. Arbour was a judge of the Ontario Court of Appeal at the time of her appointment. She had not practiced as a courtroom attorney, but rather was a law professor at the prestigious Osgood Hall Law School at York

University teaching criminal law, procedure, and evidence for over a decade before her appointment to the Canadian bench in 1987. Like Goldstone, she was based at the Hague tribunal and visited Arusha and Rwanda occasionally for court appearances in important cases. The prosecutor's office at the Arusha tribunal was, however, run for all practical purposes by deputy chief prosecutor Bernard Muna, an ebullient Cameroonian lawyer and opposition politician who had served as president of the Cameroon Bar Association for many years.

Arbour's tenure as chief prosecutor was marked by three important events in the work of the tribunal. The first was the arrest in Nairobi, Kenya, of several accused ringleaders of the Rwandan genocide in July 1997, which I discuss in chapter 7. This was an important development that, coming on the heels of the start of courtroom trials in early 1997, was a major boost to the tribunal. Prior to this, important, preliminary investigative work had gone on behind the scenes for much of 1996, together with a number of important arrests of indicted war criminals, most notably in Cameroon. From the very beginning, the Arusha tribunal was successful in fulfilling what was seen as a cardinal mission of the ad hoc UN war crimes tribunals—apprehending and bringing to justice the truly high-ranking perpetrators of genocide, crimes against humanity, and war crimes. That these achievements were recorded in the difficult work environment in which the court was located is perhaps a testament to the doggedness of the Arusha court, despite a slow rate of prosecutions at this stage of its work.

The second major event of Arbour's tenure was her effort, at first unsuccessful, to implement the prosecutorial equivalent of the big bang theory. Arbour sought to join 29 accused persons in a single trial. Her goal was to establish, *à la* Nuremberg, that the Rwandan genocide was at its core a conspiracy by the Rwandan government and military high command at the time. She also argued that such a joint trial would quicken the tribunal's judicial pace. But the judges were not persuaded about the feasibility of trying such large numbers of defendants in a single trial, its potential dramatic and psychological effect notwithstanding. The judges were not opposed to joint trials in principle, and the prosecution was ultimately successful in winning judicial approval of its "joinder motions," permitting the joint trials of several defendants in smaller groups. This enabled Arbour's successor to proceed against the defendants in thematic groups where there was initial evidence of conspiracy or common purpose,[6] resulting in subsequent joint trials of the "Cynagugu Group"[7] of military and civilian defendants from that region of Rwanda who were alleged to have carried out the killing together, the "Butare group" of six defendants that included Pauline Nyiramasuhuko, the first woman in history to be indicted and prosecuted for violations of international humanitarian law, the "military trials" of senior military commanders such as Colonel Bagosora, and the "media trial" of three former Rwandan media executives. Several years later, in the context of a strategy to finish the work of the tribunal, this policy of joint trials was reversed by one of Arbour's successors because experience had shown that such trials were often practically complicated and took longer than single-person trials.[8]

The third marker of Arbour's term as prosecutor was the beginning of a strategy to prosecute sexual crimes such as rape that were committed during the Rwandan genocide. There is no reliable estimate of how many women were raped during the massacres. But they surely number over 200,000. In Butare alone, there are over 30,000 rape survivors.[9] These women are the "walking dead." Many of them would rather have been killed than have the stigma of rape attached to their persons. Their shadow has hung heavily over the Arusha tribunal, and has been a significant source of pressure by victim–survivor groups on the court. Today, despite a few high-profile convictions and prosecutions on rape counts, victims and women's groups in Rwanda and around the world believe the Arusha tribunal's prosecution strategy has not sufficiently highlighted this dimension of the genocide. (As we shall see later, women's groups in Rwanda played a role in the politics of the removal of Arbour's immediate successor from the Arusha tribunal.) Part of the problem with this strategy is that, while rape clearly was a major component of the strategy of genocide in Rwanda and has fuelled the rise of HIV/AIDS in that country, many of the "big men" on trial in Arusha were not thought to have been directly involved in sexual violence. Rather it was the *interhamwe*, the foot soldiers of the genocide, who were widely culpable, and the small fry were not the tribunal's priority for arrests and prosecutions. A number of the tribunal's defendants have been charged with rape on the basis of superior responsibility for the acts of their subordinates, including rape.

In 1996 and 1997, this important sociological dimension of justice for Rwanda confronted the tribunal, and it fell on Arbour as the chief prosecutor to lead the response. A high-profile visit to the tribunal's headquarters at Arusha in March 1997 by Hilary Rodham Clinton, then America's first lady, also contributed to a higher profile for the issue of women and sexual violence in Rwanda. Accompanied by her daughter, Chelsea, Clinton addressed a workshop on sexual violence that Arbour's office had organized, and also addressed Rwandans via a radio link from Arusha.[10] Arbour created sexual assault teams in the investigations section of her office in 1996 and 1997, dedicated to unearthing evidence of rapes and sexual violence. This evidence was in plain sight: the "*enfants non-désirés*" (unwanted children) or "the children of hate" from forced pregnancies induced by rape abounded. But it was a difficult task to reach behind the psychological trauma and cultural taboos to discuss these matters with affected women, much less obtain evidence that would stand up in a court of law. Although critics have described Arbour's efforts in reaction to public pressure as "token," and the consistency of the tribunal's work in this area is certainly subject to perfectly valid questioning, the sexual assault teams had several competent and dedicated members, many of them young African women lawyers well grounded in gender issues.[11] A major problem the tribunal faced in this area was that the prosecution's effort was necessarily incomplete. The tribunal's judicial process included the critical process of support and protection for witnesses in the trials. This task is that of the office of the tribunal's registrar, to which I will come in a moment. It was the reforms initiated by the registrar, then, that was to integrate the prosecution's sexual crimes investigations more effectively into the trials and offer the possibility of major impact by the tribunal in this area.

Two weeks after indicting Slobodan Milosevic for crimes against humanity and war crimes at the Hague tribunal, Louise Arbour resigned from her post at The Hague and Arusha in June 1999 to take up a seat on Canada's Supreme Court. She certainly chose her moment—when the ovation, and in some quarters the consternation, was loudest. She was secretly discussing the offer from Canada's prime minister with his senior officials even as she was putting finishing touches to the Milosevic indictment, insisting that the appointment not be made public until the timing, from her perspective, was right.[12] The pattern is somewhat similar to Goldstone, in which high service to country and prosecuting war criminals in international courts sometimes have exerted a pull in both directions. In any event, Arbour was reportedly feeling the strain of the prosecutor's job and yearned for her family and her country. A Supreme Court appointment was the perfect path back home. Carla Del Ponte, then attorney general of Switzerland, was appointed the chief prosecutor of the Arusha and Hague tribunals in August 1999.

Del Ponte was an experienced prosecutor. She had not been a judge, unlike Goldstone and Arbour, and was used to addressing a courtroom from the prosecutor's side of the aisle. The former Swiss attorney general had spent most of her professional career pursuing the "bad guys" of society with a single-minded goal—putting them behind prison bars. Her appointment as chief prosecutor of the Arusha and Hague tribunals was a natural progression. Both her critics and targets at home were pleased to see her leave Switzerland. A profile of Del Ponte described her as "a woman with a tough crusading reputation", who would need all those qualities as she pursues those accused of war crimes in the Balkans and in Rwanda.[13]

Del Ponte served as Swiss attorney general from 1994 until her appointment to the Arusha and Hague tribunals. She was born and educated in Lugano, the Italian-speaking portion of Switzerland, and is famous for her pursuit of the Sicilian mafia and investigations into money laundering through Swiss banks. Bombastic and stubborn, Del Ponte is known for blunt speaking, and appears unperturbed by her reputation as someone with scant regard for the niceties of diplomacy. She is proud that she has "never served anyone or anything but the law." Her critics have noted that, while being a war crimes prosecutor certainly requires unswerving focus and no small degree of *chutzpah*, the role also calls for discretion in a framework of justice that is just as political as it is legal, and is demonstrated through political and diplomatic acumen.[14] In this light, Del Ponte has been unfavorably compared with Arbour.[15] The "Carla factor" was to have serious implications for her work in Rwanda, as we shall see in a later chapter.

## HONEST BROKER

The most influential official in the Arusha tribunal has always been its registrar, though this fact is obscured from public view because the role is one largely exercised behind the scenes. Appointed by the UN secretary general and serving as his personal representative in an international judicial institution that is a subsidiary organ of the Security Council, the registrar is the international tribunal's chief administrative officer, responsible for the tribunal's finances (provided by the UN General Assembly) and personnel (appointed by the secretary general). It is this role, that of the UN's representative in an international court with an operational mandate, that is the source of the registrar's influence.

The registrar is also the international court's chief legal officer, neutral as between the prosecution and the defense, and his office is charged with providing legal and other support for the judges of the tribunal and the tribunal as a court of law. In this context, the registrar directs witness protection and support, the assignment of defense counsel under the tribunal's legal aid program, and oversees the enforcement of the tribunal's sentences in prisons in various countries. He is also in charge of the tribunal's institutional external relations with governments and other entities. Described by the tribunal's rules of procedure as its "channel of communication," the registrar is the only official who can speak for the tribunal as a whole—the chief prosecutor cannot pronounce himself on institutional matters concerning the defense or the judges who sit in judgment over the cases he brings to trial; nor can the judges be seen as taking sides between the opposing parties of the prosecution and the defense. The registrar is thus the man in the middle—the "honest broker" between the parties before the tribunal. Inevitably, then, he is the go-to man. The position is really a combination of the clerk of the court in American judicial system, *le greffer* in French, continental system, and the registrars in English common law jurisdictions who frequently go on to become judges themselves, and much more. Not surprisingly, it requires a mix of legal skills, managerial competence, and diplomatic *savoir faire*.

Into this daunting range and depth of tasks was Andronico Adede of Kenya appointed as the founding registrar of the ICTR by then UN secretary-general Boutros Boutros-Ghali in September 1995. Adede was a senior international lawyer in the UN legal affairs department in New York at the time he was picked for the job, and had earlier served as legal adviser to the International Atomic Energy Agency in Vienna. He stayed only 15 months in the Arusha tribunal job, resigning in February 1997 in the wake of the management crisis that rocked the tribunal in its early days and was the subject of a scathing report by the UN's internal watchdog, the Office of Internal Oversight Services (OIOS).[16] While Adede, who holds a doctorate from the Fletcher School of Law and Diplomacy at Tufts University, appeared from the audit report to have lacked management abilities compared to his recognized legal skills and keen intellect, the roots of the tribunal's early administrative difficulties could be traced to the decision to establish its seat at Arusha. This was not because the tribunal was located in Africa, which was a political imperative, but rather because of *where* it was located in Tanzania. The wisdom of hindsight is always luminous: had the international tribunal been cited in, say, Dar es Salaam, Tanzania's more developed capital city, many of its now-forgotten teething problems could have been averted.

Upon Adede's resignation, Annan picked the Nigerian-born jurist Agwu Ukiwe Okali (figure 3.2) as the tribunal's new registrar in March 1997. Okali, who studied law at the London School of Economics and Harvard Law School where he obtained a doctorate in legal philosophy in 1971, was also a career UN official. He had served in the

**Figure 3.2** Agwu Ukiwe Okali, UN Assistant Secretary-General and Registrar, International Criminal Tribunal for Rwanda (1997–2001) addressing a press conference at UN Headquarters in New York.

UN's legal affairs department in New York for five years in the late
1970s after working as a corporate staff attorney at the Connecticut
General Insurance Corporation (CIGNA), before moving to the
UN's Human Settlements Program in Nairobi. Okali thus had a
strong advantage: he was a skilled manager—he was not just a lawyer,
but had actually *managed* something and people. Like many, he knew
that the tribunal was in an early childhood crisis that it could ill
afford. He felt the eyes of Rwanda and much of the world on the
institution—with a critical skepticism that made the task even more
daunting. He arrived in Arusha to take up his post the day before
Mrs. Clinton's visit with a determination to turn the institution
around in concert with his fellow principals. In chief judge Laity
Kama, he found a partner, for both men shared a keen appreciation of
the potential political impact of the tribunal's work, and the factors
that created low expectations of an international war crimes tribunal
seeking justice in Africa.

The UN official embarked on institutional administrative and quasi-
judicial reforms, which, combined with parallel reforms by the judges in
the tribunal's judicial rules, put the institution on a much firmer and
more effective footing to render justice for Rwanda. Although the
administrative reforms were of fundamental importance, to the extent
that it facilitated the increased effectiveness of the court's main function
of justice, I will not dwell on them because they are somewhat outside
the focus of this book, which is about the politics of justice. These
administrative changes will thus be noted only briefly before turning to
the registrar's innovations that had more political implications vis-à-vis
the international court's relations with Rwanda. For Okali's priorities
were two-fold: the first was to deal with dispatch with the administrative problems—no easy task considering that, as he told *The New York
Times*, Arusha in early 1997 was not a place "where you could walk
down the street and buy computer parts"[17] (the reality there is different
today, buoyed as the small town's economy is by the massive infusion of
capital that followed the influx of hundreds of UN personnel paid in
U.S. dollars). His second priority was to correct the obvious disconnect
between the tribunal and Rwandan society, with its judicial procedures
distant and seemingly irrelevant to ordinary Rwandans. If the whole
point of "political justice" was to help Rwanda build a new, more tolerant society in which the ideology of genocide was to be banished for-
ever, what was the point of the international tribunal if, in the words of
Gerald Gahima, former Rwandan attorney general and a frequent critic
of the tribunal, "few people know about it, let alone care"?[18]

Within months of his arrival, Okali, a businesslike man with a
strong sense of professionalism, had managed to establish a new work

ethic at the tribunal. He ordered the construction of two additional high-tech courtrooms that made simultaneous trials by the tribunal's three trial chambers possible, the institution of an integrated Internet communications system, and a modern legal reference library that generated several innovative products, including the first-ever comprehensive CD-ROM of cases before an international war crimes tribunal and a quarterly bibliography of international criminal justice. These innovations were at the time well ahead of what was obtained at the Hague tribunal for war crimes in the former Yugoslavia and the International Court of Justice at The Hague. A follow-up assessment of the Arusha's tribunal's management by the UN internal inspectors concluded that all areas of the tribunal's operations had experienced substantial improvements. While this assessment was judicious and measured in its tone, to the staff on the ground in the tribunal, the transformation was akin to one between night and day. When the tribunal's judges handed down two path-breaking judgments in late 1998 (see chapter 4), the tribunal regained its confidence in full, and a certain stirring was felt in the institution's impact in Rwanda. But there was too much ground to cover here. The gaps between the tribunal and Rwanda were fundamental, structural, and physical. The impositions that Rwanda resented were really beyond the tribunal's ability to fully remedy. This was not for lack of effort. For a while, relations between the tribunal and Rwanda thawed, due in large part to Okali's efforts. But, as we shall see in chapters 5 and 6, ultimately, from Rwanda's perspective, the "temperature" at which it modulated its relations with the Arusha tribunal—"warm," "cold," or somewhere in between— were determined by its strategic interests. The personalities that were its interlocutors were relevant, but only up to a point.

When Okali took up his post at Arusha in March 1997, the Rwandan government in Kigali was largely dismissive of the institution. Rwanda's victims were running out of hope that they would see justice done for the genocide at the international level. The prosecution's work, which resulted in the subsequent arrest of important figures in the country's previous government, also contributed in no small measure to the beginning of a new era in which the Rwandan government began to recognize that the international tribunal indeed had some value.

## Bringing Victims In

Okali felt a special need to address the standing of the victims of the genocide in the Arusha tribunal's judicial process. It was clear that they felt marginalized from the process; their trauma as victims largely ignored in a process that, in its design, took little account of sociological, cultural, and psychological factors. One of Okali's first actions was to signal the importance the tribunal judicial support structure would henceforth attach to gender issues by creating and staffing a new unit for "gender issues and assistance to victims of the genocide." The unit's purpose was to complement the tribunal's judicial process by providing legal and psychological counseling and limited rehabilitation assistance to victims and survivors, mostly women.[19] The second step Okali took in this direction was to propose for adoption by the tribunal's judges a new procedural rule that would facilitate the establishment of a form of restorative justice through a victim-oriented assistance program, albeit in a limited form. The proposal was adopted and the new procedural rule, Rule 34 (ii), provides that the tribunal's victims and witnesses support unit shall "ensure that [victims and witnesses] receive relevant support, including physical and psychological rehabilitation, especially counselling in cases of rape and sexual assault." This was a precedent-setting breakthrough in war crimes justice in general,[20] but particularly good news for the thousands of Rwandan women who had been dehumanized by gang-rapes during the genocide. The way was now finally open for them to participate in the quest for justice at Arusha in a manner that spoke to their psychological needs as victims, and in a framework that made the "foreign" justice of the international tribunal somewhat adapted to be contextually relevant.

The restorative dimension of justice was subsequently carried on by the registrar's office, but in a restricted manner that focused on legal and psychological counseling. Most of the women who were witnesses at trials in Arusha and were rape victims were poor, rural folk. Virtually all had never been in a formal court of law, not to speak of an international courtroom with strange gadgets, procedures, and judges of different nationalities in intimidating red robes. To compound matters, these victims had to fly in an airplane to another country to testify, always with the stealth and undercover methods dictated by the tribunal's witness protection program in a small, densely populated country where everyone knew everyone else. It was dangerous enough if anyone in their local communities (where several *genocidaires* were still at large) noticed that they had "gone to Arusha" to testify about events that were unspeakable in their culture. Rape was a crime that no one dared utter the name of. These women were also distrustful of people of other ethnic or racial groups—not surprising in light of the events of 1994. They needed counseling. And for the many infected by the HIV/AIDS virus, who was to pay for the drugs for their treatment? This was a politically loaded issue, especially when it is considered that the international tribunal covers the complete medical expenses of the defendants on trial for the crimes of which these women were victims.[21]

In a legal and policy paper he first circulated in December 1997 and updated in June 1998, Okali laid out his conceptual argument for a victim-oriented restorative justice for Rwanda, to be undertaken not by the tribunal's judges, who in the context needed to focus on the trials, but by the office of the registrar.[22] The registrar argued a threefold legal justification for such a program. The first was that of general principles of justice in which legal philosophers had identified two main strands of justice—retributive justice, which the tribunal was already pursuing with vigor, and restitutive justice, which seeks to restore the victim to as close a state as his former position as is possible, and which he was now proposing. He argued that, within the scope allowed by its remit, the tribunal had an "inherent mandate" as a court of justice to render restitutive justice for the victims of the genocide and other violations of international humanitarian law who were involved in the tribunal's judicial process. The tribunal's registrar noted that, although the statute of the ICTR made no reference to the restitution of property and compensation, the tribunal's procedural rules made by its judges made elaborate provisions concerning these two forms of restitutive justice.[23] This meant, in Okali's view, that unless "one is prepared to maintain that these provision are unauthorized and *ultra vires* [beyond the powers of the tribunal], one must accept that the judges of the tribunal in adopting them consider the matters regulated therein to be inherent in the notion of justice and therefore *within* the mandate conferred by the tribunal as a court of justice . . ."[24]

Second, he argued that the tribunal's policy goal as stated by the Security Council in creating it, that its prosecutions would contribute to national reconciliation and the restoration and maintenance of peace, could be more effectively achieved by adding the restitutive justice program to the tribunal's retributive judicial response to the crimes in Rwanda. Third, Okali stressed the point of moral and practical necessity. At the time this debate was raging in the tribunal and the circles of persons closely familiar with its work, the tribunal's Voluntary Contributions Trust Fund, established by the UN General Assembly for voluntary contributions to supplement the tribunal's regular budget, had approximately $7 million in it, much of it unspent as of then.

Three years after the genocide, large numbers of survivors had received little or no material assistance. Requests from witnesses at the tribunal, in the post-testimony period, to the Arusha tribunal to alleviate their material plight were frequent (and of course, went unmet). This resulted in a potential backlash from victims feeling "used" as witnesses by the tribunal to establish the guilt of their erstwhile tormentors for purposes of retributive justice and then "discarded."[25] Moreover in Okali's words, "Constant comparison continues to be made in Rwanda between the desperate plight of the victims and survivors and the perceived 'luxury' under which the accused are maintained—including very costly medical treatment—at the tribunal's detention facility in Arusha—often sarcastically dubbed the "Arusha Hilton.""[26]

On these grounds, Okali staked out his policy advocacy for a limited restorative justice program to be funded from the tribunal's Trust Fund, to be implemented mostly by nongovernmental organizations (NGOs) already active in assistance programs to victims in Rwanda. The program aimed to provide financial support to these NGOs for the physical and psychological rehabilitation of victim witnesses through medial care, especially for female victims of rape, to provide victims with legal counseling about the tribunal's work, and to support small-scale revenue-generating activities that would enable them to meet the basic costs generated by their participation in the tribunal's legal processes.[27] Okali was careful to stress that the tribunal's restitutive justice program was neither a generalized economic and social assistance for the people of Rwanda nor a compensation program for the genocide.[28]

There is no question, of course, that a wider compensation program for the victims of the Rwandan genocide, administered by a separate entity other than the Arusha tribunal, would have been a helpful response to the genocide, especially as a complement to the retributive justice of the tribunal. The tribunal's judges, almost certainly inspired by the debates generated by the registrar's initiative, have recommended that such a reparation fund be created for Rwanda's victims.[29] NGOs such as the International Crisis Group[30] have supported the idea. However it has not happened. Reparations as a form of justice are a sensitive subject, whether for the victims of the Holocaust in some European countries or the Japanese–Americans who were interred during World War II (who have received compensation), or for the so far unsuccessful demand by some African and African American interests for recompense for the institution of slavery. It raises complex political, moral, and strategic questions that require enormous amounts of political will to surmount. It remains to be seen if that level of will exists—or can be generated—in the case of Rwanda. This particular example is complicated by the fact that the genocide was committed not by an outside power, but by a Rwandan government that lost a civil war in which it committed genocide, its high officials now in the dock in Arusha.

The case that reparations have the potential to help heal Rwanda's wounds appears strong. In a report to the UN Security Council in 2004, the secretary general lent his support to the idea of compensation and reparation as part of transitional justice, including in the case of Rwanda:

> No single form of reparation is likely to be satisfactory to victims. Instead, appropriately conceived combinations of reparation measures will usually be required, as a complement to the proceedings of criminal tribunals and truth commissions. Whatever mode of transitional justice is adopted and however reparations programs are conceived to accompany them, both the demands of justice and the dictates of peace require that something be done to compensate victims. Indeed, the judges of the tribunals for Yugoslavia and Rwanda have themselves recognized this and have suggested that the United Nations consider creating a special mechanism that would function alongside the tribunals.[31]

And recognizing that trials alone are not an adequate response to violations of international humanitarian law, the report of the International Commission of Inquiry on Darfur has recommended the establishment of a Compensation Commission for the atrocities committed in Sudan's western region.[32]

But despite the strength of the argument for reparations, it is clear that political considerations determine the instances in which the victims of international crimes get reparations. The political questions are: *who* should pay, *why* and *for what* are they paying, and *how much*? And there are practical difficulties that beset attempts at material reparations. "Difficult questions include who is included among the victims to be compensated, how much compensation is to be rewarded, what kinds of harm are to be covered, how harm is to be quantified, how different kinds of harm are to be compared and compensated and how compensation is to be distributed."[33] The current government of Rwanda has established a trust fund for assistance to the victims and does the best it can. But Rwanda is a poor country, relying on foreign aid for two-thirds of its budget, and the government's best effort is not good enough. If outsiders are to set up such a fund, it might be seen as admission of a *legal* responsibility to intervene to stop the genocide.

The international society is not divided on whether its response to the Rwanda genocide was a *moral* and *political* failure. Statesmen from Kofi Annan to former U.S. president Bill Clinton have expressed their regret at this failure. But would the society of states go so far as to pay reparations to Rwanda's victims *because* it failed to intervene to stop the slaughter? Such a scenario is an unlikely one. A compensatory fund could, however, be created as a purely humanitarian gesture and not couched in the language of justice. Indeed a provision that such a fund does not give rise to legal claims would almost certainly be a part of the framework for such a fund.

In the absence of such a mechanism, the Arusha tribunal is constrained to limit any initiative in the area of restorative justice within the ambit of the tribunal's mandate and objectives. As it happened, when the idea of a victim-oriented justice at the Arusha tribunal was first mooted by Okali, it was met with skepticism from some quarters, though it was of course music to the ears of Rwanda's victims. These critics had a much more restrictive view of the tribunal's mandate and objectives: the court's business was simply to prosecute the defendants in its docket and nothing more. Thus Rule 34 was a lifesaver for the concept, for it provided the legal cover and legitimacy that was necessary beyond the moral argument.

Although the program was well underway by 1999, it was not until September 2000 that it was formally launched in Rwanda.[34] The ceremony was held in the village of Taba, chosen for its symbolic significance because its former mayor Jean-Paul Akayesu had been the tribunal's very first convict two years earlier. The event also coincided with the anniversary of the Nuremberg judgment. Criticism of the restitutive justice program was quick to follow the Taba event. Akayesu's defense counsel before the tribunal, the Canadian lawyers John Philpot and Andre Tremblay, fired off an angry letter to Okali challenging the legality of the tribunal's effort at restitutive justice. The letter read in part

> [Y]our statements and press release betray the stated purpose of the tribunal to indict both sides in the conflict. You are no doubt aware that the Rwandan Patriotic Front murdered selectively in cold blood 126 Hutu civilians in the same locality, Kamonyi, Taba commune on June 28, 1994. If and when restitutive justice were to become legally part of the Tribunal Statute, would it not be appropriate to provide restitution [to] the families of Hutu victims killed in Kamonyi by the RPF or to the millions of Hutu who have suffered from the ten years of war since October 1, 1990?

We also understand from your press statements that the ICTR is participating with the Rwandan Government in the creation of a Peace Village in Taba. In addition to the stigmatising of our client while his case is before the Appeals Chamber, the term "Peace Village" is rather ironic in the Rwandan warrior state led by the RPF: ten years ago the Rwandan Patriotic Front invaded Rwanda and since October 1, 1990, there has been unending war: four years of war against Rwanda, war on the Rwandan Hutu population from 1994 to present, and two wars against Zaire and the Congo with countless millions of deaths.[35]

Not surprisingly, Akayesu's lawyers made no mention of the genocide that claimed the lives of hundreds of thousands of Rwandans—Tutsis and moderate Hutus. They highlighted instead the alleged crimes of the Rwandan Patriotic Front (RPF). Their letter is symptomatic of how the defendants on trial at Arusha—and their lawyers in some cases—see the events of 1994 through very political lenses. This overall political perspective is of course germane to the question of justice and reconciliation in Rwanda, as we shall see in later chapters.

Three days after the date of Philpot's letter, Okali responded. He avoided any discussion of Rwanda's political and military travails of the past decade, confining himself to the substantive legal issues Philpot had raised.[36] The registrar refuted Philpot's claim that Okali's comments in Taba recalling Akayesu's conviction by the trial chamber had prejudiced his appeal, noting that Akayesu's conviction was factual and a matter of record. That fact did not operate as a "gag rule" that made reference to such a conviction inappropriate. "If indeed it were" Okali wrote, "there will be many inmates of prisons throughout the world who should be, not in prison but at home, since their convictions are under appeal."

On the validity of the victim-support program, Okali stressed in his reply that Rule 34 mandated the tribunal's registrar to ensure that victims and witnesses receive relevant support. He then de-linked the program from the question of Akayesu's guilt or innocence: "There would still be victims of the events of 1994 in Rwanda—500,000 dead or whatever figure one chooses to accept—and these would still be widows and orphans needing assistance *even if all of the persons currently charged in connection with these events were to be found innocent*" (emphasis Okali's). The registrar clarified that facilitating the restitutive justice program, which in any case was to be run not by tribunal's staff but by NGOs, did not compromise the neutrality of the registry, which continued to support both the prosecution and the defense at the tribunal. "Neutrality does not mean passivity or lack of action; nor does 'impartial services' mean no services to anyone."

Moreover, he argued, the restitutive justice was extended to all victims, whatever their ethnic political affiliation or whether they were prosecution or defense witnesses.

In 1998, Okali had taken his advocacy for restorative justice to the negotiations by over 150 states on the establishment of a permanent ICC. In March of that year, he addressed the plenary meeting of the representatives of states negotiating the creation of the Court, making the case for the inclusion of restorative justice in the Court's statute and specifically proposing the establishment of a trust fund from which reparations would be paid to victims of crimes within the Court's jurisdiction.[37] These proposals met a warm reception from NGOs actively lobbying country delegations in the corridors of the meeting, and from a number of states. The Rome Statute of the ICC provides for reparations for victims through restitution, compensation, and rehabilitation,[38] and makes provision as well for the establishment of a trust fund for victims for these purposes.[39]

Some analysts have argued that reorienting criminal trials so that the victim, rather than the defendant, occupies center stage erodes due process by creating an apparent presumption of the defendant's guilt.[40] This argument is not persuasive. The logic of restorative justice—that the victim needs to be healed by the restorative process—does not have to dispense with any of the due process rights of the defendant. When we consider the context of mass crimes such as genocide and crimes against humanity, there is surely something incomplete about an international criminal justice system in which the rights of a defendant appear to be more important than those of hundreds of thousands of victims and survivors of the most heinous crimes. This, of course, has much to do with the dominance of common law principles in the framework of the Arusha tribunal. It also engages the analysis by Jose Alvarez about the mind-sets of international lawyers who sit in faraway diplomatic capitals and craft the framework of justice for societies in transition. Few of these lawyers have real knowledge about these societies—or even care to. As we will see later, the impact of international justice must be ultimately assessed with the contextual relevance of that effort as a significant measuring rod. A fair trial should not be one that recognizes just the rights of the defense while casting victim–survivor witnesses into outer darkness, there to dwell in unmitigated agony. A UN report has observed that victims "were often treated by legal systems with less dignity and compassion than perpetrators."[41]

Despite the criticisms the victim-support program received, some reflecting genuine concerns, others politically motivated, there has been no successful challenge to its legal foundation or its policy and practical relevance to the objective of the Arusha tribunal. Thus the program continues, with efforts by Okali's successor to expand its operational activities.

Another major initiative put in place by Okali during his tenure at office was that of a media outreach program to Rwanda. The physical distance between the tribunal and Rwanda made such an initiative imperative. Like the restorative justice program, it was funded out of the tribunal's trust fund. And like that initiative, it was actually begun in 1998 and launched formally in Kigali only in 2000 (in fact, the day before the launch of the victim-support program). Under the program, the tribunal established an ICTR Information Centre called *Umusanzu mu Bwiyunge* (Contribution to Reconciliation) in the Kinyarwanda language and located at the center of Kigali. The Rwandan government, as a sign of support for the international tribunal, donated the building to the international court. There a library, a video center, computers, and copies of the tribunal's judgments (including Kinyarwanda language versions) are provided for public access. The Centre has received progressively increasing patronage from Rwandans, recording more than 20,000 visitors in 2003.[42]

Other aspects of the outreach program have included radio broadcasts to Rwanda of the judgments of the tribunal by Rwandan journalists sponsored by the Arusha tribunal, and the tribunal sponsorship of survivors' groups, Rwandan judges, and parliamentarians to Arusha for visits and seminars on international humanitarian law and the work of the tribunal. The Hague tribunal has a similar program. The Arusha tribunal's outreach program was of course a vast improvement on the near-total information vacuum that hitherto existed between the tribunal and Rwanda. To that extent, it is a major accomplishment by the international tribunal. Both tribunals' outreach efforts are, however, far from reaching their full potential—in the case of Rwanda, for reasons that will be discussed when we come to the question of the tribunal's image.

Okali completed his four-year tenure as registrar of the Arusha tribunal in March 2001. Annan appointed Adama Dieng, a Senegalese human rights expert who served as secretary general of the International Commission of Jurists in Geneva and as a UN expert on human rights in Haiti. Dieng inherited an operation that had been set on a very firm footing, with the necessary systems put in place during Okali's tenure. Deploying vast contacts within the African political leadership class, Dieng has sought to expand on the theme of the tribunal's significance not just globally, but for the African region in particular.

# CHAPTER 4

# UNCHARTED WATERS: JUDGING GENOCIDE

Jean Kambanda admits that there was in Rwanda in 1994 a widespread and systematic attack against the civilian population of Tutsi, the purpose of which was to exterminate them. Jean Kambanda acknowledges that following numerous meetings of the Council of Ministers between 8 April 1994 and 17 July 1994, he as Prime Minister, instigated, aided and abetted . . . massacres and killings of civilians, in particular Tutsi and moderate Hutu.

—International Criminal Tribunal for Rwanda, judgment and sentence of Jean Kambanda

From the normative perspective of international humanitarian law—laying down the law, punishing its transgressors, and setting new standards—the Arusha tribunal's impact has been huge. The court's judges have handed down historic verdicts that have set far-reaching precedents for other international war crimes tribunals and national courts on a global scale. And for the first time in Africa, "big men" that typically held sway in their national political environments, occasionally through genocidal massacres, were held accountable by a court of law. Those verdicts themselves have much political significance as I explained in the Introduction, but of course they do not remove the other political and strategic factors that are also embedded in the framework of the international tribunal.

As is frequently the case, when faced with the prospect of accountability, the perpetrators of the genocide have sought to diminish their personal responsibility. A town mayor who had admitted to war crimes investigators who caught up with him in Zambia in 1996 that he had presided over a meeting where genocidal commands were issued now feigned amnesia in the dock; confronted with his previous testimony, he became incoherent. The head of the government that organized Rwanda's genocidal slaughter owned up to his role but later claimed in court that he was a puppet of an extremist military high command (as was argued in defense of the Japanese emperor Hirohito at the Tokyo war crimes trial). And hate media journalists accused of genocide sought to diminish responsibility by recounting how they took risks to save a number of Tutsis from massacres even as they campaigned to exterminate the group (what Nicholas Kristof has described, in an analogy with the Jewish Holocaust, in a slightly different context as "the Raoul Wallenberg of Rwanda"[1]).

While the Nuremberg trials clearly had a major impact in Germany, it is the subject of much debate whether its courtroom legacy in Arusha and the Hague has had a similar effect in the societies whose conflicts they were set up to help resolve. This is still an open question. The impact of the ad hoc tribunals on the development of international law is not in doubt. But, as will be discussed in later chapters, whether that is the main reason these courts were created (in other words, to serve the experimental intellectual urges of an international legal and diplomatic elite, rather than being configured to address the real needs of conflict-ridden societies) is an important factor in assessing the courtroom legacy of the United Nation's (UN) war crimes tribunals for Rwanda and Yugoslavia. It may be premature to measure the political impact of these tribunals, just as the internal political impact of Nuremberg in Germany has taken decades to ossify. But it can safely be said that were they to be ultimately judged successful, the price has been high, and their replication in future in the pure form in which they now exist at The Hague and in Arusha is extremely unlikely.[2]

## THE MAYOR

Fifty years after the Genocide Convention, the crime that previously had no name was punished for the first time in an international court sitting in Arusha. *Prosecutor v Jean-Paul Akayesu* was the tribunal's first trial. Akayesu was formerly mayor of the Rwandan town of Taba. He had fled to Zambia after the genocide, and was arrested there in 1996 and transferred to the international tribunal's detention center in Arusha. The defendant was not one of the numerous "big fish" in the tribunal's custody. Rather he was part of what the American journalist Bill Berkeley has inimitably characterized as "the indispensable middle management" of the genocide.[3] Ranged against Akayesu during the 18-month trial was prosecuting counsel Pierre-Richard Prosper, who examined him and meticulously presented evidence of the mayor's crimes. Prosper was later to become the U.S. ambassador at large for War Crimes Issues. On September 2, 1998, with about 100 international and local journalists present in the courtroom, the International Criminal Tribunal for Rwanda (ICTR) delivered the first-ever judgment for the crime of genocide by an international court (figure 4.1). Kofi Annan, the UN secretary general, issued a statement hailing the tribunal's historic judgment. Around the world, the media and human rights campaigners reported that a landmark judgment had taken place.

**Figure 4.1** Jean Paul Akayesu, the first person to be convicted for genocide by an international war crimes tribunal.

**Figure 4.2**   Judge Laity Kama presiding over a trial at Arusha.

The tribunal, presided over by the late Senegalese judge Laity Kama (figure 4.2), had to address the question whether the widespread and horrendous massacres that took place in Rwanda in 1994 constituted genocide. This was no mere academic exercise, but rather one with important implications in contemporary international affairs. For "genocide" is an emotive, loaded word, a label frequently and loosely attached to widespread killings. The word, a combination of the Greek derivative *geno*, which means "race" or tribe, with the Latin derivative *cide*, from *caedere* ("killing"), was coined by the Polish international legal scholar Raphael Lemkin in the 1940s in his influential book *Axis Rule in Occupied Europe*.[4] Lemkin's Jewish family had perished at the hands of Hitler's forces during the German occupation of Poland. Inspired by his personal tragedy, Lemkin coined this word out of a desire to mark Hitler's crimes as being of an order totally different from, say, "barbarism" and "vandalism"—in effect, beyond the pale.[5]

The Arusha tribunal's statute[6] provides a definition of genocide that replicates that in the Convention on the Prevention and Punishment of Genocide (Genocide Convention), adopted by the UN General Assembly on December 9, 1948. According to Article 2(2) of the statute, "Genocide means any of the following acts committed with intent to destroy, in whole or in part, a national, ethnical, racial or religious group as such: (a) Killing members of the group; (b) Causing serious bodily or mental harm to members of the group; (c) Deliberately inflicting on the group conditions of life calculated to bring about its physical destruction in whole or in part; (d) Imposing measures intended to prevent births within the group; (e) Forcibly transferring children of the group to another group."

The tribunal found that, contrary to popular belief, the crime of genocide does not require the actual extermination of a whole group, but is committed once any of the acts mentioned above are done with the intent to wholly or partially destroy the group.[7] It also identified the special intent to destroy groups for who they are, that makes the crime of genocide so unique.[8] So although genocide often involves mass slaughters of large numbers of victims, the determining factor of whether it has occurred is not how many were killed, or whether *all* the intended victims were actually killed, but the intention behind the slaughter.

*Akayesu* interpreted for the first time how the definition of the crime of genocide in the Genocide Convention should be applied to a practical situation. The tribunal found Akayesu, former mayor of the Rwandan town of Taba, guilty on nine counts of genocide and crimes against humanity. He was absolved of six counts of war crimes— violations of Article 3 common to the Geneva Conventions—largely because a strong enough connection between his duties as a civilian mayor and the then ongoing civil war was not established. Akayesu was subsequently sentenced to life imprisonment on October 2, 2000, and his appeal against conviction and sentence was dismissed by the tribunal's Appeals Chamber on June 1, 2001.

The tribunal reasoned that since the special intent to commit genocide was to be found in the intent to wholly or partially destroy a national, ethnical, racial, or religious group, the precise meaning of these social categories needed to be defined. Relying on the preparatory work of the Genocide Convention, the judges of the Arusha tribunal found that a common criterion in these four groups protected by the Convention was that of sociological destiny: the members of the group belong to it automatically, by birth, in a continuous and in often "irremediable" manner.[9]

Based on the decision rendered by the International Court of Justice in the *Nottebohm* case, the *cause celebre* on questions of citizenship and nationality, the Arusha tribunal ruled that: A national group is defined as a collection of people who are perceived to share a legal bond based on common citizenship, coupled with reciprocity of rights and duties; an ethnic group is generally defined as a group whose members share a common language or culture; the conventional definition of racial group is based on the hereditary physical traits often identified with geographical region, irrespective of linguistic, cultural, national or religious factors; and the religious group is one whose members share the same religion, denomination or mode of worship.[10]

The application of these seemingly abstract legal definitions to the situation in Rwanda was complicated by the fact that the Tutsi population did not fit neatly into any of these definitions. They did not have a language or culture that was any different from the rest of the Rwandan population. Both Tutsis and Hutus spoke Kinyarwanda. Generations of intermarriage had in many cases wiped out any hereditary physical traits that formerly distinguished Tutsi from Hutu, as had a system of classification based on ownership of cattle. Thus the absurd conclusion that could have been drawn from this situation is that the Tutsi are not a protected group under the Genocide Convention, and so genocide, as legally defined by the Convention and the ICTR Statute, had not occurred in Rwanda.[11]

Adopting innovative legal reasoning, the judges of the international tribunal asked themselves "whether it would be impossible to punish the physical destruction of a group as such under the Genocide Convention, if the group in question, although stable and membership is by birth, does not meet the definition of any one of the four groups expressly protected by the Genocide Convention." The judges answered in the negative. In their view, it was important to respect the intention of the drafters of the Genocide Convention, which was clearly to ensure the protection of any stable and permanent group.[12]

The tribunal ruled that the Tutsi were a stable and permanent group for the purpose of the Genocide Convention, relying for this conclusion on the clear identification of the Tutsi as an "ethnic" group in official classifications of Rwandan society. This identification was maintained by, among other means, ethnic classifications of all Rwandans in their national identity cards before 1994. This addition of stable and permanent groups, whose membership is largely determined by birth, to the rubric of the four protected groups in the Genocide Convention will influence future cases of genocide.[13] There are clear parallels with the massacres of black Africans in the Darfur region in Sudan in 2004: the perpetrators and the victims were both Muslims. If the killings are to be confirmed as genocide, it will be necessary to answer the question: are the Muslim black Africans a stable, permanent and identifiable group in the context of Sudan? A judicial response to the atrocities in Darfur will necessarily be guided by the distinctions developed in *Akayesu*.

The *Akayesu* verdict has set precedents for the Hague tribunal judging the crimes committed in the former Yugoslavia, and the International Criminal Court. The Hague tribunal handed down its very first conviction for the crime of genocide on August 2, 2001 in the case of Radislav Kirstic, the military commander of Bosnian Serb forces in Srebrenica, known as "the Butcher of Srebrenica." That tribunal has handled mostly cases of war crimes (grave breaches of the Geneva Conventions of 1949 and violations of the laws or customs of war) and crimes against humanity, and there had been considerable debate over whether the events in the former Yugoslavia constituted genocide or were simply extreme cases of "ethnic cleansing"—a phrase that Samantha Power has called "a euphemistic halfway house between crimes against humanity and genocide."[14] Applying the relevant tests to the *Kirstic* case to determine whether or not genocide had taken place, the Hague tribunal in its judgment concluded that "by deciding to kill all men of fighting age, a decision was taken to make it impossible for the Muslim people of Srebrenica to survive. Stated otherwise, what was ethnic cleansing became genocide."[15]

The Akayesu case similarly blazed a trail in international humanitarian law in the area of sexual crimes against women. As in most armed conflicts, civil or international, many women, in this case those of Tutsi origin, were systematically raped during the Rwandan genocide. Rape, in and of itself a crime in virtually all national jurisdictions, comes alive in the jurisprudence of the Arusha tribunal as an intrinsic aspect of genocide and crimes against humanity.[16]

Akayesu was not initially indicted for sexual crimes. But the testimony of two female witnesses in the course of the trial contained graphic references to sexual violence against Tutsi women during the genocide—often accompanied by degrading language against the victims. In *Akayesu*, witness testimony established that some of these rapes had occurred in the location of the mayor's office (the *Bureau Communale*). Akayesu urged on his subordinates in their ravishing sprees, reportedly commenting: "Now don't ask me what a Tutsi woman tastes like." These testimonies led Louise Arbour, the tribunal's chief prosecutor at the time, to investigate the matter further. Arbour amended the indictment during the trial, bringing additional charges of rape as a crime against humanity and rape as a war crime against Akayesu. Various nongovernmental organizations had also been pressing for greater attention to sexual crimes in prosecutions at the Arusha tribunal, including by way of an *amicus curiae* ("friend of the court") brief.[17]

In its verdict, the tribunal found Akayesu guilty of crimes against humanity (rape) as charged in one of the fifteen counts of the indictment. This verdict revolutionized the case law on sexual violence crimes in international humanitarian law in three ways. First the *Akayesu* judgment was the first time an individual had been convicted of rape as a specific crime against humanity by an international tribunal. The importance of this advance is brought into sharper perspective by the fact that there was no mention of rape in the Nuremberg Charter. Reference was made to rape in the judgment of the International Military Tribunal for the Far East because evidence was presented of atrocities committed upon women in Nanking, the Philippines, and other locations, but rape and sexual violence were not charged as specific crimes. Rather they were lumped together as Crimes against Humanity—Inhumane Treatment. In the apt words of former U.S. ambassador at large for War Crimes Issues David Scheffer, "this situation resulted in a blur. Rape was lost in the barbarous mass of the overall crimes. It became a passing reference in a tale of horror. In the end, no one knew whether rape in time of conflict could be prosecuted as a separate, substantive crime standing on its own merits in international law . . . but today, we find ourselves in an enormously stronger position to investigate, document and prosecute rape and other forms of sexual violence . . . And it all started quietly within the International Criminal Tribunal for Rwanda."[18]

Second *Akayesu* provided for the first time in legal history a definition of rape as a crime under international law. The tribunal stated:

> The Chamber must define rape, as there is no commonly accepted definition of this term in international law. While rape has been defined in certain national jurisdictions as non-consensual intercourse, variations on the act of rape may include acts which involve the insertion of objects and/or the use of bodily orifices not considered to be intrinsically sexual. The Chamber considers that rape is a form of aggression and that the central elements of the crime of rape cannot be captured in a mechanical description of objects or body parts . . . The Chamber defines rape as a physical invasion of a sexual nature, committed on a person under circumstances which are coercive. Sexual violence, which includes rape, is considered to be any act of a sexual nature which is committed on a person under circumstances which are coercive.[19]

This definition of rape has been cited in subsequent cases in the Arusha tribunal and the Hague in the latter tribunal's judgments in the *Furundzija*,[20] *Celebici*,[21] and *Kunarac*[22] cases. Some observers have criticized it as too sweeping a definition, a case of judicial activism that has brought the goals of the feminist movement under the umbrella of international legal protection. If that is so, it would be no different from the inclusion of the rights of other groups under the tent of international law. In any event, what *Akayesu* did was to demonstrate how international law has taken a larger view of what constitutes criminal mass atrocity than domestic law.

The third and perhaps most important manner in which the sexual violence dimension of *Akayesu* advanced international humanitarian law was by ruling that rape was an act of genocide and thus a genocidal crime. As noted earlier, the tribunal found that rape was systematically used as a weapon in the campaign to destroy Tutsi women. They were violated precisely because they were of Tutsi ethnicity. Many were killed in the process of these rapes, the clear intent of which was to kill or inflict mental or bodily harm as part of the process of destroying an ethnic group in whole or in part.

Rape was not specifically charged as an act of genocide in the indictment against Akayesu. Yet based on the overwhelming evidence in that case, the judges at Arusha followed the proof of facts to their logical, ultimate conclusion in their decision: rape as genocide. The ICTR, in ruling that rape was genocide, did just what the International Military Tribunal at Nuremberg (IMT) did when it criminalized aggressive war without any pre-existing law: it expanded international law to right wrongs in a historical and moral context.

But women were not exclusively victims in the Rwandan genocide. Some are alleged perpetrators too. The ICTR became not only the first international criminal tribunal to indict a woman, but also the first to charge one with rape. In *Prosecutor v Pauline Nyiramasuhuko and Arsene Shalom Ntahobali*,[23] the first accused, Rwanda's Minister of Women and Family Affairs in 1994, is on trial for genocide and crimes against humanity (including rape) under the principle of superior responsibility: she stands accused by the prosecution of having ordered and presided over rapes by members of killer squads under her command, including her son, the second accused.[24]

These developments in the trials before the Arusha tribunal demonstrate its achievement in providing a road map for the prosecution and adjudication of sexual crimes in international humanitarian law. In doing so, the tribunal raised sexual crimes against women from the status of mere offences against honor[25] and that of a spoil of war to a substantive place in the code of conduct in war. Has it, however, deterred rapes in war? The systematic rapes of African women in

Darfur point to a negative answer. But the *Akayesu* decision at the Arusha tribunal— and others like it at the Hague tribunal—have established a framework for meeting the challenge of this ageless crime.

## THE PRIME MINISTER

From the standpoint of legalism, a major aim of the Arusha and the Hague tribunals was to bring to justice the political and military leaders who planned, instigated, and commanded the genocide, crimes against humanity, and war crimes in Rwanda and the Balkans. As a matter of policy, the prosecution organ of the Arusha tribunal had a track record of focusing its investigative and prosecution energies mostly on such high-ranking accused persons and suspects—the big fish. Reflecting the imperatives of political justice, these individuals were carefully chosen and cut across various spectrums of Rwandan society's erstwhile leadership: senior military commanders and politicians, senior civilian administrators, the clergy, and senior media practitioners accused of inciting and sustaining the mass killings in Rwanda with hate propaganda.[26] Neither the Nuremberg trials nor those at The Hague for war crimes in the Balkans has matched this array and diversity of defendants at the Arusha tribunal.

In this pantheon of senior figures tried by the Arusha court, the most senior individual has been Mr. Jean Kambanda (figure 4.3), prime minister of Rwanda and head of its interim government from April 8, 1994 until he fled the country in mid-July 1994—the three months during which the genocide occurred. Kambanda, now 50, an economist and former banker who became an extremist Hutu politician, was appointed head of government by a clique of extremist military officers who took temporary charge in Rwanda following the death of its president Juvénal Habyarimana in a plane crash on April 6, 1994, when the genocide commenced. As the killings erupted, Kambanda traveled around the country promoting the massacres. He made incendiary speeches that amplified the slaughter, distributed weapons to the militias that carried out most of the massacres, and inspected the "work" done by the foot soldiers of the genocidal killing machine. In one of his famous hate speeches, he upbraided Hutus who sat on the sidelines during the killings: "You refuse to give your blood to your country and the dogs drink it for nothing."

Kambanda was arrested by the Kenyan authorities in July 1997 on the basis of a formal request submitted by the tribunal's chief prosecutor. The former premier was then charged with genocide, conspiracy

Figure 4.3   Former Rwandan Prime Minister Jean Kambanda at his sentencing for genocide.

to commit genocide, inciting genocide, complicity in genocide, and crimes against humanity. The indictment charged that as prime minister, Mr. Kambanda exercised *de jure* and *de facto* authority and control over the members of his government, senior civil servants including *prefets* (regional governors) and senior officers in the military; and that he presided over meetings of the Council of Ministers, attended by Pauline Nyiramasuhuko, Eliezer Niyitegeka, and Andre Ntagerura[27] among others, in which the massacres of the civilian population were discussed. He was also accused of inciting massacres of Tutsi and moderate Hutu at public meetings and through the media.

In a dramatic development, Kambanda had earlier pleaded guilty to the six counts in his indictment at his initial appearance before the tribunal on May 1, 1998. He had also signed a plea agreement negotiated with the tribunal's deputy chief prosecutor Bernard Muna by his court-appointed defense counsel, Michael Oliver Ingliss. Technically speaking, the "plea agreement" is not identical to a plea bargain in the American or other legal systems: the prosecutor could not promise a lighter sentence in return for Kambanda's cooperation, as sentencing was the sole province of the tribunal's judges and could not be negotiated. Although he provided in-depth information to the prosecution on the planning and execution of the genocide, and promised to testify in future cases, he later reneged on these promises for motley political and personal reasons including, no doubt, a sharp sense of disappointment at the severity of the sentence he ultimately received despite having cooperated with the tribunal.

Kambanda agreed in the plea agreement that he was pleading guilty because he was in fact guilty, and acknowledged full responsibility for the crimes with which he was charged.[28] He explained in the third person the motivation for his guilty plea: "the profound desire to tell the truth . . . his desire to contribute to the process of national reconciliation in Rwanda," and his consideration that his confession would contribute to the restoration and maintenance of peace in Rwanda.[29]

On September 4, 1998, just two days after its verdict in *Akayesu*, the tribunal convicted Kambanda on all counts in the indictment against him and sentenced the former prime minister to life imprisonment for his crimes. The ICTR thus became the first international tribunal in history to punish a head of government for genocide, trumping sovereign immunity.[30]

The judges of the international tribunal made clear in the judgment and sentence that despite the ordinarily mitigating factor of a guilty plea, they considered the combination of the gravity of the offence and Mr. Kambanda's high position of authority to be overridingly aggravating factors:

> The heinous nature of the crime of genocide and its absolute prohibition makes its commission inherently aggravating . . . The crimes were committed during the time when Jean Kambanda was Prime Minister and he and his Government was responsible for the maintenance of peace and security. Jean Kambanda abused his authority and the trust of the civilian population. He personally participated in the genocide by distributing arms, making incendiary speeches and presiding over cabinet and other meetings where the massacres were planned and discussed. He failed to take necessary and reasonable measures to prevent his subordinates from committing crimes against the population.[31]

Jean Kambanda's subsequent appeal against his judgment and sentence, in which he requested for a trial or, in the alternative, a reduction of his sentence, was unanimously rejected and his sentence confirmed by the tribunal's appellate chamber on October 19, 2000.[32] He is currently serving his prison sentence in a high-security jail in the West African country of Mali.

*Kambanda* had tremendous political and other significance.[33] It was the first confession by an individual for the crime of genocide, 50 years after the Genocide Convention. It confirmed that the criminal enterprise that was Rwanda's genocide was a state-sponsored plan aimed at wiping out the country's ethnic minority.[34] In so doing, it shattered a budding revisionist movement that sought to portray the slaughter of nearly one million victims as merely collateral damage from the civil war. The genocide, then, was not just a crime of hate; it was a crime of state as well. And *Kambanda* was to become a precedent cited by human rights groups in the 1998 case in which the United Kingdom's House of Lords ruled that Gen. Augusto Pinochet, former head of state of Chile, was not immune from prosecution for international crimes such as crimes against humanity, torture, and hostage-taking, overruling a lower court.[35] As the first head of government to be convicted for genocide, the Kambanda verdict set the stage for a legal progression to the 1999 indictment of Slobodan Milosevic at the Hague tribunal.

## THE JOURNALISTS

The role of the media in every society is a unique and powerful one. It does not matter whether the society in question is an open or closed one, a democracy or a dictatorship. Rwanda was no different. It is not overstating the case to say that without the progressive mass indoctrination of hate by extremist media in Rwanda between 1990 and 1994, the proportion, ferocity, and efficacy of the mass slaughter of minority Tutsi in 1994 would have been far less so. The civil war provided a perfect cover for an appeal to misbegotten sectional patriotism, and the media, in the form of the *Radio Television Libre des Milles Collines* (RTLM) and the *Kangura* ("Awake!") newspaper, became the sprinklers that watered the soil for the genocide.

In the first trial of media executives since that of Julius Streicher at Nuremberg, the ICTR became the first contemporary international tribunal to prosecute media hatemongers. The case was aptly named the "media trial." More formally, it was *Prosecutor v Ferdinand Nahimana, Jean-Bosco Barayagwiza, and Hassan Ngeze*.[36]

The RTLM was established in 1993 as a privately owned radio station in which the then Rwandan president Habyarimana was the largest shareholder. It was created in order to get around the limitations faced by the state-owned Radio Rwanda—which, though a political mouthpiece as well, could not promote a genocidal agenda that would be directly traceable to the government at a time it was negotiating with opposition political and military forces. RTLM, then, was the journalistic equivalent of a private army.

Ferdinand Nahimana and Jean-Bosco Barayagwiza were key share-holders of RTLM, while Hassan Ngeze was the founder and editor-in-chief of *Kangura*. All three were political and ethnic extremists who abhorred Tutsis and belonged to racist Hutu political parties. Nahimana, 54, was a professor of history and dean of the Faculty of Letters at the National University of Rwanda. Prior to founding the RTLM and becoming a member of its "steering committee" (board of directors), he was director of the Rwandan Office of Information, which included Radio Rwanda. Nahimana was the moving spirit behind the creation of RTLM and its principal ideologue.

Barayagwiza, 54, a slight, mild-looking man with horn-rimmed glasses and a scholarly air, was also a member of the steering commit-tee of RTLM. A career diplomat educated in international law at the State University of Kiev in Ukraine, he joined the Rwandan Ministry of Foreign Affairs in 1977 and rose to become its director of political affairs. Around 1990, he added partisan politics to his career dossier. He founded the Committee for the Defence of the Republic (CDR), the most virulently extremist party in the country at the time, one which officially excluded Tutsis from membership. Incongruously he was also the author of a book on human rights and, in one of the para-doxes of state sovereignty, had been seconded by the then Rwandan government to the senior position of director of the cabinet to the secretary general of the then Organization of African Unity in the Ethiopian capital of Addis Ababa (dissolved in 2002 and succeeded by the African Union, and currently headed by Alpha Konare, former president of Mali).

Hassan Ngeze, 47, was a journalist by training. He established *Kangura* in 1990. A quixotic, unstable personality with a flair and bombast akin to that of the Nazi Herman Goering at the Nuremberg trial, Ngeze had attempted suicide while in pretrial detention at Arusha. True to type, he also managed to operate an external website—against the tribunal's detention rules—on which he lam-pooned the tribunal and ran regular commentary on his trial.[37] The three defendants were charged with in separate indictments but were tried jointly in order to establish their common conspiracy. They were charged on counts of genocide, conspiracy to commit genocide, and crimes against humanity (persecution and extermination). Nahimana and Barayagwiza also faced charged of crime against humanity of murder.

In the run-up to the genocide and during the massacres, RTLM broadcasts explicitly urged the extermination of Tutsis. The names of Tutsi individuals and their families, as well as Hutu opponents of the

Habyarimana regime were broadcast on the radio, a signal for them to be killed by extremist Hutu militias. In an RTLM broadcast on April 25, 1994, for example, Nahimana told his listeners that "the war of media, words, newspapers and radio stations" was a complement to bullets in resisting the Tutsi enemy.[38] Another broadcast, by RTLM journalist Kantano Habimana, urged:

> They should stand up so that we kill the *inkotanyi* [a derogatory name for Tutsis] and exterminate them . . . the reason we will exterminate them is that they belong to one ethnic group. Look at the person's height and his physical appearance. Just look at his small nose and then break it.[39]

In testimony during the trial, one witness described the effect of RTLM broadcasts as being "to spread petrol throughout the country little by little, so that one day it would be able to set fire to the whole country."[40]

Ngeze, for his part, had earlier published the "Hutu Ten Commandments" in *Kangura* in December 1990. He warned his fellow Hutu to beware Tutsi women whom he described as spies for Tutsi soldiers, and branded a "traitor" any Hutu who married a Tutsi woman or kept one as a mistress. Other commandments forbade Hutus to enter into business partnerships with Tutsis, and urged Hutus to be "firm and vigilant towards their common Tutsi enemy."[41]

The ICTR judges recalled the *Streicher* case at Nuremberg, in which Streicher's newspaper *Der Stümer* was found to have "poisoned" the minds of thousands of Germans and fueled their support for the Nazi Party's policy of persecution and extermination of Jews. In that case, evidence was presented of numerous articles penned by Streicher or published by his newspaper, in which he called for the extermination of Jews. In one such article, Streicher wrote: "If the danger of the reproduction of that curse of God in the Jewish blood is to finally come to an end, then there is one way—the extermination of the people whose father is the devil."[42]

John Floyd, Ngeze's American defense counsel, argued that *Kangura*'s anti-Tutsi tirades were protected speech. He proposed that U.S. law, known for its strong protection of free speech, should be adopted as a standard by the international tribunal. The tribunal dismissed Floyd's argument. International law was its point of reference—national laws on freedom of expression varied widely while international standards against discrimination were well codified. Moreover, the judges noted, even U.S. domestic law recognized incitement to violence, threats, and certain other expressions as being beyond the boundaries of protected free speech.[43] "Freedom of expression and freedom from discrimination are not incompatible principles of law," the tribunal ruled. "Hate speech is not protected speech under international law."[44] Establishing an important linkage in Rwanda's crimes of hate, the judges also noted that the portrayal of Tutsi women as *femme fatales* and agents of enemy forces by *Kangura* and RTLM set the stage for the widespread sexual attacks on them, which formed an intrinsic aspect of the genocide.[45]

The ICTR convicted Nahimana, Barayagwiza, and Ngeze on the counts of conspiracy to commit genocide, genocide, incitement to genocide, and crimes against humanity (persecution and extermination). All three were found not guilty of the murder charge of crimes against humanity, with which they had been also charged. Nahimana and Ngeze were sentenced to life in prison, and Barayagwiza to 35 years in prison. The judges had pointed words for the convicts on judgment day, which reflected the power of the media, power they had abused: "The power of the media to create and destroy fundamental human values comes with great responsibility. Those who control such media are accountable for its consequences . . . Without a firearm, machete or any physical weapon, you caused the deaths of thousands of innocent civilians."[46]

This verdict has important consequences for the balance between free speech and hate speech. There has been no genocide in modern history, from the Holocaust to Bosnia and to Rwanda, where the massacres have not been preceded or accompanied by the constant denigration of the victim as "the other." It is largely such propaganda that makes large scale massacres justifiable in the minds of the perpetrators. The historic ruling also has implications for the struggle for press freedom, as it could be deliberately distorted by dictatorships seeking to quash press freedom in the many countries around the world where "insulting the president" is a journalistic offense. As the *New York Times* put it in an editorial on the Arusha tribunal's judgment: "These verdicts pose no threat to journalistic free speech, as defense lawyers tried to argue. RTLM was not offering drive-time political chatter—it was acting as a radio dispatcher of murder, knowingly helping squads of killers locate their victims . . . Ngeze, Nahimana and Barayagwiza were not challenging government propaganda, exposing corruption or expanding political debate. They were organizing the physical extermination of a people."[47]

## COUNSEL FOR THE DEFENSE

There is a widespread belief that the Arusha tribunal was created to serve as an automatic conveyor belt to dispatch its defendants to lifetimes in jail. But throughout its 10-year history, the tribunal has ensured fair trials for the erstwhile powerful men in the dock—perhaps, some observers believe, well in excess of what is fair for the defense without becoming unfair to the other interests of justice. But there are both political and legal dimensions to the question of what exactly a fair trial is.

The first of these is that of the wording of the tribunal's statute. The international tribunal, according to its statute, was established "to *prosecute* the persons responsible for the genocide and other serious violations of international humanitarian law" in Rwanda and neighboring countries in 1994 (emphasis added). Is the use of the word "prosecute" rather than, say, the more neutral "adjudicate" responsibility for the crimes, or "bring to justice" the perpetrators, indicative of a tilt in favor of the prosecution arm of the tribunal? Where then is the "equality of arms" between the prosecution and the defense that is the hallmark of a fair trial?

Yes, say the defendants at Arusha, their lawyers, and their sympathizers to the first question. "It doesn't exist," they answer to the second. Let us briefly dispose of the first question. To say that creating an international tribunal to prosecute the 1994 genocide is an indication of bias, is to deny some important realities. To begin with, it is an incontestable fact that the ultimate crime was committed in Rwanda in 1994. The genocide was not collateral damage in the civil war. It was calculated, cold-blooded mass murder of Tutsis because they were Tutsis, and of those Hutus who were tolerant of the idea of an integrated society where the two groups could coexist. The verdicts discussed earlier in this chapter have established this historical fact. *Kambanda* proved that genocide was government policy. A revisionist movement that sought to deny the genocide, much like denials of the Jewish holocaust, was active in the first few years after 1994, and appeared to have strong support in the Canadian region of French-speaking Quebec.[48] It was from that geographical axis that several defense lawyers for the accused Rwandan Hutu extremists on trial at the ICTR were to make their way to Arusha in the early years of the tribunal to mount something of a political last stand using the forum of a court of law.

Second these crimes were committed by persons, not phantoms. To say, then, that these persons were to be prosecuted by an international court set up precisely for that purpose is not inconsistent with a fair trial. It is, in fact, a statement of the obvious, for if a single murder—or serial murders—is expected to invoke the full weight of the law, why then would the planners and directors of the state-sanctioned murder of a million people, virtually all innocent civilians, go scot-free? One consideration to bear in mind, of course, is that Rwanda is a country in which the rule of law practically did not exist before the genocide. It was a despotic one-party state in which for many years the Minister of Interior (in charge of internal security) was also the Minister of Justice—meaning that there was no real separation of powers between the executive and the judiciary and those who often meted out massive human rights abuses in the name of the state were the very same persons who were supposed to "judge" such violations. Thus the genocide was only the culmination of a deeply entrenched culture of impunity super-imposed on a culture of order. Aloys Ntabakuze, a codefendant with Theoneste Bagosora in the "military trial," is alleged to have assured extremist Hutu soldiers and militias to massacre Tutsis as he dispatched them on mass murder assignments: "No one will prosecute you."

Third, all defendants at the Arusha tribunal are presumed innocent unless and until proved guilty. The individual guilt of a defendant must be established beyond reasonable doubt—a high burden of proof for the prosecution, and one it is not always able to discharge. Three defendants—two of them former high-ranking officials[49]— have been acquitted at the tribunal after a full trial, to the dismay and irritation of the Rwandan authorities and victims groups. In one case, the then chief prosecutor Carla Del Ponte withdrew the indictment against Leonidas Rusatira, a former Rwandan army colonel, because the evidence was found, on further scrutiny, to be weak. Anyone found guilty by the tribunal has thus been convicted on the basis of solid proof of their culpability. Moreover four persons, including Kambanda, have confessed their crimes through guilty pleas.

At first glance, it might appear to present a perception of unfairness that the office of the prosecutor is one of the three organs of the international tribunal but the defense is not. Not being part of the tribunal's official structure was an understandable and deliberate omission given that the defense would have otherwise had to become tribunal officials—in effect, civil servants. This might have posed significant problems of its own for perceptions of the independence of the defense. As it is, the defense is on the outside looking in. The upshot of all this is that the defendants in one of the tribunal's early trials, *Prosecutor v Clément Kayishema and Obed Ruzindana*, argued that there was no equality of arms as between the prosecution and the defense, citing the relatively vast human and other resources available to the former. Not so, the tribunal's judges ruled. Equality of arms did not mean equality of material resources, but equality of opportunity for both parties to make their case before the court.[50]

Against this backdrop, the Arusha tribunal has consistently ensured a credible defense for its defendants, conscious that the absence of a robust defense for persons accused of genocide and other grave crimes would leave the tribunal a kangaroo court in history's judgment. The purpose has been precisely to ensure equality of arms. While the accused may engage a defense lawyer at his own expense, the Arusha tribunal, like that at The Hague, has a comprehensive legal aid program by which it assigns defense counsel to "indigent" defendants and bears the costs of that defense. This program is administered by the office of the tribunal's registrar under the tribunal's rules of procedure.[51] All defendants at the tribunal have claimed indigent status. The tribunal lacks the financial tracking expertise that would enable it to verify these claims more credibly, a process that would involve detailed investigations of money trails in numerous countries.[52] Small surprise, then, that the legal aid program eats up a significant chunk of the tribunal's budget—the total budget for defense counsel at Arusha for the financial years 2002–2003 was $22 million, with the tribunal paying for the more than 80 defense counsels involved in the trials.[53] In my view, this expense is not just financial, but also the *political* cost of a fair trial.

This is also one of the most controversial and problematic areas of the process of judging genocide at the Arusha tribunal. These problems have arisen because in some cases the defendants and their counsel are brought together more by shared political persuasions relating to the genocide, the Hutu–Tutsi divide, Rwandan politics in general, and personal considerations than by truly professional ones.

But the greatest problems in this area in the tribunal's early years arose from orchestrated attempts by some defendants, their lawyers, and political sympathizers to manipulate the legal aid regime of the tribunal for subjective interests, including the obvious purpose of delaying trials. The bone of contention in many cases has been whether a defendant who cannot pay for his legal defense but has a right to have counsel assigned to him or her, has an additional right to choose or impose particular counsel at the tribunal's expense.

*Akayesu* was the main case where this matter played out in 1998, leading to much controversy in the media. The tribunal's then registrar Agwu Okali was portrayed by the defendants and their supporters as biased against the defendant. The portrayal was one of a weak defendant on trial for genocide at the mercy of a powerful international tribunal that was prosecuting the Hutus who had lost the war and would not even allow Akayesu the "basic" right to choose who would defend him. In reality, however, Akayesu had made five requests for changes of his defense lawyers since he was arrested in Zambia and transferred to the tribunal in 1995, based on a "lack of confidence" in them. All these requests were honored by the registrar.[54] His frequent changes of defense lawyers cost the tribunal over $500,000 in legal aid fees.[55] When Akayesu asked for yet another change of lawyer, the registrar declined to assign him new counsel of his choice. Akayesu made the question of lack of his choice of counsel a main ground of his appeal. In its verdict on Akayesu's appeal, the tribunal's appellate chamber ruled that the right to free legal defense for an indigent defendant does not confer a right to counsel of such a defendant's choosing.[56] The latter right, the appellate judges ruled, "is guaranteed only for an accused who can bear the financial burden of retaining counsel." The judges recalled that while the tribunal's practice was for the registrar to choose a lawyer from a list of available counsel who meet the tribunal's criteria, he is not necessarily bound by the wishes of an indigent defendant. "Indeed," the tribunal ruled, "[the registrar] has wide discretion, which he exercises in the interest of justice."[57]

The legal finality of the appeals judges' ruling came more than two years after Akayesu and several other detainees had gone on a hunger strike over their "right" to choose whatever counsel they liked, changing their lawyers at whim—and have the tribunal pay the bill because they were indigent defendants. The hunger strike is a favorite political tool of detainees on trial at the Arusha tribunal. On October 30, 1998, Akayesu had ended his one-week hunger strike with a letter to the tribunal's registrar affirming that he would utilize "the established procedures" of the tribunal to pursue his request for a different lawyer. Political and media controversy also emerged in the wake of a decision by Okali to freeze the assignment of French and Canadian lawyers as defense counsel at the Arusha tribunal for one year. The controversy was fueled by the defendants' allegations that their rights had been abridged by the registrar's decision. The decision was in fact inspired by a need to break the back of the negative impact some of these lawyers were exerting over the judicial process through tactics such as "frivolous motions" that delayed the trials on flimsy grounds. A subsequent review by an expert group to review the Arusha and Hague tribunals appointed by Kofi Annan found these tactics to be a major stumbling block to the efficiency of both tribunals and recommended corrective actions.

The ruling by the appellate panel of the Arusha tribunal vindicated the registrar's position that an indigent defendant has a right to be assigned counsel by an international tribunal, but no right to select the counsel to be assigned to him. That is the law of the tribunal. But the political struggles had already taken place in the media, in the detention facility of the tribunal, and in the capitals of Europe and North America. And, in practice and reality, the defendants get the lawyers they want assigned to them most of the time.

The Arusha tribunal also established important precedent in situations, such as the Milosevic trial at the Hague tribunal, where an accused person declines to be represented by counsel. At The Hague, Mr. Milosevic declined to formally appoint a lawyer or accept the assignment of one by the tribunal to represent his interests. The tribunal initially appointed three lawyers as "friends of the court" to assist the tribunal in protecting Milosevic's interests, but not to work with the defendant directly. After several months of legal arm-wrestling between Milosevic and the tribunal, in which a subsequent decision by trial judges to appoint a defense counsel for him in the interests of justice was affirmed by the tribunal's appeals court, Milosevic is in practice back to defending himself with bombast and political arguments.[58]

Clearly Milosevic, who sees the tribunal as "a political tool financed by NATO to punish him" and has insulted the tribunal as "a joint criminal enterprise," has stared down the Hague tribunal by watering down the impact of the decision to appoint defense counsel for him.[59] At the Arusha tribunal, this scenario came up in the media trial of Jean-Bosco Barayagwiza. Unlike the Milosevic case, Barayagwiza's attempts to manipulate the tribunal failed. At Arusha, the tribunal scaled this hurdle by adopting a new procedural rule stipulating that a trial chamber may, in the interest of justice, instruct the registrar to assign counsel to represent the interests of the accused.[60] This new rule formalized a power the tribunal previously exercised as an "inherent power."

In *Barayagwiza*, a trial chamber had instructed the registrar of the tribunal to assign counsel to represent the interests of Barayagwiza, one of three defendants in a joint trial.[61] The defendant, who was indigent and was assigned a lawyer to defend him, ceased cooperating with his defense counsel in 1999 in a move clearly designed to obstruct the progress of his trial. Charging that the Arusha tribunal was in the pocket of the "dictatorial, anti-Hutu regime in Kigali," he boycotted his own trial after a certain point in the proceedings, raising questions amongst tribunal attorneys about whether he should be brought to the hearings by force, if necessary in handcuffs. This is a scenario that, in many national jurisdictions, would be a no-brainer: such a defendant would be hauled to court in manacles. But here we have an international war crimes tribunal where human rights sensitivities are deeply entrenched. While the Arusha tribunal judges were unwilling to go so far, by having the registrar appoint a standby lawyer to represent Barayagwiza's interests, they ensured that his case continued and he could not disrupt the trial. Giacomo Calderera, an Italian lawyer, was appointed by the registrar to represent Barayagwiza's interests. He executed his duties to the court despite Barayagwiza's petulant refusal to cooperate with him, arguing that the tribunal had foisted "the Italian mafia" on him.

To be sure, a defendant at the Arusha and Hague tribunals has the right to defend himself under tribunal rules. But bearing in mind that a war crimes defendant might have a variety of reasons for opting to defend himself, not least of which is the desire to make a political mockery of the proceedings and cast them as a "show trial," the court is bound to ensure other interests involved in a criminal trial, including, but not exclusively, those of the defendant.[62] These include the need for an expeditious trial and the interests of the victims and the public to see justice done.[63]

What is clear, however, is that the question of what is a fair trial for violations of international humanitarian law is not infrequently one of perspective. Those perspectives often include a mix of politics and sheer vanity. At the Arusha tribunal, many of the defendants are well-educated men who profess a sound grasp of international human rights law. Barayagwiza, for example, was an extremely prolific pamphleteer before he was silenced by his conviction. And at the Hague tribunal, defendant Vojislav Šešelj, a rabidly nationalist politician and former law professor at Belgrade University, miffed at a judge's suggestion that he should request legal counsel for his defense, exclaimed in court: "I have never met a better lawyer than I am in my whole life."[64] Of Milosevic, who has a law degree, it has been commented that the former Serb leader "by the end of his trial will have earned himself several years of advocacy experience."[65] From whichever way such scenarios are approached by a war crimes tribunal, they demonstrate the competing tensions between the right of an accused to defend himself and the overall interest of justice. And it illustrates the deeply political nature of war crimes trials.

## PRISONS FOR THE CONVICTED

As the Arusha tribunal's first verdicts approached in 1998, the question of where defendants who might be convicted would serve their prison sentences weighed increasingly on the minds of tribunal observers. Indeed it was the logical next challenge to be met, for enforcement is essential to the efficacy of retributive justice. What good is a court of law and justice if its prison sentences could not be served in the four walls of a jail? In national jurisdictions, this question does not arise because prisons are a basic element of criminal justice systems. When it comes to war crimes justice at an *international* level, however, the enforcement of prison sentences cannot be taken for granted. There are no "international prisons" established by states or international institutions to enforce the verdicts of supranational courts that lack the sovereign prerogatives of states.

It is not as if this scenario was unforeseen. According to the tribunal's statute its prison sentences are to be served in Rwanda or in any other countries that have indicated to the Security Council their willingness to accept convicted persons. The imprisonment is to be served in accordance with the laws of the host country, subject to supervision by the international tribunal.[66]

For several years the international tribunal did not regard Rwanda as a practical destination for its convicts for a number of reasons. Chief among these were considerations such as the security and safety of such convicts. Under Rwanda's domestic Genocide Law, many of the persons convicted by the Arusha tribunal would be Category A convicts—the architects of the genocide—and thus eligible for the death penalty. But the Arusha court cannot impose the death penalty, and life imprisonment is the harshest sentence it can hand down. From the Rwandan perspective in the early years of the Arusha tribunal, this situation was not only seen as unfair, but was seen as *injustice*. In the face of such a fundamental philosophical divergence between Rwanda and the Arusha tribunal, the former was not seen as offering an agreeable environment for enforcing the tribunal's sentences.

Moreover incursions into Rwandan territory by the extremist Hutu militias based in the Democratic Republic of Congo (then Zaire) after the Rwandan Patriotic Front (RPF) won the war and took power in Rwanda were still persistent at the time. Thus there was a heightened atmosphere of insecurity in some parts of Rwanda. What if, then, a convict of the international court was jailed in Rwanda for life or a term of years and an aggrieved survivor decided to take "justice" in his own hands and assassinate such a convict in breach of prison security? Or what if, in another scenario at the time, the extremists-in-exile staged a raid on prison facilities to secure the release of a convict who would be one of their own? In late 1998, with feelings still running high on both sides of the political/ethnic divide, these were not implausible scenarios. Either way it would be a major scandal for the Arusha tribunal, denting its credibility irreparably.

A second concern, more openly acknowledged, was that there were no prisons in Rwanda that met international human rights standards. As would be expected in any country faced with mass crime on the scale of a genocide that claimed nearly a million lives and was executed by hundreds of thousands of individuals, let alone a poor country such as Rwanda, its prisons were overwhelmed by the sheer numbers of persons held on accusations of participating in the genocide. At one time, an estimated 125,000 persons were in pretrial detention in prison facilities originally built to accommodate a few thousand detainees or prisoners at any one time. The space constraints were so bad that detainees and prisoners took turns sleeping on the limited floor space while others stood. International human rights standards of detention recommend that a prisoner or detainee should occupy a cell alone, a standard ignored in some developed countries and in many developing ones. But it was precisely these standards that prevailed in the Arusha tribunal's UN Detention Facility at Arusha where the defendants were held throughout the pretrial and trial periods. In these circumstances, the practical prospects of sending the international tribunal's convicts to jail in Rwanda remained a distant one at the time. Recent developments, however, have brought that prospect somewhat closer.

In 1998, then, the tribunal had little choice but to look to countries other than Rwanda to provide prisons for its convicts. African countries were favored as a matter of policy. The tribunal's position, without excluding non-African countries from consideration, was that since deterring future genocides, eradicating the culture of impunity, and contributing to the maintenance of peace in the region were the larger goals of the tribunal, persons convicted by the tribunal should as far as possible be imprisoned in African countries.[67] Both Judge Kama and Registrar Okali held this position. From this perspective, it was seen as less than ideal that individuals should commit genocide in Rwanda and go to distant prisons in, say, Finland. Moreover the countries with which the Hague tribunal for Yugoslavia had concluded agreements to enforce its own sentences were predominantly European. Thus the sociopolitical and cultural context was justifiably important in the Arusha tribunal's policy calculus. If the tribunal was to have any hope of influencing an evolution in Africa toward a culture of accountability and respect for human rights, it made perfect sense to begin by having erstwhile political leaders and military commanders convicted of grave international crimes imprisoned in African jails for the genocide of Africans.

Okali launched negotiations with some African countries, which resulted in the conclusion of agreements between the UN and the West African countries of Mali (February 1999) and Benin (August 1999) and the Southern African Kingdom of Swaziland (August 2000) to provide prisons to accommodate the tribunal's convicts. These agreements were important breakthroughs for the tribunal. And they were possible not just because of the efforts of the tribunal's registrar, but also because the leaders of these countries recognized the political value of the tribunal's mission. Alpha Omar Konare, then president of Mali, is a progressive African statesman with a strong track record of respect for human rights. It was no surprise when in 2003, having served two terms as the democratically elected president of his country, he was unanimously elected the founding chairman of the Commission of the African Union, the successor organization to the Organization of African Unity. Mathieu Kerekou of Benin is a former dictator who, in a remarkable epiphany, was converted to the virtues of democracy after having been removed from office by a Sovereign National Conference in 1990 as the first wave of democratization swept through the African continent. Even more remarkably, Kerekou later returned to office through the ballot box in 1996 with 84 percent of the vote. King Mswati III of Swaziland, a British public-school educated monarch, has sought to achieve a balance between his kingdom's progress and retaining its distinctive cultural mores. All three leaders, in offering their cooperation to the UN tribunal, were categorical in their condemnation of the Rwandan genocide and their acknowledgment of the tribunal's potential role in the continent.

These agreements, however, did not take away a practical problem—the need for prisons that meet international standards. With the exception of Swaziland, prisons in Africa fell far short of these standards. Converting the prisons offered by these countries into high security, well constructed, and equipped facilities required money. In the case of Mali, where six convicts of the Arusha tribunal including former Rwandan prime minister Jean Kambanda and Akayesu are serving their jail terms, the UN's budget committee in New York had to approve, at the tribunal's request, financial resources that funded the necessary upgrade of a prison in Bamako. The Arusha tribunal has concluded additional agreements on the enforcement of its prison sentences with France (March 2003), Italy (March 2004), and Sweden (April 2004).

It is politically significant that the ICTR and Rwanda negotiated—but have not signed as of this writing—an agreement in 2004 to send ICTR convicts to prison in Rwanda. A modern prison constructed in Rwanda with aid funds from the European Union has apparently been earmarked for this purpose.[68] Three points should be noted about this development. First it is strongly related to a plan to complete trials at the Arusha tribunal by the end of this decade and hand outstanding cases over to Rwandan courts. This linkage notwithstanding, there is a technical distinction between enforcing the tribunal's prison sentences in Rwanda, which is a decision that can only be made by the judges of the international tribunal, and the handover of cases for prosecution, an arrangement largely within the prosecutor's domain and necessitated by the new sunset clause for the tribunal (see chapter 6). The latter requires far more elaborate policy and legislative action such as the removal of the death penalty from Rwanda's statute books as a condition precedent.

Second, negotiating the possibility of Arusha tribunal convicts serving time in Rwanda is part of the tribunal's continuing efforts, now led by Dieng, to improve relations with Rwanda. The more likely scenario is that the only international tribunal defendants that will wind up in Rwandan jails are those whose cases will be handed over to Rwanda for trial in its national courts. For the reason below, the tribunal is unlikely to actually send prisoners it has convicted to Rwanda for imprisonment.

Third, the negotiations between registrar Dieng and Rwanda triggered strong protests from the Rwandan defendants at Arusha, leading the judges to clarify that they are the ones who designate where a convict is actually sent to serve his or her prison sentence, the existence of agreements with various countries notwithstanding. From the political perspective of the defendants, there could be no worse fate than returning to Rwanda a prisoner. The real question, however, is whether in light of the limitations imposed on the tribunal's relevance to Rwanda by its physical distance, sending convicts to Rwandan jails at this point would not in fact be the best outcome for the Arusha tribunal, the justice it seeks, and for Rwandan society. Should this outcome be determined (in effect) by the defendant? The balance of justice ought to dictate that it should not.

# CHAPTER 5

# A BAPTISM OF FIRE:
# THE BARAYAGWIZA AFFAIR

We try to keep politics out of it, but over the years I've seen how
hard it is.

—Carla Del Ponte

On November 3, 1999, the appellate court of the Arusha tribunal,
presided over by the respected American judge Gabrielle Kirk
McDonald, delivered a procedural decision[1] in the *Barayagwiza* case
that became the most controversial in the tribunal's history and
provoked an epic clash between the strategic interests of the Rwandan
government—backed by Rwandan popular opinion—and the judicial
independence of the Arusha tribunal. The decision was based on an
appeal by Jean-Bosco Barayagwiza (figure 5.1) against the ruling of a
trial bench on his request to be released from pretrial detention. He
argued that he was entitled to that remedy on account of serious
violations of his fundamental rights: he had been detained far too long
without trial in Cameroon (where he was arrested) and in Arusha after
he was transferred to the tribunal from Cameroon. The trial panel of
judges had rejected Barayagwiza's argument[2] and he appealed.

The appellate chamber agreed with the defendant that his rights had
indeed been violated. It allowed the appeal unanimously, dismissed
the charges against Barayagwiza "with prejudice" to the prosecutor,
ordered the immediate release of Barayagwiza, and by a vote of four
to one, directed the tribunal's registrar to return Barayagwiza to
Cameroon and hand him back to that country's authorities. Outraged,
Rwanda's government suspended cooperation with the international
tribunal, and a major diplomatic, political, and judicial crisis ensued.

**Figure 5.1**    Jean-Bosco Barayagwiza at his trial for genocide.

Two facts are important as background here. First Barayagwiza was indeed an extremist politician and a kingpin in the planning and execution of the genocide. As of 1999, however, he had not been put on trial, much less found guilty, and thus was entitled under the tribunal's procedures to a presumption of innocence.

Second the appellate chamber ruling in *Barayagwiza* came against the backdrop of an earlier and similarly controversial ruling by the tribunal in the *Ntuyahaga* case. There the international tribunal's chief prosecutor had made a policy decision to drop charges against Maj. Bernard Ntuyahagu, a former officer in the Rwandan Government Forces at the time of the genocide, who had actually turned himself in to the international tribunal in Tanzania and was subsequently indicted. The prosecutor's decision was based on apparent understandings with Belgium that the latter would prosecute Ntuyahaga on the basis of concurrent jurisdiction for the murder of 10 Belgian peacekeepers in Rwanda in 1994.

A judge of the tribunal had earlier confirmed just one count (responsibility for participation in the murder of the 10 Belgian soldiers) out of several the prosecutor had brought against Ntuyahaga, which suggested that the initial evidence against the accused was weak. Deeming such a trial not worth the effort, and Ntuyahaga in any case not being a "big fish," chief prosecutor Louise Arbour in an exercise of prosecutorial discretion filed a motion requesting leave from the bench to drop the case after a charge had formally been brought.

But the trial judges did not follow her script. They granted the prosecutor's request to drop the charges against Ntuyahaga, but declined to hand him over to Belgium or any other national jurisdiction (including Rwanda) because the Arusha tribunal's jurisdictional primacy precluded that alternative.[3] This decision dashed Belgium's hopes and Rwanda's expectations to see Ntuyahaga tried. A messy battle for the custody of the now technically "free" defendant ensued between Belgium and Rwanda,[4] with the latter criticizing the tribunal's ruling.

The tribunal's registrar, Agwu Okali, had received no further guidance from the judges on exactly how—and to whom—to "release" Ntuyahaga, who, meanwhile, filed an urgent motion requesting a stay of the trial chamber's order for his "immediate and unconditional release." Naturally fearful for his personal security if he were to be released into the wild, Ntuyahaga wanted to remain in custody until proper arrangements had been made to implement the court's order. Having made several discreet but unsuccessful attempts to find a neutral third country willing to accept the former defendant, Okali was left with little choice but to release Ntuyahaga in the Tanzanian capital of Dar es Salaam at the latter's written request.[5] Okali thus instructed the tribunal's small Beechcraft plane to drop Ntuyahaga, armed with some cash provided by the tribunal and a letter from the tribunal's registrar addressed to United Nations (UN) member states requesting safe passage to Ntuyahaga's destination, at Dar es Salaam airport on a clear morning. Otherwise Ntuyahaga was left to his own devices with the hope that he would come to no harm. But the judges' order to release the former defendant had been technically executed, and the tribunal declared the matter closed as far as it was concerned.[6]

The problem was that Ntuyahaga had no destination, as no country had agreed to take him in. He first went to a Scandinavian embassy to ask for asylum, but was turned away. He promptly went underground, but was arrested hours later by the Tanzanian security services, who reportedly found him brooding over a bottle of beer in a bar in Dar es Salaam. A new legal and diplomatic dilemma quickly emerged: would Tanzania hand Ntuyahaga over to Rwanda or Belgium, both of which wanted him for trial? Tanzania, which is opposed to the death penalty that would be Ntuyahaga's possible fate should Rwanda obtain custody and the former soldier be convicted by a Rwandan court, was loathe to hand him over to a European country and offend the political sensibilities of a fellow African state. As a middle course, it decided to try Ntuyahaga in a Tanzanian court.[7] It is against the backdrop of these legal, political, and diplomatic consequences of a judicially ordered release of an accused person who had not been acquitted in a proper trial that we can now see the Barayagwiza saga. This time, however, the defendant was one that had a far greater political significance in the scheme of things.

## BONE OF CONTENTION

There were several issues in dispute between Barayagwiza and the international tribunal's prosecutor, as well as a somewhat complicated chronology of events. Since the objective of this chapter is to examine the broad political and conceptual implications of this case rather than the comprehensive details of the legal dispute, it will suffice to review only the major issues here.

The main point of dispute was whether or not the prosecutor of the international tribunal was responsible for Barayagwiza's arrest and detention during a 19-month period between his arrest and detention in Cameroon in April 1996, and November 19, 1997 when he was transferred to the tribunal's detention under a procedural rule that allowed the prosecutor to request a state to arrest and hand over a suspect to the international tribunal prior to a formal indictment.[8] The defendant's right to be informed promptly of the charges against him, his right to challenge the legality of his arrest and detention; the delay between the tribunal's request to Cameroon for the transfer of the appellant from that country and the actual transfer; the length of the appellant's provisional detention; and the delay between Barayagwiza's arrival at the tribunal's detention facility in Arusha and his initial appearance before the tribunal (another 3 months) were among the contentious points in this case.[9]

As reconstructed in their appellate decision,[10] on April 15, 1996, the authorities of Cameroon arrested and detained a number of suspects, including Barayagwiza, in connection with the genocide and crimes against humanity in Rwanda in 1994. These arrests were carried out in response to international arrest and extradition requests issued separately by the Rwandan and Belgian governments in 1994.

Two days later, on April 17, the Arusha tribunal's chief prosecutor indicated her interest in proceeding against Barayagwiza. On May 6, 1996, she asked Cameroon for a three-week extension of the detention of the defendant and the other suspects. But on May 16, 1996, the international prosecutor informed the Cameroonian authorities that she would prosecute four of the detainees, but not Barayagwiza.

On October 15, 1996, the prosecutor, in response to a letter from Barayagwiza complaining about his detention in Cameroon, informed him that she was not responsible for his detention there. The Court of Appeal of Cameroon resumed its hearings on Rwanda's extradition request for Barayagwiza and the other suspects, and on February 21, 1997 ultimately rejected the Rwandan extradition request and ordered the release of Barayagwiza and his fellow suspects. The same day, the Arusha tribunal prosecutor requested Barayagwiza's provisional detention. The former Rwandan politician was promptly rearrested. At the prosecutor's request in conformity with the tribunal's rules, Arusha tribunal judge Lennart Aspegren of Sweden on March 3, 1997 signed a judicial order for Barayagwiza's arrest and his transfer to the tribunal. Barayagwiza was not transferred to Arusha, however, until November 19, 1997, following a presidential decree signed by President Paul Biya of Cameroon on October 21, 1997. On February 24, 1998, Barayagwiza filed a motion for the nullification of his arrest and detention. In dismissing his motion, a trial panel of judges headed by Tanzania's William Sekule upheld the prosecutor's arguments and ruled that Barayagwiza's provisional detention was justified. His initial arrest in Cameroon was at the behest of Rwanda and Belgium and not that of the international tribunal's prosecutor as Barayagwiza claimed; and the prosecutor's reversal on proceeding against Barayagwiza was an exercise of prosecutorial discretion and was not discriminatory.

The tribunal's prosecutor admitted that the delay in transferring Barayagwiza after the tribunal's request was indeed prolonged, but argued that this delay could not be imputed to her office because custody involved "care and control." Since Barayagwiza was not in the tribunal's custody until his transfer to Arusha in November 1997, the legality of his detention was a matter for the laws of Cameroon and beyond the competence of the Arusha tribunal's appellate chamber.[11] The prosecutor also argued that her change of heart on prosecuting Barayagwiza did not create any "prescriptive claims" against eventual prosecution for crimes as serious as genocide and other violations of international law.

## THE DECISION

The appellate judges made a number of findings and discussed international human rights standards as a basis for their eventual ruling. First they found that there were two periods in which Cameroon detained Barayagwiza clearly at the behest of the international tribunal at Arusha and for most of which he was not promptly charged: from May 17, 1996 until June 16, 1996, a 29-day period that violated the 20-day limit under Rule 40 of the tribunal's rules; and from March 4, 1997 until Barayagwiza's transfer to the tribunal's detention unit on November 19, 1997. While it accepted that pretrial detention is lawful, the appeals bench was of the view that such pretrial detention should not be unreasonably extended, and relied on the UN Human Rights Committee's interpretation of the International Covenant on Civil and Political Rights (ICCPR) in several cases.[12] Evidence was adduced of concerns expressed by Judge Laity Kama, the president of the tribunal, about the prosecution's tardiness in bringing charges against Barayagwiza.[13] The appellate judges concluded that the delay in indicting the appellant violated the 90-day limit set out in the tribunal's rules.

The appellate chamber then addressed the 96-day delay between Barayagwiza's transfer to Arusha and his initial appearance before the international tribunal. This, it also found, violated the statutory requirement of the tribunal (based on international human rights standards) that an accused person should "be brought promptly before a judge" following arrest. While the practices of individual states differ and there is no specific number of days stipulated in this context, in states with a human-rights–conscious judicial system, this period is normally interpreted in terms of days rather than weeks, let alone months. The appellate chamber thus found a 96-day delay a violation of Barayagwiza's rights.[14]

A review then followed of the appellant's right to be promptly informed of the charges against him in the early days of his detention in Cameroon, an alleged failure of the tribunal to consider his writ of *habeas corpus* (a writ used to challenge the validity of a person's detention[15]) and the prosecutorial diligence of the prosecution. Of much significance is the legal context in which the appellate judges reviewed these issues—that of the "abuse of process" doctrine, under which a lawful judicial proceeding may be terminated after an indictment has already been issued if improper or illegal procedures are deployed in pursuit of an otherwise lawful process.[16] This is a discretionary power as the judges stressed. The Arusha tribunal's appellate chamber invoked the doctrine as summarized in a decision in the British House of Lords: "[A] court has a discretion to stay any criminal proceedings on the ground that to try those proceedings will amount to an abuse of its own process either (1) because it will be impossible (usually by reason of delay) to give the accused a fair trial or (2) *because it offends the court's sense of justice and propriety to be asked to try the accused in the circumstances of a particular case*"[17] [emphasis added by ICTR Appeals Chamber].

Going further in search of authority, the appellate chamber then asserted the notion that courts have "inherent supervisory powers" to dismiss prosecutions in order to remedy a violation of the rights of an accused person, deter future misconduct, and guard the integrity of the judicial process.[18] The Arusha tribunal judges found that authority in a string of constitutional cases in the U.S. appellate courts and the U.S. Supreme Court.

The appeals court further ruled that Barayagwiza's detention for 11 months before he was informed of the general nature of the charges the tribunal's chief prosecutor was planning to bring against him was a violation of his rights, although only 35 days of that period were clearly attributable to the tribunal. It deplored the tribunal's failure to hear the appellant's *writ of habeas corpus* (a Latin phrase meaning "produce the body"). The judges then set forth a stinging rebuke of the prosecutor's breach of duty of prosecutorial diligence in taking necessary steps to bring the *Barayagwiza* case to trial quickly.[19] "The crimes for which the Appellant is charged are very serious" the appellate judges acknowledged. "However, in this case the fundamental rights of the Appellant were repeatedly violated. What may be worse, it appears that the Prosecutor's failure to prosecute this case was tantamount to negligence. We find this conduct to be egregious and, in light of the numerous violations, conclude that the only remedy available for such prosecutorial in action and the resultant denial of his rights is to release the Appellant and dismiss the charges against him."[20] The appellate court did not stop here, but went to dismiss the indictment against Barayagwiza "with prejudice to the Prosecutor," thus ensuring that the prosecutor could not in any event bring charges against Barayagwiza before the tribunal. "Nothing less than the integrity of the tribunal is at stake here," the judges wrote in their decision. "To proceed with the Appellant's trial when such violations have been committed would cause irreparable damage to the integrity of the judicial process. As difficult as this conclusion may be for some to accept, it is the proper role of an independent judiciary to halt this prosecution, so that no further injustice results."

## RWANDAN FURY

The appellate ruling was greeted with incredulity in Rwanda. There settled in Rwandan public opinion a belief that the decision in *Barayagwiza* was part of a "judicial conspiracy" against the Rwandan government. This conspiracy theory was predicated on the fact that the ruling was issued one day before Judge McDonald (figure 5.2) left the appellate bench at The Hague and Arusha, having earlier announced her resignation from both tribunals.

The Rwandan government's decisive political response was not long in coming. First Kigali denied the chief prosecutor a visa she requested from the Rwandan Embassy in Brussels to visit the country immediately after the decision and meet with Rwandan authorities. Carla Del Ponte of Switzerland (figure 5.3) had been appointed chief prosecutor of the International Criminal Tribunal for the Former Yugoslavia (ICTY) and the International Criminal Tribunal for Rwanda (ICTR) in September 1999, just two months earlier, following Louise Arbour's resignation from the post in order to take up a new appointment at the Supreme Court of Canada. For Del Ponte, this was surely a baptism of fire.

Rwanda accompanied the visa denial with announcements that it was suspending its cooperation with the international tribunal unless the decision was reversed. This was no mere rhetoric. As international criminal justice is constructed, it cannot function without the practical support of states. The international tribunal could not be effective without Rwandan's cooperation—more than 90 percent of all prosecution witnesses at the tribunal came from there. As the place where the genocide was committed, the bulk of the investigations to establish evidence in cases before the Arusha tribunal have been conducted on Rwandan territory.

In truth, Carla Del Ponte did not need a visa to go to Rwanda.[21] Visas for visiting officials of the tribunal were normally issued on arrival at Kigali airport. But in the circumstances, requesting a visa was a way to test the reaction she would receive in Rwanda. This was one example of the "brinksmanship"[22] that pervaded the whole affair. "Everyone agrees this is a tragedy of justice," said Gerald Gahima, then attorney general of Rwanda in reaction to the ruling.[23] "And until the UN shows us concrete steps to, first and foremost, reverse that ruling in the Barayagwiza decision and ensure that nothing like this happens again, we don't see any reason for meeting Del Ponte."

These clear threats to the international tribunal were indicative of the *political* leverage Rwanda had over the tribunal, for the reasons set

**Figure 5.2** Judge Gabrielle Kirk McDonald taking her oath of office as head of the Appeals Chamber of the ICTR.

out in the previous chapter. Until the *Barayagwiza* decision, however, the noncooperation card had never been played explicitly. In fact, just weeks earlier on October 19, 1999, a team of senior Rwandan officials comprising Gahima, Rwandan ambassador to Belgium and the

**Figure 5.3**   Former ICTR Chief Prosecutor Carla Del Ponte in court at the Arusha tribunal.

European Union Jacques Bihozagara, and Rwandan military prosecutor Lt. Col. Andrew Rwigamba had met with Del Ponte and (separately) Judge McDonald at The Hague. Affirmations of mutual cooperation were exchanged between the chief prosecutor and the Rwandan delegation.[24] Judge McDonald, for her part, emphasized that her departure notwithstanding, she remained committed to justice in Rwanda.[25] But now, Rwanda felt its political and societal interests threatened by a purist judicial ruling by the international tribunal, and responded with the political tools at its disposal as a sovereign state.

Several countries, including the United States, intervened with the Rwandan authorities. The United States remonstrated with Kigali that its strong reaction, though understandable, was not the best approach to the situation. It was not until Washington informed Kigali that the international prosecutor would challenge the appellate decision, and that the United States would provide evidence of its intercession with Cameroon's leader to authorize Barayagwiza's transfer to the tribunal, that Rwanda began to soften its position in private, though not in public.[26] This, of course, had now become the major objective of Carla Del Ponte's planned trip to Kigali—to discuss with the Rwandan authorities her intention to seek a reversal of the ruling and a strategy to achieve that objective. She had already scheduled a courtesy visit to Rwanda,[27] her first since her appointment, but developments on the ground had now radically altered the rationale for the visit. At this point, the strategy that had begun to evolve in the prosecutor's office was to seek a reconsideration of the Appeals Chamber decision under a procedural rule that allowed for a review of appellate decisions in certain circumstances. In this case, the secret legal trump card was to be details of efforts made by the U.S. Department of State to have President Biya of Cameroon authorize Barayagwiza's surrender to the tribunal in line with the ICTR prosecutor's March 4, 1997 requests. The whole point was to demonstrate that the ICTR, with the assistance and political support of the United States, had made attempts to have Cameroon hand over Barayagwiza, but that Cameroon was "moving at its own pace."[28]

Following the intercession of a number of influential governments, the visa question was finally resolved with an elegant diplomatic compromise: the chief prosecutor applied for a visa not to visit Rwanda as such, but to visit her office in Kigali from which, under the Memorandum of Agreement between the UN and Rwanda, the Rwandan government could not exclude her.[29]

Meanwhile tribunal registrar Okali was engaged in judicial and political diplomacy on several fronts.[30] There was a flurry of telephone calls and meetings with interested parties, capitalizing not just on his official role, in which he was neither a judge nor a party to cases before the tribunal, but on his credibility with the Rwandan government and civil society. That cachet rested largely on his previous efforts to improve relations between the tribunal and Rwanda, and on his well-known advocacy for victim-oriented justice at the international tribunal. But first there was the matter of executing the appellate judges' decision that the registrar should "make the necessary arrangements" to deliver Barayagwiza back to Cameroon. Under the tribunal's procedural rules, where an accused person is held for more than 90 days without a formal charge, he would have to be returned to the country where he was arrested, in this case Cameroon.

Judge Mohammed Shahabuddeen of Guyana had dissented from the appellate chamber's order that Barayagwiza be returned to Cameroon. Presciently Shahabuddeen, who had the reputation of being the sharpest legal mind in a group that included some outstanding jurists, framed the issue thus:

> it is considered that Cameroon has a duty to accept delivery of the appellant, or that, at any rate, Cameroon has some legal basis for doing so. Has it? A possible argument is that the direction to the

Registrar . . . can be supported by Cameroon's obligation to cooperate with the Tribunal. But also possible is an opposing argument that state obligation to cooperate with the Tribunal does not extend to assisting the Tribunal to correct its own errors . . . No doubt, Cameroon was at fault in not transferring the appellant to Arusha as speedily as it should have done in compliance with Judge Aspegren's order of 4 March 1997. Nevertheless, with full knowledge of that, the Tribunal did later issue an indictment and arrest warrant for the appellant. Thus, the Tribunal really wanted to have the appellant transferred to Arusha. This being so, and Cameroon having eventually made the transfer, why should it be under a duty to take back the appellant from the Tribunal?[31]

All of this, it turned out, was academic. Okali dispatched a small team of the tribunal to the Cameroonian capital of Yaounde to formally deliver a copy of the appellate court's decision to the government and, more importantly, to discuss the Cameroonian government's role in its implementation. It was, he recalls, "a typical third world experience."[32] In the former senior UN official's recollection:

Unfortunately, if perhaps not surprisingly, no decision could be made or action taken by anyone until the Big Man [President Biya] had spoken, and no one apparently dared press him on it. Indeed, given that, from what one heard, the President remained perpetually in his hometown and one, including his Ministers, could only go to see him on invitation, it was never clear if the matter really ever reached him personally. The [ICTR] delegation, after a period of stay in Cameroonian capital came back without any formal response by the Cameroonian authorities—I don't believe any was ever received in fact. This, of course put paid to any idea of implementation of the Appeals Chamber decision in so far as this involved Cameroonian participation.[33]

On the Rwandan front, Okali engaged the country at a number of formal and informal levels to nudge them toward a more pragmatic and less emotional view of the situation. He visited Kigali and met with the then vice president Kagame and other senior Rwandan officials. His message to the Rwandans was this: their anger, even outrage, over the decision was perfectly understandable, even to a large extent justifiable.[34] But it was important, he had argued, that Rwanda not express its outrage in a manner that would in fact be inimical to its own ultimate strategic interest. This would certainly be the outcome if Rwanda's actions either destroyed the tribunal or rendered it so limp that the institution had to be disbanded.[35] (Here one should note that the tribunal's dependence on Rwanda's cooperation—at least in those early years of the tribunal's existence—having been acknowledged, Rwanda's leaders also recognized that they too needed the tribunal if justice was ever to be rendered in response to the genocide. Joseph Mutaboba, Rwanda's ambassador to the UN at the time conceded as much.[36])

Okali deployed the "additionality" argument as his meeting with Kagame continued: deficient and inefficient as the Arusha tribunal might appear from Rwanda's standpoint, it was making possible the prosecution of the otherwise out-of-reach ringleaders of the genocide apprehended in various countries at its request. Moreover considering the mischief-making potential of these fugitives (already apparent in the neighboring Democratic Republic of Congo), it was infinitely better for such political figures to be in detention at the tribunal than "out there" in their countries of refuge. Okali had the impression that these pragmatic arguments were well appreciated by the Rwandan leader.[37]

## RECONSIDERATION

On November 19, 1999, Chief Prosecutor Carla Del Ponte put into action her legal strategy to obtain a reversal of the Appeals Chamber's decision rendered two weeks earlier. She filed a notice of her intention to request a "review" of the appellate chamber's decision of November 3, 1999.[38] With Judge McDonald's departure from the tribunal, Judge Claude Jorda of France had become the presiding judge of the ICTR Appeals Chamber. Otherwise the composition of the bench remained the same as it was under McDonald: Judges Shahabuddeen, Lal Chand Vohrah of Malaysia, Wang Tieya of China, and Rafael Nieto-Navia of Colombia.

Del Ponte's notice invoked the statute of the tribunal and procedural rules,[39] which permit an application for a review of an appellate decision within one year on the basis of new facts. Those facts must be such as could not have been discovered with due diligence. If it is proven that the new facts would have had decisive impact on the decision, the Appeals Chamber is required to review the judgment, hold a hearing between parties, and pronounce a further judgment. This is an important point, for it demonstrates that there was indeed a legal basis within the tribunal's framework from which the prosecutor could at least attempt to obtain a reversal of the appellate decision in *Barayagwiza*. All too often commentary on this case has proceeded as if the decision to review the first appellate ruling was a politicized one in travesty of legal rules.[40] This, of course, is without prejudice to whether or not the prosecutor's motive was political, a matter I will come to in a moment. In her notice, the prosecutor noted that she had "no objection" to the Republic of Rwanda appearing before the tribunal as a "friend of the court" as Rwanda had asked for in a request filed with the tribunal on the same day as the prosecutor's notice—indicative of the close collaboration between the prosecutor and the Rwandan authorities on this issue.

On November 22, 1999, Jean-Bosco Barayagwiza filed a response to the prosecutor's notice.[41] He argued that the prosecutor's intention was not to produce any "new facts" but rather to review her arguments and reopen the proceedings by introducing "additional facts." He invited the Appeals Chamber's attention to his position that the prosecutor had a political motive, under pressure from the Rwandan government, to have an opportunity to challenge the decision, prolong his "ordeal," and introduce political elements in the judicial proceeding in order to pressure the appellate judges and please the Rwandan government.[42] Such a political motive, he argued, ought not to be tolerated by a UN tribunal that is supposed to protect human rights, including those of the accused.[43] Barayagwiza then urged the appellate chamber to dismiss the prosecutor's notice and the Rwandan government's request to appear in the case.

Barayagwiza did not get his way, for the tribunal gave the prosecutor leave to request a review of the November 3 decision, a procedural ruling that also led the appellate judges, at the prosecutor's request, to suspend the order to release the appellant pending the determination of the review process. In her motion for review of the November 3 decision,[44] the prosecutor introduced several new facts in order to establish that Barayagwiza had knowledge of the nature of the charges against him during his detention in Cameroon, and catalogued efforts made by the tribunal's former registrar, Andronico Adede, to obtain the transfer of several detainees including Barayagwiza. These efforts included at least four trips to Yaounde by Adede between April 1996 and January 1997. And it emerged that Cameroonian judicial officials had in fact drafted and submitted a draft decree ordering Barayagwiza's surrender to the ICTR to the country's presidency in March 1997 (following the tribunal's issuance of a Rule 40*bis* order for Barayagwiza's transfer to Arusha). This draft decree remained in the presidency, unsigned, until October 1997.

That delay was not coincidental, and a report submitted to the Arusha tribunal by Judge Mbale of the Cameroon Supreme Court suggested that scheduled elections in the country contributed to the delay in handing over Barayagwiza. It was only when the U.S. government exerted pressure on President Biya that the Cameroonian leader signed the decree. The fact, nature, and process of that diplomatic pressure were what the ICTR prosecution sought to utilize in proving its efforts to obtain custody of Barayagwiza. In September 1997, Deputy Chief Prosecutor Bernard Muna had asked David Scheffer, then U.S. ambassador at large for War Crimes Issues, for assistance in obtaining Barayagwiza' surrender to the Arusha tribunal. Baffling though it appears, there was apparently no feedback from Scheffer to Muna on what steps the former took, for the prosecution now asserted as a central "new fact" that it had now been informed that Ambassador Scheffer contacted the ambassador of the U.S. in Yaounde, and requested him to intervene in the matter. Shortly thereafter, a Presidential Decree authorizing the transfer of the Appellant was signed.[45] This critical American diplomatic intervention and its role in securing Barayagwiza's surrender demonstrated that Cameroon was deliberately resisting the tribunal's judicial orders, the prosecutor argued. This was all the more so because such extraterritorial judicial orders are perceived by states as an encroachment of their sovereignty, a problem exacerbated in 1996–1997 by the tribunal's relative infancy and the novelty of international judicial intervention.[46] Regarding the defendant's writ of *habeas corpus*, the prosecutor contended that it fell through procedural cracks in the tribunal as a result of the failure of Barayagwiza's defense counsel to respond to a letter from the tribunal's registry offering a date for a hearing of the motion. This was, as well, a new fact, and the absence of diligence on the part of the defense could not be laid at the feet of the prosecution.

Moreover the prosecutor contended that the appeal judges would not have dismissed the indictment with prejudice to the prosecutor had it considered the likelihood of "abundant proof" of human rights violations for which it alleged Barayagwiza was responsible, as well as the rights of the victims.[47] These two points were at the heart of the matter, politically as well as legally, but it did not appear that way in the prosecutor's request for a review. Indeed they appeared to have been added as an afterthought. This may have been a tactical move, however, to stick to the technical requirement of new facts rather than larger issues of the overall justice of the case.

In conclusion the prosecutor, among other requests, asked the Appeals Chamber to review its November 3 decision, stay the execution of the directive to release Barayagwiza, schedule an oral hearing on the prosecutor's motion for review, and send Barayagwiza's case back to a trial panel for trial. The appellate judges granted a stay of execution on the release of Barayagwiza and scheduled an oral hearing for February 15, 2000.

At that hearing, an affidavit sworn by Ambassador Scheffer regarding the diplomatic intervention of the United States in Cameroon was introduced, with Scheffer present in the courtroom. Rwanda was represented by its then chief prosecutor Gerald Gahima who presented its arguments. The thrust of Rwanda's case was that this was a unique situation. No doubt, respect for the rights of accused persons was a requirement of a free and fair judicial process. However the tribunal's mandate, its obligation to prosecute the perpetrators of genocide and other serious violations of international humanitarian law, meant that releasing Barayagwiza, one of the alleged planners and instigators of the genocide, without prosecution constituted

> grave failure on the part of the Tribunal to perform its obligations under international law and will have adverse effects on the process of national reconciliation and the maintenance of peace in Rwanda by facilitating a culture of impunity . . . In the event that the Tribunal chooses not to prosecute the Appellant itself, the Government of Rwanda respectfully requests that the Tribunal release Appellant into the custody of the Government of Rwanda for trial before the national courts of Rwanda . . .

> To create a balanced remedy, the Appeals Chamber should weigh each of these important factors: the rights of the Appellant, the role of the Tribunal in promoting justice and accountability and in contributing to the process of national reconciliation in Rwanda; the position of Rwanda as the *locus delictus* of the alleged crimes and therefore the only jurisdiction besides the Tribunal that is specifically given authority by the Genocide Convention to try the Appellant for genocide; the severity of the Appellant's alleged crimes; and the rights and interests of the surviving victims of the genocide.[48]

Rwanda's argument then addressed specific aspects of the findings and conclusions of the appellate court's November 3 ruling with arguments that, from an objective standpoint, were persuasive and eminently sensible. Indeed the Rwandan brief was brilliant, as much for its substance as for a balanced, judicious tone that belied the steaming cauldrons of public opinion and diplomatic fencing outside the courtroom. It is said that precedent is the life of the law, but it is also often the case that each party to an adversarial proceeding can find opposing precedents that support its case. Thus where the McDonald appellate chamber relied on numerous British and American decisions supporting its interpretation of the abuse of process doctrine and the weight to be given to the rights of the accused, Rwanda's submissions relied on American and South African case law authority that suggested that "procedural delay in prosecuting an accused is not per se a basis for releasing the defendant. Instead, any such delay simply triggers an inquiry into a possible violation of the right of the accused to a speedy trial and, if appropriate, the nature of the measures that should be taken to remedy that violation."[49] In short, Rwanda's argument was that setting an alleged architect of the genocide free on a technicality without a substantive trial was not "justice," and there were other ways open to the court to remedy violations of Barayagwiza's rights without undermining accountability for genocide.

Yet impressive as Rwanda's arguments were, they were a sideshow. What stood out from the day's courtroom proceedings was Prosecutor Carla Del Ponte's statement at the hearing. Del Ponte, in a fiery performance, bluntly told the appellate judges, not in a legal proposition but in an appeal to political facts of life, that "whether we like it or not, we must come to terms with the reality that our ability to continue our investigations depends on Rwanda." Without Rwanda's help, "we might as well open the doors to the prison. It is my hope that Barayagwiza will not be the one to decide the fate of this tribunal."

Del Ponte thus opened her legal case with a political argument. This was undoubtedly the most controversial statement in the appellate hearing. It drowned the otherwise strong, subsequent points she had made: that there were indeed new facts that would have influenced the original decision had they been known at the time; that the crimes Barayagwiza was accused of were also a violation of the rights of the victims and survivors of the 1994 genocide—and that the real travesty would not be bringing him to trial, but a failure to do so.

Del Ponte's ill-advised political opening phrases were made from her viewpoint as a prosecutor who, in this context at least, had convergent strategic interests with the Rwandan government. Popular perception notwithstanding, it is doubtful that this was the deciding factor in the Appeals Chamber's subsequent decision, for, as we shall see shortly, there were indeed strong factual grounds on which the appellate judges reached a conclusion different from their November 3 decision. To the extent it can be said that "political" factors were at play, it was the matter of the tribunal's *framework* that was actually at play, and not the rather hyperbolically expressed matter of the very existence of the international tribunal hanging in the balance. This analysis is supported by the fact that few people, certainly not Carla Del Ponte, expected the Appeals Chamber to come to a radically different decision from that handed down on November 3, 1999. What Del Ponte undoubtedly did was to make a good faith effort to demonstrate to Rwanda her commitment to the rights of the victims. Her statement above was admittedly a rather dramatic manner of making her point. And the situation should also be seen against the background that Barayagwiza's experience was not unique. There were a number of other detainees of the tribunal whose rights had undoubtedly been infringed by prolonged pretrials detentions. It was known that these defendants, bolstered by the November 3 decision in *Barayagwiza*, were preparing to flood the tribunal with motions for their own release on similar grounds. Had they succeeded in being released in large numbers on technical grounds, it would have been a fatal blow to the tribunal. What Del Ponte was playing for, in fact, was the more limited outcome of getting the Appeals Chamber to revoke the dismissal of the charges "with prejudice" to the prosecutor, based on the new facts she had presented.[50] Thus armed with a new decision that altered the first, she could proceed anew against Barayagwiza before the international tribunal—or, at the very least, ensure that the defendant was prosecuted in a national court with jurisdiction.

As it turned out, the appellate chamber in its review ruling on March 31, 2000 found the information now before it demonstrated that Barayagwiza knew of the general nature of the charges against him by May 3, 1996 at the latest, bringing the number of days he spent in detention without being informed of the reasons to 18 at most. While the appeals judges found that even this period violated the appellant's rights, "this violation is patently of a different order than the one identified in the Decision [of November 3, 1999] whereby the Appellant was without any information for 11 months."[51]

Moreover, Judge Mballe's report confirmed that the Arusha tribunal prosecutor's request pursuant to Rule 40 *bis* was transmitted immediately to President Biya for the leader's assent to a legislative decree for the surrender of Barayagwiza. Mballe's interpretation of the matter was that Biya signed the decree only on October 21, 1997 in order to halt continuing pressure from Rwanda to extradite Barayagwiza to that country. U.S. ambassador Scheffer's affidavit was also of central importance in the view of the appellate judges. The picture from these two pieces of information squarely contradicted the Appeals Chamber's determination of November 3, 1999 that "Cameroon was willing to transfer the appellant" to Arusha. Cameroon's evident unwillingness to transfer Barayagwiza to the international tribunal was a new fact that would have had a significant impact on the Appeals Chamber's initial decision to release Barayagwiza.[52] Furthermore the appellate chamber found that the violation of the appellant's rights while in Cameroon were no fault of the ICTR prosecutors, and new facts were established to show that what was adjudged a 96-day delay in bringing the appellant before a judge following his transfer to Arusha was in fact a 20-day lapse—a violation of the appellant's rights though it remained.[53] The prosecutor was thus not as much to blame for Barayagwiza's "ordeal" as it had appeared from the November 3 decision.

In conclusion, the tribunal's appeals court found that "the new facts diminish the role played by the failings of the Prosecutor as well as the intensity of the violation of the rights of the Appellant. The cumulative effect of these elements being thus reduced, the reparation ordered by the Appeals Chamber now appears disproportionate in relation to the events. The new facts being therefore facts which could have been decisive in the Decision [of November 3], in particular as regards the remedy it orders, that remedy must be modified."[54]

The appeal judges allowed Barayagwiza's appeal regarding the violation of his rights (to the extent now established), but rejected the appellant's application to be released. He was now to face a substantive trial on the basis of the charges against him. Barayagwiza was entitled to a remedy at the judgment following his trial as follows: (1) if found not guilty, he would receive financial compensation, (2) if found guilty, his sentence would be reduced to take account of the violation of his rights.[55] Thus it was that, upon Barayagwiza's conviction in December 2003 following his trial, the judges noted that he would ordinarily have been sentenced to life in prison, but taking into account the appellate decision of March 31, sentenced him to 35 years. Moreover with credit given for the 8 years he had already spent in detention, his actual sentence became 27 years. From the standpoint of what the justice of this controversial case should be, Rwanda's argument was right on the mark.

## POLITICAL OR "POLITICIZED" JUSTICE?

That, then, was the conclusion of the *Barayagwiza* saga: an even-handed decision by the appellate chamber, a substantive trial that found the defendant guilty, but took account of the unquestionable violation of his rights. Which brings us back to the controversy that surrounded this case: was the outcome law, justice, or politics?

The two central issues here are (1) the constant tensions between procedural and substantive justice that confront most courts in countries with judicial systems that place significant value on the former, and (2) following from this, just what kind of courts are the Arusha and Hague tribunals? Both questions are linked. In fact, the answer to the second determines the outcome of first. Initially, I address the tension between procedural and substantive justice. Barayagwiza, not surprisingly, condemned the second decision of the appellate court. He requested his court-assigned lawyers, Carmelle Marchessault of Canada and David Danielson of the United States, to cease representing him because the Arusha tribunal was subservient to the "dictatorial anti-Hutu regime in Kigali," and claimed that he was ready to face the charges against him in an independent and impartial tribunal of any democratic state that respected the procedural rights of an accused person.[56] Ultimately Barayagwiza fired his defense lawyers and stopped attending his trial in protest, and the tribunal appointed Giacomo Calderera of Italy to represent his interests for the rest of his trial.

The demands of substantive justice (holding the accused accountable for alleged acts of genocide) and those of procedural justice (safeguarding the defendant's rights against unlawful or prolonged arrest or pretrial detention) are both indispensable norms of a justice system that functions well.[57] There are those who see this in a much wider context than *Barayagwiza*—as a product of the historical struggle to establish norms of civil liberties in many societies. Without a doubt, Judge McDonald appraised the situation from this standpoint. This is not surprising, considering her antecedents on the American bench (McDonald is an African American who fought for civil liberties at the bar and on the bench in the United States), nor was she alone in reaching the first decision of the appellate chamber in *Barayagwiza*.

Courts in criminal cases constantly have to choose between the demands of procedural and substantive evidence (reflected in issues such as the admissibility of evidence seized in an unauthorized search or obtained by coerced confession, and the Miranda rules in the United States).[58] It depends, then, on which justice a particular court chooses to emphasize.[59] Reference was made to this point earlier in the discussion of Rwanda's *amicus curiae* submission to the Arusha tribunal in *Barayagwiza*.

It is also the case, however, that respect for the rights of the accused does not automatically mean an unconditional release of the defendant/appellant in a case such as this, for one can wonder if full justice has been done, or whether such a decision does not give a lopsided weight to technicalities over substance. The issue for debate is not that Barayagwiza's rights were upheld, but rather the *extent* of the remedy. Justice, surely, must mean that persons accused of crimes as grave as genocide should have their day in court, as Barayagwiza was wont to assert was his desire. A trial is not tantamount to a conviction, and the tribunal has so far acquitted three persons following substantive trials, on each occasion much to the displeasure of Rwanda's authorities and citizens. Moreover it is pertinent to note in regard to the "procedural justice" argument that one of the strongest demands that Barayagwiza not escape justice, whether before a national court or the international tribunal, came from Amnesty International.[60]

What is clear from the November 3 ruling is that the appeals judges were intent on delivering a stinging rebuke to the tribunal's prosecution branch. That there were prosecutorial lapses is demonstrated by the lenient construction by the Jorda appellate chamber of the requirement that a new fact should not have been known to the party seeking to establish it at the time of the decision that is up for review. In any event, the McDonald court's decision was a wake-up call not only to the prosecutor but to the tribunal as an institution, of the importance of procedural justice regarding pretrial arrest and detention. Far greater care has been taken on such matters since then, doubtless in light of experience.

We now turn to the second issue: the nature of international criminal tribunals. This was the most important underlying issue in *Barayagwiza*. And it was highlighted early in the controversy when Joseph Mutaboba, Rwanda's ambassador to the UN at the time, addressed a press conference on the controversial case in New York. Mutaboba noted that two *special* courts had been created to bring war criminals to justice. But "then [the Arusha tribunal] said; 'Let's work as a *classic* court' " (emphasis added). That, he concluded, was wrong. And there's the rub. Is the tribunal a "special court," and if so, what makes it different from a "classic" court, and should that have any implications for procedural justice? And if it does, was Joseph Kanyabashi, questioning the legitimacy of international judicial intervention, not on strong ground in his claim that the establishment of the tribunal violated the principle that the rights of individuals before the law should not be violated by special courts in special circumstances? These are critical questions, the answers to which lead us more accurately to what war crimes tribunals *really* are, not what we may wish to believe they are. They answer the issues of the raison d'être and framework of such courts.

The Arusha tribunal was created because genocide and other mass atrocities happened in Rwanda and claimed nearly a million lives. These are not exactly misdemeanors, and they were committed by persons, not phantom entities. Barayagwiza has been adjudged one of the culprits. That is why Security Council resolution 955 provides that the Arusha tribunal was established "for the sole purpose of prosecuting persons responsible for genocide and other serious violations of international humanitarian law" in Rwanda. If this is the case, then it follows that the tribunal and others like it are not ordinary courts in, say, the Old Bailey in London, or in Tokyo or Pretoria. What this means is that considerations of what on the face of it may appear to be technical matters of procedural justice must bear in mind the tribunal's raison d'être and resolve such matters within that framework. Respecting that framework means that where the prosecutor has brought an indictment, there ought to be, at the very least, a trial of the accused to determine his or her guilt or innocence except in cases where the prosecutor drops the charges.

No doubt, particular judges, such as the respected McDonald, may on the occasion deviate from this overarching framework. But as well-intentioned as such an emphasis on procedural justice may be, the result in *Barayagwiza* teaches lessons to all—that when it comes to these kinds of crimes, the expectation of a political community, whether the Security Council in New York or a rural community in Rwanda, is part of the mix in that nebulous term "justice". This is what those who interpret the nature of international war crimes tribunals from a political impact perspective have in mind when they argue that there simply should be no room in such tribunals to free on technical terms (before a substantive finding of guilt or innocence) a person charged with genocidal slaughter, because setting such a person free has political consequences[61] (as Mutaboba reminded journalists at his New York press conference, Barayagwiza had been found liable for human rights abuses in a civil suit filed against him in the Southern District of New York in 1994[62]). Indeed such analysts and practitioners argue that international criminal tribunals must move away from technicalities, which are mainly a characteristic of Anglo-Saxon legal culture.[63] All of this, however, is only one aspect of the framework issue regarding war crimes tribunals. The other, and perhaps more important one—to whom does the framework apply in reality?—will be discussed in the next chapter.

It is important to address the question of whether the first appellate chamber decision in *Barayagwiza* was "wrong" and the second "right." There is no simple answer to this question, for it cannot incontrovertibly be asserted that the decision of November 3, 1999 was *not* justice.[64] Regarding the second appellate ruling of March 3, 2000, from the analysis presented earlier it can be seen as a case where the court opted to emphasize substantive justice far more than the procedural. In that sense, there are those who believe it was not any more *right* than the first decision.[65] Certainly it was a common sense approach to the problem, and one more in accord with the tribunal's raison d'être.[66] From this perspective, it is wrong to ascribe to it a politicized motivation—a "caving in" to Rwanda's protests at the first decision, pure and simple. The circumstances, though, make this inference plausible, even if inaccurate. The international tribunal's appeals judges were fully aware of this impression. In a separate declaration appended to the March 31, 2000 decision, Judge Rafael Nieto-Navia rose to the stout defense of the international tribunal and his judicial brethren:

> I refute most strenuously the suggestion that in reaching decisions, political considerations should play a persuasive or governing role, in order to assuage States and ensure cooperation to achieve long-term goals of the Tribunal. On the contrary, in no circumstances would such considerations cause the Tribunal to compromise its judicial independence and integrity. This is a Tribunal whose decision must be taken, solely with the intention of both implementing the law and guaranteeing justice to the case before it, not as a result of political pressure and threats to withdraw cooperation being exerted by an angry government.[67]

If this was a response to Carla Del Ponte's "political declaration" at the appellate hearing, the prosecutor was to receive a robust political response from Rwanda as she sought to apply the tribunal's framework to both parties to the Rwandan conflict.

# CHAPTER 6

# CARLA DEL PONTE "AXED"

It was a case of two simultaneous truths.

—Yifat Susskind

As we have seen in chapter 3, when the International Criminal Tribunal for Rwanda (ICTR) was established in 1994, its statute prescribed that the chief prosecutor of the Hague tribunal would also be the chief prosecutor of the Arusha tribunal.[1] Thus for much of the past decade, the two tribunals had a common prosecutor. On August 28, 2003, the Security Council decided that the Arusha tribunal should now have its own full-time prosecutor, splitting the chief prosecutorial post and effectively removing Carla Del Ponte as chief prosecutor of the Arusha tribunal against her wishes.[2] Del Ponte (figure 6.1) was nevertheless reappointed as chief prosecutor at The Hague.

There was a combination of factors, some institutional, others of a raw political nature, that led to the chief prosecutor's ouster from her prosecutorial role in Arusha. Taken together, these factors were all ultimately political, to the extent that they demonstrate how the great powers determine the framework of war crimes tribunals. And the decision was the outcome of a *political* process in the Security Council. Mixed with what is, from an objective standpoint, a potentially beneficial impact on the effectiveness of the tribunals, the decision was also taken to serve medium to longer term strategic interests of the great powers to shorten the lifespan of the war crimes tribunals for Rwanda and the former Yugoslavia. Carla Del Ponte's prosecutorial policies had become inimical to those interests. Her convictions about her statutorily guaranteed "independence" as a prosecutor clashed with

**Figure 6.1** Carla Del Ponte, Prosecutor of the International Criminal Tribunal for Rwanda, 1999–2003.

the reality that it was the Security Council—the tribunal's parent organ and a political body—that called the shots.

It is widely believed, certainly by Del Ponte herself, that she was removed as the prosecutor of the Arusha tribunal as a result of a diplomatic campaign waged by the Rwandan government in reprisal for her attempts to investigate war crimes committed by the Rwandan Patriotic Front (RPF) troops in 1994 and bring charges against some of those soldiers (all of whom were Tutsi) before the tribunal. However the officially stated reason for her removal from the post had to do with expediting the efficient implementation of the road map to wrap up the work of the Arusha and the Hague tribunals by 2010. In that context, there were valid questions about the continued viability of having one prosecutor for two separate war crimes courts located thousands of miles apart. Management problems in Del Ponte's prosecutorial office at the Arusha tribunal also appear to have become intertwined with the "completion strategy" question. I shall examine briefly the structural background issue of a single prosecutor for the international tribunals at The Hague and Arusha, followed by the completion strategy question, and then the "Rwanda factor."

## YOKED TO THE HAGUE

A root problem that had faced the prosecutorial function of the Arusha tribunal was the structural one of an international war crimes tribunal situated in Arusha and another at The Hague having a single chief prosecutor in the first place. This odd arrangement was made against the backdrop of a highly politicized selection process for the chief prosecutor of the Hague tribunal several months earlier, when eight individuals were nominated unsuccessfully in succession for the position and the Russian Federation vetoed five of these candidates in the Security Council.[3] The Hague tribunal had been established in May 1993, 19 months earlier than the Arusha tribunal. It was not fully appreciated in the early days of 1993–1994 just how complicated and time consuming the trials at both war crimes tribunals would become. There was also a certain view that both courts would benefit from the development of a common prosecution strategy, standardized procedures, and case law, developed in the then newly emergent system of international criminal justice and facilitated by their having a single chief prosecutor.[4]

But this is an apolitical view, or an apolitical rationale for a politically inspired construct. The counterfactual is that the Arusha tribunal having been established largely out of guilt and then only because the

Hague court existed as a precedent, there was a perhaps unconscious instinct to situate it in the shadow of The Hague by having the latter's court's chief prosecutor supervise prosecutions at Arusha. Moreover it was clear that in the establishment of two international tribunals by the Security Council, international judicial intervention had emerged as a major new dimension in world politics alongside diplomacy and the use of force. It was strategically important at the time to centralize control of that instrument in one person who would be accountable to the Security Council.

Furthermore setting common jurisprudential standards is a task for judges, not prosecutors. The two tribunals have appellate courts that are technically separate but are composed of the same judges. As most verdicts at the trial level are appealed, the appellate chambers were expected to ensure that there were no embarrassing contradictions in the jurisprudence that was being established for the first time since Nuremberg. All of this is to make the point that having one prosecutor for both tribunals was neither essential nor, in retrospect, logical—a rough equivalent is to argue that because the Nuremberg and Tokyo tribunals were established by the same group of allied states, they should have had the same prosecutor for separate war crimes tribunals in two continents.

There also was a fundamental, practical question: could one chief prosecutor oversee prosecutors at The Hague and Arusha at the same time? As Professor Cherif Bassiouni notes: "The choice of a single Prosecutor was particularly ill advised because no person, no matter how talented, can oversee two major sets of prosecutions separated by 10,000 miles. The idea that one can shuttle between The Hague, Netherlands and Arusha, Tanzania as part of a normal work schedule is nothing short of absurd."[5]

Even in the early days of the tribunals, Judge Goldstone had a difficult time heading the prosecution functions of both.[6] And as an internal investigation by the United Nation's (UN) Office of Internal Oversight Services (OIOS) found 10 years after the Arusha tribunal was created, the expected synergy from having a common chief prosecutor for the two courts did not materialize, leading the internal watchdog to conclude that "consideration needed to be given to the International Criminal Tribunal for Rwanda having its own Prosecutor."[7]

As we have seen, at the time that tribunal was established in 1994, Rwanda criticized the strong—and subordinate—institutional link to the Hague tribunal of the prosecutorial office of the Arusha court, a tribunal that was formally separate and independent from the Hague tribunal.[8] Argentina would also have preferred a tribunal with its own appeals chamber and prosecutor but "understood the reasons why the present solution was accepted," and was pleased to see that as a compromise, a deputy chief prosecutor was to be appointed for the Arusha tribunal.[9]

The greatest political impact of the original design that yoked the Arusha tribunal to the one at The Hague through one prosecutor based at The Hague was that the arrangement appeared decidedly "colonial." It created a strong impression of the war crimes tribunal in Africa as an appendage of the one in Europe, reinforcing a view that the "African" tribunal was not really as important in the eyes of global policy makers as its "European" counterpart. The Rwandan government certainly felt that justice for their citizens was not as high a global priority as justice in the Balkans.[10] Thus the Arusha tribunal appeared second class in relation to the Hague tribunal by reason of its having a "part-time chief prosecutor" based at The Hague and preoccupied with the trials of its Slobodan Milosevic and other Balkan war crimes defendants.

When Arbour was the chief prosecutor of both tribunals, Bernard Muna, her deputy for the ICTR, essentially ran the prosecution and enjoyed a large degree of delegated authority. Upon Arbour's departure, Muna's relationship with her successor, Del Ponte, soured progressively as the latter whittled down Muna's role and insisted on centralizing decision making for the Arusha tribunal's prosecutions at The Hague. Del Ponte eventually recommended the non-renewal of Muna's appointment—effectively removing Muna from his position in 2001; the deputy chief prosecutor's position (and that of chief of prosecutions) were then subsequently left unfilled for nearly two years, creating grave management problems for war crimes prosecutions for the Rwanda half of her office.[11]

Carla Del Ponte had been aware of the criticisms of neglect of Rwanda war crimes trials by a Hague-based chief prosecutor. Her visits to Arusha and Kigali (about four times a year) still did not remove an impression of a distant prosecutor who ran the Arusha tribunal prosecution team by remote control from The Hague, parachuting into East Africa at intervals to put in the occasional court appearance. This "parachute" factor was of course generated largely by the fundamental problem of how the tribunal was designed. But what if the chief prosecutor had chosen to relocate to Arusha, either partially or full-time shuttling to The Hague? Del Ponte, as noted above, was well aware of the political sensitivity this issue was already generating when she took up her post. That was as good a time as any to make a decision about where to live, and she made a decision to live in The

Hague. As the Rwandans have pointed out, with not a little irony per-haps, the statute of the Arusha tribunal vested its chief prosecutor position and that of the older Hague tribunal in the same official, but did not stipulate that the prosecutor had to live in The Hague. If that official had chosen to live in Arusha and visit The Hague occasionally, then perhaps the Rwandan government would not have been as both-ered as it was because its own national interests were the ones being harmed by the subsisting arrangement.[12]

All of this notwithstanding, in the early summer of 2003, there was nothing in the public domain to indicate that the Security Council was considering a restructuring of the post of chief prosecu-tor of the Arusha and Hague tribunals, although senior Rwandan offi-cials had long made clear their displeasure at the existing situation. Moreover back in 1999, the Expert Group that Kofi Annan had appointed at the UN General Assembly's request to review the func-tioning of the Arusha and Hague tribunals had concluded that mid-way through the life of the tribunals, there was "no compelling reason" to recommend the appointment of a separate prosecutor for the Arusha court.[13]

But as Del Ponte approached the completion of her initial four-year appointment as chief prosecutor of the two UN war crimes courts in September 2003 and a renewal was up for consideration by the Security Council, Secretary General Kofi Annan wrote a letter to the Council recommending the appointment of a separate prosecutor for the ICTR. It was on the basis of that recommendation that the Council split the previous single prosecutor position into two[14] and in a subse-quent decision,[15] appointed former Gambian attorney general and Supreme Court judge Hassan Bubacar Jallow chief prosecutor of the ICTR. Annan's letter anchored his recommendation on the need for efficient completion strategies for both tribunals. The Security Council's decision agreed with this rationale, with the Council noting that it was "convinced that the International Criminal Tribunal for the Former Yugoslavia (ICTY) and the ICTR can most efficiently meet their responsibilities if each has its own Prosecutor."[16]

## EXIT STRATEGY

Several UN member states have become increasingly tardy in financing the ad hoc tribunals for Rwanda and former Yugoslavia,[17] although the costs of both tribunals do not amount to more than a tiny fraction of global military spending by the Western powers that contribute most of the tribunal's costs.[18] This is an indication that the real reason for the pressure for a completion strategy may be that, after a decade, the tribunals are close to discharging their core mandates, and their continued existence exerts pressure for international judicial intervention in other, politically inconvenient situations where juridical intervention is not perceived as a matter of state interest by the great powers. There is, of course, the quite valid need to avoid "mission creep." The tribunals had no "sunset clause" that assured a date for the completion of their work, a situation that Brazil had expressly criticized during the statements in the Security Council that followed the vote that established the ICTR.[19] The cases before the two ad hoc tribunals initially moved at a plodding pace, largely because they had too few judges and crowded dockets. After a decade of existence, it was obvious that if nothing drastic was done, hearings would continue for another 15–20 years—a situation that would make a mockery of the phrase "ad hoc tribunals." It became imperative to establish an end date—initially called an "exit strategy" but later changed to the more politically correct phrase "completion strategy"—for the ICTY and ICTR to wrap up their trials. For Rwanda, where the ICTR prosecution relied mostly on witness testimonies (unlike the Nazi trials where there was a long trail of documentary evidence, or the former Yugoslavia, where Western powers had satellite images of mass graves and communications intercepts of the conversations of Serb military commanders), the accuracy of recollections from memories of events that occurred more than a decade ago, was an additional concern. The Security Council has set a cut-off date of end 2008 for trials and 2010 for appeals for both international tribunals. To achieve that target, all investigations by the prosecution were to be completed by the end of 2004.[20]

For the United States, the main financial and political supporter of the two courts, there might have been even more strategic reasons to shorten the lifespan of the tribunals: America's critics were making good use of the inconsistency in principle between American support for the ad hoc tribunals and its vigorous opposition to the International Criminal Court (ICC). In reality, however, the ad hoc tribunals were set up to deal with specific regional conflicts and did not pose as much of a strategic threat to America as the ICC, which covers many more countries by treaty arrangement and thus aims to be universal. Even then, an attempt had been made to bring charges against U.S. troops for alleged war crimes committed during NATO bombing in Kosovo in 1999—an incident that infuriated American policy makers and strengthened their resolve against the ICC.

Thus both ad hoc, UN Security Council created tribunals and the ICC were institutions that reflected the same principle (that of supranational justice administered by international institutions) and were different only as a matter of specifics. An overly extended life span for the Hague and Arusha tribunals had become inconvenient, and consistency of position from an American foreign policy perspective had to be established. The U.S. war crimes ambassador Pierre-Richard Prosper (figure 6.2) articulated the year 2008 as the completion date for the work of the tribunals.[21] An important factor in U.S. policy is also that of a general shift in preference from top–down, international prosecutions to the establishment of accountability by national courts for violations of international humanitarian law.[22]

It is also an interesting coincidence that this policy shift followed the terrorist attack of 9/11 and the launch of a war against terrorism in which the United States is loathe to accept that terrorists can be tried by international tribunals rather than by American courts.[23]

**Figure 6.2**   Honorable Pierre-Richard Prosper, United States Ambassador at Large for War Crimes Issues. Prosper was the ICTR lead prosecutor in the Akayesu trial.

All of this, of course, is just one example of how the framework of international war crimes tribunals is molded largely by the national interests of individual, powerful states. Prosper faced criticism for his proactive policy push for a specific end date for the work of the tribunals, with some critics complaining that his statements called the independence of the ad hoc tribunals into question—a criticism that glosses over the political reality that the tribunals are ad hoc, were created by the great powers, and their lifespan is thus dependent on the political decisions of those powers.[24] Prosper was not telling the tribunals how to decide specific cases before them. He was, rather addressing their continued institutional existence—a thoroughly political question that lies squarely in the purview of sovereign states in the UN Security Council.

Against the background of an exit strategy that called for a significant pruning of numbers of investigations in order to meet a cut-off date of 2004, Carla Del Ponte was initially politically tone-deaf. She saw her role as an independent prosecutor as one of investigating, indicting, and prosecuting accused war criminals as long as there were any at large. If only things were so straightforward, and if the pursuit of *genocidaires* and war criminals happens outside a political context, maybe this would be a feasible approach to the challenge. As late as November 2001, addressing the Security Council, Del Ponte outlined her intention to launch a further 136 investigations at the ICTR to bring her investigative mandate to an end by December 2004.[25] This was an "outer universe," as the chief prosecutor explained that several factors affected whether or not investigations resulted in actual prosecutions—some of the suspects may be dead, not all investigations succeeded in gathering substantive evidence, and some of the accused persons simply could not be traced.[26]

Despite these caveats, some members of the Security Council, the judges of the Arusha tribunal, and even some of Del Ponte's staff in Arusha and Kigali were uneasy with such a large scope of investigative targets.[27] Knowing how slowly the wheels of justice turned, there was no realistic prospect of completing so many investigations of war criminals by the end of 2004. Moreover not a few of her colleagues believed that many of the additional suspects Del Ponte was bent on pursuing were persons who ought to be no priority for an international tribunal that hitherto had focused mainly on apprehending the "big fish." But Del Ponte now sought to establish what she called "the local face of the genocide" by indicting persons who, though only of minimal significance in the planning of nationwide massacres in the national context, were important ringleaders at local levels. Her belief that she should investigate and propose indictments as long as there were targets was resolute, but some members of the Security Council became progressively concerned at her purist approach to her role. By July 2002, reluctantly responding to the political pressure from states, Del Ponte revised her investigations program for the ICTR from 136 new suspects to 14, with 10 ongoing investigations, making a total of 24 projected new indictments.[28] In May 2003, however, the number of new investigative targets increased to 26.[29]

## AT THE SECURITY COUNCIL

What, then, happened in the capitals of members of the Security Council, and in New York regarding the future of the ICTR chief prosecutor? The U.S. ambassador Prosper provided this rationale for the removal of Del Ponte:

> The management of the OTP [office of the Prosecutor] was severely lacking from the very beginning, exacerbated by the fact that the prosecutor was based at The Hague. There were all the problems [between Del Ponte and] the deputy prosecutor. Everyone was afraid to make a decision because it had to be cleared at The Hague—and that's no way to run an office. The set-up was inherently inefficient. That was a driving factor. The next part was the completion strategy. Because the [prosecutor's] office was inefficient, the chances of our reaching a completion strategy were reduced. So we put the two together and decided that this [removing Del Ponte] was the best way to go.[30]

U.S. foreign policy, then, played a critical role in Del Ponte's ouster. But the human rights expert Aryeh Neier has noted that the United Kingdom also played a key role in the process of splitting the position of chief prosecutor for the Hague and Arusha tribunals and appointing a separate prosecutor for the latter.[31] Carla Del Ponte has asserted as much in discussing the split and her removal from the Arusha court.[32] The United States was drafting the Security Council resolution on a decision on Del Ponte's mandate when it came up for review in August 2003. America's initial strategy, led by Prosper, had been to deny the chief prosecutor a full four-year appointment. Rather Del Ponte's joint appointment for the Hague and Arusha tribunals would be extended for one year only, with the possibility of yearly renewals.[33] This strategy was designed to be used as a leverage to ensure that the completion strategy followed a script written by the great powers, especially by the United States.[34]

It was at this point that Britain, according to Prosper, suggested that splitting the prosecutorial functions of the two tribunals would enhance the efficiency of the Arusha court.[35] Washington's initial response was cautious. It did not oppose the proposal, and in fact eventually warmed to it. But the United States still felt committed to its original approach. As it "shopped" its draft of a resolution around to members of the Security Council, however, Washington found that it was "not getting any traction" on its proposal for a one-year extension, but "everyone was getting excited about the proposal for a split" of the prosecutor's functions.[36] The United States then swung behind the British proposal. It still toyed with the idea of renewing Del Ponte's mandate at The Hague for one year, with roll-overs while approving a new chief prosecutor at Arusha for a full four-year term. The possibility was discussed by several diplomats, but it proved too complicated and was dropped.

While national diplomats in various capitals and in New York were talking quietly to themselves about Del Ponte's future, Secretary General Kofi Annan, who had perhaps the most accurate picture of the institutional problems that had trailed Del Ponte's tenure as chief prosecutor of the Arusha tribunal (the chief prosecutor is appointed by the Security Council, but on the recommendation of the secretary general), was coming to his own conclusions about the position. Keenly aware that, in his words, "the question of the separation of the prosecutor function has been around for quite a long time,"[37] he concluded that the completion of Del Ponte's four-year term presented the perfect opportunity to solve the problem once and for all. Annan was motivated largely by the logistical problems that confronted a prosecutor in directing prosecutions in two tribunals thousands of kilometers apart, the need for undivided attention to both the cases at Arusha and the Milosevic trial at The Hague, and the Security Council's judgment that the time had come for the ICTY and the ICTR to each have its own prosecutor if the work of the two tribunals was to be completed in good time.[38] The negotiations among members of the Security Council were low-key, but it was Annan's letter of July 28 to the Council recommending a split that sealed Del Ponte's fate.[39]

But the Swiss-born prosecutor would not go quietly into the good night. She was determined to retain her dual position. She flew to New York in late July and held two tense meetings with Annan. Following their initial meeting, the secretary general agreed to give

Del Ponte a chance to lobby Security Council members to renew her appointment at both tribunals, which was to expire on September 15.[40] On July 29, Del Ponte met Annan again to brief him on her discussions with members of the Council before returning to Europe. Sensing that what she termed a "political" decision on her fate had already been made, she made a proposal she thought could save the day and take the sting out of the looming decision to relieve her of her Rwanda post: Del Ponte informed Annan that if her post was to be split, she would rather be prosecutor of the ICTR than the ICTY. She asked if she could choose between The Hague and Kigali.[41] "No," she recounted that Annan responded. "The trial of Milosevic is too important to be left in the hands of someone else."[42] It is doubtful that Carla Del Ponte's request was anything more than a tactical ploy to hold on to her double-barreled title. Few believe she had any real desire to give up The Hague for Arusha. Leaving the UN Headquarters building after her meeting with the secretary general, political reporters in tow, Del Ponte was asked about the encounter by television journalists. "No comment," she responded. "Ask the secretary-general." But she was to tell the media later that Annan was "inflexible" and "I realized there was no room for negotiation."[43]

## Rwanda's Campaign

Although Rwandan officials disavowed any role in Del Ponte's removal from her post,[44] she attributes her ouster largely to pressure by Rwanda's government on various members of the Security Council in response to her attempts to investigate war crimes committed by the RPF.[45] Circumstantial evidence points to a concerted diplomatic lobby by Rwanda to have Del Ponte consigned to The Hague as ICTY prosecutor and a separate prosecutor appointed for the ICTR. In addition to New York, Del Ponte believes part of that campaign took place at the annual summit of African heads of state and government in Maputo, Mozambique, in July 2003, bringing the African members of the Security Council on board.[46] The relative weight of the Rwandan campaign vis-à-vis the other factors discussed earlier is difficult to determine. That it had some influence on some key member states of the Security Council is not in doubt. Less certain is whether the Rwandan campaign's influence on the great powers was predicated on the order-based, strategic argument that derives from a perceived need to ensure the stability of Rwanda's government, as Del Ponte and many observers believe, or on the institutional reasons discussed earlier. It is more likely that, for certain states at least, both factors were important. While both factors were important for Rwanda, the political sensitivity created by the appearance of one of two equal international war crimes receiving unequal treatment was more persuasive to most states on the Council. One commentator put it most aptly: "It was," he said, "a case of two simultaneous truths."[47]

Rwanda's relationship with the Arusha tribunal has always been one of shifting moods, guided by what the country considers its strategic interest. Its leader, President Paul Kagame, is widely respected as a cerebral, strategic soldier and political leader who has a clear vision for his country. His credibility rests on his reputation for discipline and for having ended the genocide with the RPF's military victory. In the latter fact lies the tension in Rwanda's relationship with the international tribunal's mandate to prosecute crimes committed by both sides to the conflict. Thus despite the letter of the tribunal's statute, the RPF has consistently been sensitive to what it sees as attempts to create a moral equivalency between the genocide of nearly a million Tutsis and war crimes of relatively far lesser gravity committed by the troops that liberated the country. It has sought to ensure that the day when the international tribunal would indict RPF (and mostly Tutsi) troops would never come.

When the then ICTR registrar Okali met with Paul Kagame in Kigali in 1998, Kagame described his country and the tribunal as "partners" in the search for justice.[48] Whether that "partnership" concept includes trials of RPF troops is open to conjecture. For the Hutu opponents of the Rwandan government, the credibility of the tribunal—and the possibilities of political reconciliation—rests on whether or not the ICTR is able to punish crimes committed by RPF soldiers. Absent such accountability, they consider the tribunal the justice of the victor. It would thus be one-way accountability, despite the tribunal's mandate to prosecute both the victor and the vanquished.[49] Of course, this does not match with the notion of retributive justice as just desserts. From this perspective, the extremists regret not the massacres they planned and committed, but losing the war.

That war, as we shall see, is not over, for the extremist forces continue to foment instability and sow fear in Rwanda from their bases in the Democratic Republic of Congo (DRC). For the RPF, the Arusha tribunal's judicial process is a means to seal its military victory over the forces of genocide. In the eyes of most of its leaders, trials of RPF soldiers at the tribunal are simply out of sync with this strategic consideration.

This situation has always been a challenge for the Arusha tribunal. The nature of the institution meant that it could not function effectively—including in investigating RPF crimes—without Rwanda's cooperation because much of those investigations had to take place in Rwandan territory. Although noncooperation could trigger sanctions by the Security Council if the tribunal reported as much, in reality the guilt that states felt over their failure to prevent or halt the genocide, coupled with the close strategic relationship the United States and Britain established with Rwanda after the genocide, made resort to such a tool—at least in the early years of the tribunal's work—unlikely. In any case, the Security Council has never imposed formal sanctions on any country for noncooperation with an ad hoc war crimes tribunal. In the case of the Hague tribunal, its members have utilized individual threats of economic sanctions in the Bretton Woods institutions, membership of NATO's Partnership for Peace program, and the carrot of EU accession talks to compel Croatia's cooperation. And in order to debunk Serbian nationalist claims of anti-Serb bias, that tribunal has indicted and is prosecuting accused war criminals from all sides of the wars of the former Yugoslavia.

It was in this context that the Arusha tribunal had to proceed. And there was a tactical question: should the tribunal investigate RPF war crimes early on, when the likes of the alleged genocide mastermind Theoneste Bagosora were yet to be judged? Or should such investigations be left to the tail end of the tribunal's work? The genocide itself provided a heavy enough caseload. The provisions of the statute notwithstanding, is the prosecution of RPF troops really unavoidable? We will return to this question later.

In the beginning, however, the government of Rwanda indicated in its interactions with the ICTR prosecution that it would cooperate with investigations of alleged RPF crimes, despite its early displeasure with the framework of the tribunal. But subsequent events proved that when faced with the imminence of such inquiries, Kigali balked.[50] It soon became evident that the Rwandan authorities were not inclined to allow the investigation and possible indictment of RPF soldiers.

In the period from 1997 to 1999, Chief Prosecutor Louise Arbour and her deputy Bernard Muna embarked on a discrete conversation with the Rwandan government on this sensitive aspect of the chief prosecutor's task.[51] The response from Kagame was initially positive. The ICTR senior prosecutors wanted the government to turn over files on alleged massacres, such as the killings of the Catholic priests in Kabgayi. They sought to persuade the Rwandan authorities, including through Rwanda's military prosecutor, that cooperating with the international tribunal was in their interest.

Del Ponte's appointment as the new chief prosecutor—and the jarring note introduced by the *Barayagwiza* case—delayed these negotiations. Moreover Del Ponte's aggressive stance complicated the more cautious strategy of her predecessors.[52] Some ICTR prosecution investigators were subsequently dispatched to European countries on investigative assignments into RPF crimes. But this approach was never going to yield nearly as much as investigations on the ground in Rwanda conducted with Rwanda's cooperation.

When Del Ponte first discussed the investigations into RPF atrocities with President Kagame sometime in 2000, the Rwandan leader pledged his cooperation, but he later backtracked as a result of pressure from hardliners within the Rwandan military.[53] Their argument: their RPF government had integrated several Hutu soldiers of the former RGF into the new post-genocide national army. Not a few of these integrated soldiers had doubtless committed atrocities. If they (former RPF troops) are to be prosecuted, then the Hutus in the army would have to face trial too, they argued. If everyone who committed violations of international humanitarian law were to be prosecuted, order would be threatened.[54] In the continental political context, a coup attempt by disgruntled Tutsi soldiers who would feel threatened by ICTR indictments could not be ruled out. And such a scenario would be profoundly destabilizing to the RPF's hard-won victory—and to the country itself. Kagame had to keep his troops pacified by *not* giving in to the chief prosecutor's demands.

Del Ponte met with Kagame in Kigali again in April 2001. Again Kagame promised his government's cooperation. Rwigamba, the Rwandan military prosecutor, participated in the meeting. He told the media afterward: "We reiterated our determination to cooperate in dealing with suspects of genocide and other crimes against humanity . . . especially, on behalf of the [Rwandan] military we reiterated the same cooperation."[55]

One year later, the picture had changed, with a decidedly frosty chill emanating from the Rwandan authorities toward Del Ponte's investigations. Three specific investigations of RPF crimes were already underway, and Del Ponte was hoping to issue the first indictments before the end of the year.[56] "We have opened investigations into three massacres," she said. "I have spoken to Paul Kagame. I showed him a list of the massacres and said we will be investigating. I said that if Rwanda wants justice and peace there must be accountability on both sides."[57] But the international prosecutor noted that the Rwandan leader had not delivered on his pledge to cooperate, and most of the investigations into massacres allegedly committed by the RPF had been conducted outside Rwanda.[58]

The relationship between the ICTR prosecutor and Rwandan authorities became so tense that, in mid-2002, Rwanda suspended cooperation with the international tribunal by creating restrictions on Rwandan witnesses who had to travel from Kigali to Arusha to give evidence as prosecution witnesses in trials. This action was ostensibly based on claims by some of the witnesses—who also happened to be survivors—that they had been subjected to insensitive treatment at the hands of defense counsel. This allegation was not baseless. Although Rwandans were new to the common law adversarial system that was dominant at the international tribunal, some defense lawyers were quite insensitive in their questioning of Rwandan women who had been raped and sexually abused and were witnesses for the prosecution. But this was certainly not the real reason why Rwanda cut off the flow of prosecution witnesses, mostly victims and survivors of genocide, without whom trials could not continue. With witnesses effectively barred from coming to Arusha to testify in the hearings, several trials ground to a temporary halt.

The prospect of a prolonged suspension of trials at the tribunal evoked a scenario where the defense counsel would take legal steps to seek the release of their clients. As the tribunal's president at the time, the South African judge Navanethem Pillay, noted: "That would be justice too, you know, because you cannot hold defendants indefinitely without trial. No matter what they have done. But it is not the justice we came to Arusha to find."[59]

In these circumstances, the tribunal's judges issued judicial rulings in the cases affected by the witness crisis, reprimanding Rwanda's noncooperation and reminding the Rwandan government of its statutory *obligation* to cooperate with the tribunal's judicial work. This was to no avail. Judge Pillay formally reported Rwanda's noncooperation to the Security Council, backing up complaints by Del Ponte. The Council responded to Judge Pillay's report six months later. Nevertheless several governments, in particular the United States, privately pressed Kigali to resume cooperation with the tribunal. The flow of prosecution witnesses from Rwanda to Arusha resumed after several months, but by then Rwanda's relationship with Del Ponte had deteriorated even further.

When Del Ponte met on November 18, 2002—presumably in the course of her investigations of war crimes committed by RPF forces— with representatives of the Alliance for the Liberation of Rwanda (ALIR), an extremist Hutu opposition group based in the DRC, the Rwandan government issued a press release condemning the prosecutor in strong terms for hobnobbing with "a known terrorist organization which regards genocide in Rwanda as an unfinished business . . ."[60] The Rwandan statement continued:

> For sometime now, the ICTR prosecutor has acted in a manner clearly designed to politicize the office she occupies and indeed, she has on several occasions confessed that some of the decisions she has made were motivated by political considerations and pressure. Carla Del Ponte's meeting with a known Rwandan terrorist and genocidal organization . . . comes as a culmination of her deliberate policy of dangerously veering from the issues of justice, to a point where she is now wining and dining with people whose confessed ideology and practice is genocide. Today, the people of Rwanda have lost faith in Del Ponte's objectivity and capacity to deliver justice . . .
>
> It is in light of these shocking revelations, therefore, that the Government of Rwanda calls upon the international community and the United Nations Security Council in particular to hold her accountable for her deliberate conduct, which clearly bears grave consequences.[61]

On that ominous note, then, the die was cast. Rwanda had drawn a line in the sand. But Del Ponte was not one to be easily cowed. Barely one week later, seeking to capitalize on Rwanda's strong relations with Britain, Del Ponte responded to Rwanda's attacks against her. The occasion was a speech the international prosecutor delivered to the British Parliament's All Party Parliamentary Group on the Great Lakes Region and Genocide Prevention in London on November 25, 2002. Del Ponte reviewed the tribunal's judicial activities and described the prevailing situation in which the Rwandan authorities had withdrawn their cooperation with the ICTR. Her disappointment was expressed in measured but trenchant declarations:

> Although it has been publicly stated that the reason for the suspension of cooperation is the way witnesses are treated, the true reason is to be found elsewhere. As I indicated to the Security Council, we have good reasons to believe that powerful elements within Rwanda strongly oppose the investigation, in the execution of the ICTR mandate, of crimes allegedly committed by members of the Rwandan Patriotic Army in 1994. Despite assurances given to me in the past, no concrete assistance has been provided in response to repeated requests regarding these investigations. There is no genuine political will on the part of the Rwandan Authorities to provide assistance in an area of work that they interpret to be political in nature . . .
>
> *Only a few days ago, the Government of Rwanda released a statement accusing me of acting politically and also of abusing my office, for having met with representatives of groups opposed to the Kigali Government.*

*Without commenting further on my rights and duties as an independent Prosecutor. I wish to record my disappointment. For me, a victim is a victim, a crime falling within my mandate as the ICTR Prosecutor is a crime, irrespective of the identity or the ethnicity or the political ideas of the person who committed the said crime. Justice does not accommodate political opportunism. No one should remain immune from prosecutions from the worst crimes. The political and military leadership of Rwanda has to accept to respond to the allegations of crimes that may have been committed by their own side. If they are genuinely interested to foster true peace and reconciliation in their country and in the Great Lakes Region, they should fully and unconditionally cooperate with the ICTR.* (emphasis Carla Del Ponte's)[62]

Del Ponte was careful to stress that prosecuting the instigators of the genocide of Rwanda's Tutsis remained, "without any ambiguity," the core of the tribunal's mandate. But she raised the philosophical question of denying justice to any victim of the crimes within the tribunal's remit—genocide, crimes against humanity, and war crimes. In doing so, she evoked the debate between principle and pragmatic relativity that is at the heart of the thorny question of prosecuting the soldiers of the government that is now in power in Rwanda.

But Del Ponte, principled as she appears to be in her judicial work, has indeed occasionally introduced political considerations into judicial matters. Her opening courtroom statement in the *Barayagwiza* appellate hearing is a case in point. This is a reluctant admission of the political reality that affects her work. Given the political framework of international criminal tribunals, this is an inescapable reality. But the courtroom was surely not the place for that argument, and it must be seen for what it is: a conscious application of political tactics to ostensibly purist juridical ends. Either way, her occasional verbal appeals to politics have lent her to criticisms of double standards by her Rwandan critics. In London, she again appealed to political/strategic realities in soliciting British support: "I am particularly turning to you," she told the British parliamentarians, "as I believe that the United Kingdom is in a strong position to recall to the Government of Rwanda its obligations of cooperation. The financial aid allocated by your country to Rwanda corresponds to a very substantial part of the budget of Rwanda . . ."[63] This was a clear appeal to hegemonic power and influence in aid of the "pure" principle of justice. In the next breath, she offered the argument of legalism's imperative— justice as *policy*—against that of *strategy*, drawing parallels with the Balkan states of the Federal Republic of Yugoslavia and Croatia:

Obviously, there is always a "good" reason to justify non-cooperation. There is always some political consideration or struggle, some forthcoming election. There will always be unresolved strategic issues of genuine concern to the International Community . . . Broad concerns of this kind will occupy the minds of those who have to deal with the reconstruction of divided societies . . . My point, however, is that some "magical" or "ideal" moment will never arise for cooperating with International Tribunals. No system of justice anywhere in the world is expected to work that way. The right time concerning investigating and prosecuting crimes such as genocide, crimes against humanity, war crimes is always now, today.[64]

As the summer of 2003 approached—and with it the matter of the renewal of Del Ponte's appointment—Rwanda emphasized its position that it would try Rwandan Patriotic Army (RPA) soldiers suspected of war crimes in its own courts, and that the international tribunal at Arusha should focus on the genocide of Tutsis committed by Hutu *genocidaires*. There were three problems with this position. First, while Rwandan courts surely have jurisdiction over these crimes, the Arusha tribunal's jurisdiction is preeminent over that of national courts. Second, although Rwanda frequently claims to have tried Tutsis suspected of war crimes, or to be perfectly willing to do so, its record in this respect is spotty. As some human rights groups have observed, the Rwandan military court has tried just one senior officer, a major, for war crimes committed in 1994.[65] The officer confessed to a massacre of more than 30 people and was sentenced to life in prison, but he successfully appealed his sentence and was set free.[66] Of five others convicted of war crimes in 1994, four were privates, one was a corporal, and all were given light sentences: the corporal, convicted of killing 15 civilians, was sentenced to a two-year prison term.[67] Alison des Forges, a Rwanda expert and human rights activist whose record as a chronicler of the genocide does not easily lend her to charges of anti-Tutsi bias, commented wryly that "Rwanda has had nine years to deal with such cases, and it has not done a significant job."[68]

Rwanda's record is reminiscent of the domestic trial of German war criminals in Leipzig following World War I, when the defeated German government demanded and got a dispensation from Allied Powers to prosecute Germans accused of war crimes. Those found guilty were given ridiculously light sentences, and then set free soon afterward. The difference here is that the current government of Rwanda was the victor, not the vanquished, in the Rwandan civil war. Its behavior is consistent with a pattern that is recurrent in many other countries, including powerful states and victors in war. Few are willing to try their own war criminals, but would be happy to put on trial those of the opponent or defeated states or groups. As the colloquial

cliché goes, "he may be a son of a bitch, but he is *our* son of a bitch."
The third problem with Rwanda's position is the perception problem
it hands the international tribunal at Arusha. Should the tribunal end
up not having prosecuted any Tutsis, many will consider that it failed
to discharge its mandate in full.

Ambassador Prosper, seeking to leverage American influence with
both the international tribunal and the Rwandan government, offered
to mediate.

But first, what was Washington's point of departure on the
accountability of RPF forces for crimes committed in 1994? Was it
opposed to the Arusha tribunal undertaking such prosecutions if they
would have the effect of destabilizing Rwanda and the Great Lakes
Region as Rwanda claims they would? The prevailing assumption is
that the United States would not like to see RPF troops and commanders prosecuted at Arusha in such a scenario. Undoubtedly this
sympathy exists in a larger, geopolitical context. But the situation is
considerably more nuanced.

For Prosper, the starting position of his government was that
allegations of atrocities by RPF soldiers needed to be investigated.
"We are agnostic as to who investigates these allegations, so long as it
is done fairly and properly and it is genuine. If it is by the international
tribunal, that's fine; if it is by Rwanda, that's ok, but it is necessary to
close the chapter of 1994."[69] From this perspective, Prosper tried
to broker an agreement that recognized the international tribunal's
primacy but gave Rwanda a sense of ownership of the investigations.
In the spring of 2003, Prosper met in his eight-floor office in the
U.S. Department of State in Washington with Carla Del Ponte, accompanied by her aides, and the Rwandan delegation for negotiations on
the issue. On the Rwandan side there was the then attorney general
Gerald Gahima, Richard Sezibera, then Rwanda's ambassador in
Washington, DC, and Martin Ngoga, a Rwandan lawyer–diplomat
who was at the time Kigali's official observer at the ICTR in Arusha.[70]

Del Ponte's recollection is that she was invited to Washington for a
general discussion on cooperation between her office and the Rwandan
authorities, but to her "surprise," Prosper suggested that she let the
Rwandan government take over responsibility for investigations into
alleged crimes by the RPF.[71] But she was unwilling to pass on to the
Rwandan authorities the information she had gathered in her investigations. And, against the background of positions that Kagame had
expressed to her in their meeting in 2002, she doubted the workabil-
ity of any understanding that would be reached at this meeting, if such
an agreement was based on the tribunal maintaining the primacy of its

jurisdiction to prosecute violations of international humanitarian law in Rwanda.[72] The international prosecutor believed the Rwandan leader's current position left little or no room for a role for the Arusha tribunal in prosecutions of RPF soldiers. Against this background, Del Ponte declined to relinquish the tribunal's investigations, but agreed to Rwanda conducting its own investigations in the exercise of its concurrent jurisdiction, which would be reviewed by the international prosecutor after two or three months to assess their credibility.[73]

Over coffee, the delegations worked out an agreement whereby Rwanda would carry out some investigations of RPF suspects and submit the results to the ICTR for an assessment.[74] If they were judged to have been a credible and fair process, the tribunal would not issue indictments but support prosecution in Rwandan courts. The meeting then tried to reach an understanding on what events would actually be investigated. Thus it was a "partnership approach" toward these investigations, and all parties walked away believing they had reached an understanding.[75] This was important because the tension between Rwanda and the tribunal was, in Prosper's view, detrimental to the tribunal and "ripe for resolution," not to mention that the spillover effect of resolving the standoff would be beneficial to the political equation in the Great Lakes Region as a whole.[76]

On returning to The Hague, however, Del Ponte later telephoned Prosper and informed him that she had received advice against implementing the agreement. Del Ponte then backed out of the understanding and followed up her oral communication with a letter to Prosper.[77] A subsequent meeting that had been planned in Kigali fell through. The "deal" was dead.

Meanwhile Rwanda's campaign against Del Ponte in the Security Council was picking up.[78] The African states in the Council were by now supportive of a split. Rwandan diplomats approached the United States for more robust support. America gave it, tacitly. America's response was: "if you get the votes, we're with you."[79]

Rwanda's campaign did not put forward the core reason for its opposition to Del Ponte—its resistance to her attempts to investigate alleged RPA atrocities. Rather it dwelt on the more appealing—and objectively more persuasive—rationale that ICTR prosecutions were suffering neglect at the hands of a prosecutor who considered Rwanda part of a far-flung prosecutorial empire. "The genocide has been dealt with by a part-time prosecutor," Rwandan diplomat Valentine Rugwabiza told a Swiss journalist. "She hardly spends 30 days per year in Arusha."[80] By late July, diplomats in the Security Council and human rights groups were publicly confirming Rwanda's campaign.

"We and others have been heavily lobbied by the Rwandan government complaining about Del Ponte, saying her work has lagged behind and that she is too busy in The Hague," a diplomat from a Security Council member state told the *New York Times*.[81]

There was initial division in the Council over the proposed split of the chief prosecutor's job, although a majority of member states was clearly in favor of the approach. While Britain and the United States backed the move, some Council members, such as Germany and Spain, shared Del Ponte's view that it was too late in the day to split the prosecutor's job. "If I had to vote, I would vote for giving her an extension of one or two years on both courts," said Inocencio Arias, Spain's ambassador to the UN and the president of the Security Council for the month of July 2003. Removing Del Ponte from the Arusha tribunal "makes it look as if she did a bad job," he said. "She didn't do a bad job."[82]

Some members of the Security Council who supported the decision to split the post were nevertheless critical of what they perceived as Rwanda's political interference regarding Del Ponte. "No government, particularly the Rwanda government, should interfere in the work of the tribunal and the independence of the prosecutor," said Mexico's ambassador to the UN Adolfo Aguilar Zinser, while confirming his country's support for the decision to split the chief prosecutors post.[83] Ultimately the decision eventually won the unanimous support of the Council's 15 members, and was described by a key player in the process as "one of the easiest decisions the Security Council has made."[84]

Prosper is dismissive of the view that investigating RPF crimes, and the related consideration that such investigations may destabilize Rwanda, was behind the removal of Carla Del Ponte from her Rwanda post. "The completion strategy and management issues were the driving force," he explained. "Indicting the RPF had nothing to do with this. That's a myth."[85] It was to dispel this myth, Prosper contended, that the United States ensured the inclusion of a compromise clause in the Security Council resolution by which the post was split, explicitly calling on Rwanda, Kenya, DRC, and the Congo to cooperate with the prosecutor on investigations, "including investigations of the Rwandan Patriotic Army . . ."[86]

Although Del Ponte pronounced herself "saddened" at the Council's decision[87] but "relieved" by the wording of resolution 1503, she recounted in a media interview her version of the events that resulted in her sacking in which she laid the blame squarely on President Kagame and the primacy-of-order perspective in Rwanda. Del Ponte recounted that at a meeting she had with Kagame, the Rwandan's president insisted that it was up to his government to investigate alleged RPA atrocities while her duty was to prosecute the genocide. "This work of yours is creating political problems for me," she recalls the Rwandan leader as saying, "you are going to destabilize the country this way."[88] In Del Ponte's words, "Probably, if I had given in—if I had accepted his orders—I would still be here."[89]

The Rwandan government's concern with the stability of its domestic order is entirely consistent with state behavior in this kind of situation. There is, at the very least, a perceived, if not actual, tension between bringing members of the victorious army to justice, and order in its basic form within such a fragile polity, although whether this tension translates into actual destabilization depends on how Rwanda's Tutsis collectively react to prosecutions of RPA soldiers in a country where the society of states has clearly invested far less in pursuing even-handed justice than it has in the former Yugoslavia.

Let us imagine a scenario where the Arusha tribunal prosecutes RPF soldiers, especially if they had significant ranks and roles in the "struggle to liberate Rwanda," as that country's government officially describes the civil war, and some elements in the army, feeling betrayed, become restive and take unconstitutional steps to register their protest. What then? Would the "international community" that failed the country once now intervene in its "internal affairs"? That is most unlikely. Then again, we can imagine another scenario, one in which the Rwandan government, Mandela-like, pursues a path of forgiveness that encompasses submitting RPF troops to accountability for war crimes. If the Hutu extremists in exile in the Great Lakes Region were to respond in kind and seek political accommodation, it would have been a worthwhile move. But if they did not, and were to utilize the historical record established in those trials to further their opposition to the Tutsi-dominated government on ethnic grounds, acceptance of even-handed justice (although the crimes by both sides are not comparable in scope) would have backfired from Kigali's perspective.

These constructs for now remain hypothetical. Del Ponte, for her part, would not accept the argument that stability in Rwanda should have been prioritized over her prosecutorial functions during her tenure at the tribunal. For her, "stability must proceed from the application of justice," a liberal worldview of international justice.[90] She had, in fact, expressed to Kagame and the Security Council her position that an amendment of the tribunal's statute by the Security Council that removed the prospect of prosecuting crimes committed by RPF forces was an option[91]—although, as she surely must know, an impractical one at this point in the life of the tribunal. Absent such a decision, she would implement that mandate in its current form, which meant investigating *both* parties to the conflict.[92]

An additional element in Del Ponte's removal as chief prosecutor of the Arusha tribunal was a campaign by several Rwandan civil society groups in tandem with the Rwandan government's efforts. In a petition to the Security Council in July 2003, a group of 46 organizations in Rwanda representing women, genocide survivors, and students urged the Security Council "to strongly consider the dismal record of Prosecutor Carla Del Ponte at the International Criminal Tribunal for Rwanda when deciding on her renewal in September 2003."[93] The nongovernmental organizations (NGOs) indicted Del Ponte on the grounds that she had failed to articulate a coherent long-term prosecution strategy; lacked a comprehensive approach to the inclusion of sexual violence charges in its cases; there were undue delays in appointing key leadership and unpredictable hiring decisions that had undermined the work of the tribunal; and the care and dignity of genocide survivors had not been accorded priority.[94]

This petition focused on issues of direct relevance to the tribunal's daily work, with an emphasis on the gender aspects of justice. This dimension of the tribunal's prosecutions has long preoccupied NGOs that observe the tribunal, and for good reason: women, both as victims of rape and survivors of the slaughter, bore the brunt of the genocide. In a context in which sovereign states were the prime movers of events, the impact of the NGO campaign lay in the all-inclusive air with which it clothed opposition to the feisty Swiss prosecutor. The message it sent was: "even the grassroots organizations don't want her too."

## THE JUSTICE OF THE VICTOR?

All things considered, then, it was virtually impossible for Del Ponte's prosecutorial role at the Arusha tribunal to have survived such a determined and carefully orchestrated political onslaught by Rwanda and the great powers. Nevertheless several international human rights groups, while noncommittal on Del Ponte's individual fate, were concerned about the potential medium to longer term impact of the split of the prosecutor position on the larger question of the international prosecutor's independence from the Rwandan government. There was concern that, given the outcome in this battle between a puny "David" (a prosecutor employed by an intergovernmental organization—the UN), and a "Goliath" (a sovereign state with *effective* control of its territory), the incoming chief prosecutor of the ICTR would have little incentive to act independently of the Rwandan government and challenge the latter's strategic interests.

In a battle between liberal legalism and the realist paradigm of power, strategy, and order in world politics, will the purist view of justice pushed by Del Ponte—with legal backing from the tribunal's statute—prevail? It is more likely that the opposing view that is selective about the instruments and subjects of justice—national courts or international tribunals, *your* defendants or *mine*—that, in the words of Shinoda, "warns against inappropriate implementation of legality that ignores political considerations"[95]—will emerge triumphant. It is increasingly unlikely that the Arusha tribunal will be able to prosecute any *substantive* figure from the RPF, although the outside chance remains that it could indict a few low-level Tutsi soldiers.[96]

Hassan Bubacar Jallow, Del Ponte's successor as chief prosecutor of the international tribunal, has visited Rwanda frequently and cultivated good relations with the Rwandan government since his appointment. To date, Jallow has repeatedly and tactfully said, in response to questions on the issue, that he is "reviewing" the matter of investigations of the RPF and possible indictments. One option Rwanda has offered is essentially a rehash of its previous position: that the international prosecutor can hand over case files of such investigations for indictments and trials by Rwandan courts in the context of an imminent, larger handover of cases to its courts as the international tribunal winds down in the years ahead.[97] Given the deadlines imposed by the completion strategy and the reality he faces in the need for Rwanda's cooperation, it is unlikely that Jallow will reopen active investigations of RPF atrocities with a view to bringing charges. Such an outcome would, in effect, be victor's justice—surely not what the Security Council intended when it framed the remit of the ICTR.

The only possibility of averting this outcome is if the Security Council were to make a robust political intervention in the matter and demand, with real political will to enforce its resolution 1503, that the prosecutor indict RPF atrocities and Rwanda cooperate with trials at Arusha by handing over the persons charged. The amount of political capital this process would consume, from the perspective of Rwanda's strategic partners among the great powers, is significant. Whether it will be judged as not worth the effort remains to be seen. But perhaps, as Okali has noted, "it is a little optimistic to think that the world is ready yet for international criminal adjudication of the conduct of victorious forces in armed conflict."[98] Time will tell whether the advent of the ICC, as a supposedly independent and permanent institution, will alter this existing reality.

There are those who argue that this outcome cannot be accurately described as victor's justice, and that the tribunal is unlikely to prosecute the RPF not because it does not want to, but simply because it will not be able to gather enough evidence to do so. "Prosecutions cannot happen in a vacuum," says former deputy chief prosecutor Muna. His analysis: given the manner in which the tribunal is politically constructed, it cannot go into Rwanda and forcefully oblige Rwanda to turn over RPF soldiers. It has no SFOR (NATO's Stabilization Force that largely provided muscle for the apprehension of war criminals in the former Yugoslavia) type force. The Arusha tribunal was created at Rwanda's demand, even if Rwanda was not pleased at the outcome. The international community saw Rwanda as a partner. If this was truly a UN initiative, the Security Council would have created an enforcement mechanism. By this light, it would be wrong, then, to blame the tribunal should the institution close its doors without prosecuting any Tutsis.[99] In this view, the tribunal is, after all, an epiphenomenal interstate institution, reflecting, for better of worse, the degree of political support it has from its political master—the Security Council.

If this scenario is the one that unfolds, then the most that can be said, as not a few attorneys and policy makers even in the international tribunal's prosecutor's office argue, is that faced with these limitations, the tribunal should focus its efforts on the more heinous crimes of genocide and crimes against humanity committed against Tutsis. This would be an imperfect outcome, but we live in an imperfect world. It is possible that the feared negative impact of this "victor's justice" will be counterbalanced by power realities and the evolution of democratic governance and economic growth in Rwanda. This situation would be akin to that in which the Nuremberg trials have been criticized as victor's justice, but those flaws have not obviated the outcome 50 years later—the construction of a democratic, peaceful, and wealthy Germany, on the ashes of Nazi ideology despite, or perhaps *because of*, the victor's justice imposed by the Allied Powers.

Nevertheless the contradiction of one-sided justice would be better avoided by the Security Council. That contradiction has not been allowed to ossify at the Hague tribunal, despite initial claims by the Serbs that their leaders are on trial there because they lost the war to NATO's military superiority. In the end, behind the veil is a struggle over what version of history will prevail in Rwanda and the Great Lakes Region of Africa.

Del Ponte argued that having one prosecutor for The Hague and Arusha strengthened the hand of the holder of that office. But for what purpose was this "strength"? While the design may have strengthened the hand of the individual that held the office, it has clearly not strengthened the Arusha tribunal institutionally, as we have seen. From both institutional-efficiency and political standpoints, the decision to split the prosecutor's role for two judicial institutions that are statutorily independent is a welcome one. It frees up the prosecutor of the Hague tribunal to focus on the significant challenges that confront that court, such as the trial of Milosevic, and give prosecutions at Arusha the undivided leadership and managerial attention the equally weighty challenges at that court so clearly deserve.

# CHAPTER 7

# HOT PURSUIT: FUGITIVES
# FROM JUSTICE

Kabuga is our Osama bin Laden.
—Benoit Kaboyi, executive secretary, Ibuka

The very idea of international criminal justice is predicted on a framework in which sovereign states cooperate with international criminal tribunals, giving effect to their judicial orders and providing political and financial support. This is what oils the wheels of war crimes justice. It could not be otherwise, for the Arusha and Hague tribunals have no police forces or prisons of their own. These two tribunals, created as they are by the United Nations (UN) Security Council's enforcement powers, impose on states an obligation to cooperate with them. In the treaty-based International Criminal Court (ICC), that obligation is willingly taken on when a state signs on to the treaty regime. And for the "hybrid" courts such as the Special Court for Sierra Leone, the weak legal framework for state cooperation has had important practical consequences. That court, not having the enforcement powers of UN Security Council-created International Criminal Tribunal for the Former Yugoslavia (ICTY) and International Criminal Tribunal for Rwanda (ICTR) under the UN Charter, cannot compel the cooperation of states. Charles Taylor, the Special Court's most important indictee, is in exile in Nigeria, which has declined to hand him over to the Court.

In this chapter, I review the cooperation of states with the ICTR and their political support for the tribunal, beginning with the legal basis for that cooperation. In doing so, we will see how legal and political contexts have come together to make possible the apprehension in various states of persons indicted by the tribunal. As well, we shall see how the absence of political will in some cases has limited the tribunal's success.

## THE LAW

The legal basis[1] in international law for the cooperation of states with the Arusha tribunal is Article 2 of Security Council resolution 955. There the Security Council decided that "all states shall cooperate fully with the International Tribunal . . . and that consequently all states shall take any measures necessary under their domestic law to implement the provisions of the resolution and the Statute" of the tribunal. Article 2 also stipulates that carrying out the provisions of the resolution and statute included the obligation of states to comply with judicial requests or orders issued by the tribunal.[2] Several African and European states and the United States have provided the Arusha tribunal the cooperation and assistance envisaged in these and other statutory provisions.[3] As we have seen in the discussion on the tribunal's legitimacy, decisions of the UN Security Council are binding on member states. Article 48 of the organization's Charter obligates UN member states to support decisions of the Security Council by cooperating in their execution.

In Article 2 of resolution 955, states are requested to take any measures necessary under their domestic law to implement the resolution and the tribunal's statute. One might wonder why the provision is necessary if decisions of the Security Council are automatically binding on states. Are the decisions of the Security Council somehow, then, subordinate to the domestic laws of UN member states? Certainly the answer is no, for the reasons that follow. The first part of the answer to this seeming contradiction lies in Article 2 itself, in which the council "*decides* that all states *shall* cooperate fully with the International Tribunal" (second emphasis added). Both words are mandatory in law. The second part of the answer can be found in the nature of international law and the general problems of enforcement that attend it: in the absence of a "sovereign" in the international realm to perform similar law-making functions as in the domestic arena of states, enforcing compliance with international law is sometimes problematic, and some states (especially powerful ones) can stand behind domestic laws in attempts to avoid compliance with international law. The provision is thus a bow to the practical realities of sovereignty. And in making it mandatory for states to take necessary measures under their domestic law, the Security Council, intentionally or not, makes a practical recognition of the theories of monism and dualism in the relationship between international law and municipal law. According to the monist doctrine, international law and state laws are mutually reinforcing aspects of one system—law in general. Monists believe that all law is a single body of legal rules that are binding—whether on states, on individuals or on non-state entities.[4] Dualists believe that municipal law[5] and international law originate in fundamentally different ways, the source of state law being the will of the state itself, and that of international law being the common will of states.[6] Thus in the dualist view, international law is not automatically self-enforcing within a country's territory; it needs to be enabled, empowered, or validated by domestic legislation.

The practical impact of the monist and dualist attitudes to international law on the work of the Arusha tribunal is that it tends to condition how national institutions, including judicial institutions and law enforcement agencies, react or proact to the needs and requests of the international tribunal for judicial cooperation or assistance. States with a dualist perspective believe that, to facilitate such cooperation with the tribunal, it is necessary to adopt enabling domestic legislation. Monist states see no legal bar to cooperating with the international tribunal's requests for arrests of suspects in their territory and their transfer to the tribunal at Arusha. In practice, however, political and nonlegal considerations weigh more heavily on the degree of cooperation the Arusha court has received from states than issues of monism and dualism. This has been especially true of African countries, in particular in the early years of the tribunal. As one commentator has accurately observed: "Not one of the African states that have executed arrest and transfer orders of the Rwanda Tribunal had a legal instrument at their disposal authorizing national authorities to comply with such order."[7] Their responses have been conditioned more by political reflexes than by legal considerations—in this case, a perverse benefit from the "big man syndrome" in which the heads of state and government in some African countries are not subject to the separation of powers between the executive, legislative, and judicial branches of government. Thus it was that, as we saw in chapter 5, Barayagwiza was turned over to the Arusha tribunal by a "Presidential Decree." The adoption of domestic legislation, while it may be indicative of a dualist legal tradition, is thus not an automatic barometer of a state's ability or willingness to cooperate with UN war crimes tribunals by arresting the accused criminals sought by such courts. A number of states, all non-African, have adopted domestic cooperation acts in relation to the Arusha tribunal.[8]

Whether or not a state is monist or dualist, as the secretary general of the UN stated in the formative stages of the Hague tribunal, once an international war crimes tribunal has been set up under the UN Charter's peace enforcement powers, a binding obligation is created on all countries to take whatever steps are necessary to implement the decision.[9]

Moreover the practice of various states when it comes to facilitating the apprehension of fugitives from justice at the request of the Arusha tribunal confirms the view of one authority in international law that: "The fact that municipal courts must pay primary regard to municipal law in the event of a conflict with international law, in no way affects the obligations of the state concerned to perform its international obligations."[10] This has not prevented the occasional legal challenge in domestic courts to the arrest and surrender of persons indicted by the international tribunal, in the rare case of protracted nature.

## A Pastor in Texas: An American Surrender

The classic illustration of this tension between domestic legal standards and a state's international legal obligations to the UN war crimes tribunals in Arusha and The Hague is the case of Elizaphan Ntakirutimana, a former Seventh Day Adventist pastor indicted by the Arusha tribunal and arrested in the United States. As we have seen earlier in this chapter, the United States had applied political pressure on Cameroon to surrender an individual who had been indicted by the Arusha tribunal. It has applied similar pressure on other countries, as will be seen later when the political dimension of state cooperation is discussed. In this context, *Ntakirutimana* provided the United States with the first—and so far, only—domestic legal and political test of its commitment to the ICTR.

In 1996, the Arusha tribunal indicted Elizaphan Ntakirutimana on charges of genocide, complicity in genocide, conspiracy to commit genocide, crimes against humanity, and violations of the Geneva Conventions.[11] These charges were based largely on allegations that in April 1994 Ntakirutimana and his son Gerard, a medical doctor, had planned and executed the massacres of hundreds of Tutsis at a church complex in Mugonero in the Kibuye region of western Rwanda.[12] The victims had been instructed by the clergyman to hide in the church premises as the massacres of Tutsis unfolded across Rwanda: the Tutsis were then separated from non-Tutsis who were released, and on April 16 Pastor Ntakirutimana returned in a convoy of several vehicles and armed individuals and participated in the slaughter of unarmed Tutsi men, women, and children.[13] After the genocide, Ntakirutimana left Rwanda and eventually immigrated to the United States where he lived in Laredo, Texas, with another son Eliel, a medical doctor as well.

On September 7, 1996, the tribunal issued a Warrant of Arrest and Order for Surrender of Elizaphan Ntakirutimana, which read in pertinent part:

> To: The United States of America, I, Judge William Sekule, Judge of the International Criminal Tribunal for Rwanda, Considering the United Nations Security Council Resolution 955 of 8 November 1994 . . . and Articles 19 (2) and 28 of the Statute of the International Criminal Tribunal for Rwanda.
>
> Considering the indictment submitted by the Prosecutor against Elizaphan Ntakirutimana, and confirmed by me . . . on 7 September 1996, a copy of which is attached to this warrant of arrest, HEREBY DIRECT the Authorities of the United States of America to search for, arrest—and surrender to International Criminal Tribunal for Rwanda: Elizaphan Ntakirutimana, [who] is currently believed to be in the United States of America . . . And to advise the said Elizaphan Ntakirutimana at the time of his arrest, and in a language he under-stands, of his rights as set forth in the Statute . . . and of his right to remain silent and to caution him that any statement he makes shall be recorded and may be used in evidence.
>
> REQUEST THAT The United States of America, upon the arrest of Elizaphan Ntakirutimana, promptly notify the Registrar of the International Criminal Tribunal for Rwanda, for the purposes of arranging his transfer to the custody of the International Criminal Tribunal for Rwanda . . . [14]

This document represents the general format of warrants of arrest and surrender orders issued by the international tribunal. Arrest warrants invariably are addressed to states; they state the legal basis of the war-rant in international law (the relevant decision of the Security Council and the statute and procedural rules of the international tribunal); they enumerate the charges against the accused person; they provide for the respect of due process rights; and they provide guidance on how to initiate the actual surrender of the accused to the international tribunal.

On the basis of this warrant, U.S. federal marshals arrested Ntakirutimana, then 73, on September 26, 1996. But his transfer to Arusha was to become an obstacle course, for the Rwandan clergyman had no intention of going quietly into the good night of justice. He mounted a spirited legal battle in U.S. courts, which became an endurance test for America's commitment to the ad hoc international criminal tribunals, equally tested the country's extradition law, and delayed Ntakirutimana's effective surrender to the tribunal for three-and-a-half years.

The United States had enacted domestic legislation[15] on February 10, 1996 to establish a basis in its domestic law to implement two international agreements its executive branch of government had entered into with the Hague and the Arusha tribunals.[16] When the U.S. Federal Government filed a request at the U.S. District Court for the Southern District of Texas to secure Ntakirutimana's surrender to the tribunal in January 1997, Ntakirutimana's defense team, headed by former U.S. attorney general Ramsey Clark, opposed the motion on the basis of four main arguments: (1) that the Arusha tribunal was not legitimate as it was improperly created; (2) that extradition would be unconstitutional, there being no valid treaty between the United States and the tribunal; (3) that the U.S. authorities had not established enough evidence to meet to standards of "probable cause"; and (4) that he would not receive a fair trial at the tribunal.[17]

The U.S. government and the New York based NGO Lawyers Committee for Human Rights[18] argued that the Arusha tribunal was validly established under the authority of the UN Charter; member states of the UN should cooperate with the tribunal because they were "obligated to abide by and carry out decisions made by the Security Council"; the Agreement on Surrender of Persons was properly authorized under U.S. law and created a binding obligation to surrender Ntakirutimana under domestic law and a legal basis for extradition by either treaty or statute; and disputed the defendant's claims that he would not receive a fair trial and that the international tribunal had not shown probable cause.[19] The U.S. magistrate Judge Marcel C. Notzon ruled that the Congressional-Executive Agreement of Surrender of inductees to the Arusha and the Hague tribunals was unconstitutional and could not provide a legal basis for extraditing Ntakirutimana. Rather, Judge Notzon ruled, extradition required a treaty, and no treaty existed between the United States and the international tribunal; he then ordered Ntakirutimana's release from custody.[20]

Judge Notzon's ruling generated much publicity in the United States. Most Americans became aware of the existence and work of the Arusha tribunal for the first time, and the overriding public sentiment supported the notion that an accused war criminal could not remain in the United States and should be surrendered to face justice. The decision was also legally unsound. It displayed a lack of understanding of the status of the Arusha tribunal in international law and the basis of obligation that exists in the UN Charter (a multilateral treaty to which the United States is a party).[21] Indeed Judge Notzon ignored that core argument altogether in his decision. His legal reasoning stemmed in part, no doubt, from the ambiguous status of international law, including validly concluded treaties, in American domestic law. (It might also have been inspired by a philosophical bias against international institutions that are perceived as limiting the sphere of action of sovereign states especially that of a superpower like the United States.) American law provides that even international treaties concluded by the United States are invalid if they are unconstitutional. In other words, the U.S. constitution is asserted by some American lawyers as superseding international law in the American legal sphere—a position that goes beyond dualism to one of primacy. Louis Henkin has stated that "treaties are subject to constitutional limitations that apply to all exercising federal power," and noted that the U.S. constitution does not forbid the president or Congress to violate international law.[22] However "suspending domestic law does not relieve the United States of its international obligations."[23]

At a practical level, Judge Notzon's ruling was an embarrassing setback to the United States' political positioning in the 1990s as the leading political and operational supporter of the ad hoc international tribunals for Rwanda and for the former Yugoslavia.[24] Ramsey Clark had already echoed the challenge to the legitimacy of the tribunals. "This is the first time in our history that we've been asked to surrender a person to a tribunal and one of doubtful legality," he told the *Houston Chronicle*. "There is nothing in the UN Charter that allows for a criminal tribunal."[25]

The tribunal, for its part, took the view that it was up to the U.S. government to determine its next move, but emphasized that states, including the United States, were required to cooperate with the tribunal.[26] And the U.S. Department of State, which bore the political responsibility of ensuring the surrender of the fugitive from justice on American territory, reassured the media of its determination to ensure Ntakirutimana's eventual surrender.[27]

As decisions on extradition are not subject to appeal under U.S. law,[28] the U.S. government refiled its request for the surrender of Ntakirutimana with a different judge in the Laredo judicial division. The magistrate who was to hear the case recused himself, and the matter subsequently ended up on the docket of the U.S. District Court (a federal court) for the Southern District of Texas. There Ntakirutimana filed a writ of *habeas corpus*. Judge John Rainey denied the writ and upheld Ntakirutimana's surrender, ruling that the Surrender Agreement and the National Defense Authorization Act provided adequate constitutional basis for extradition.[29] Ntakirutimana petitioned for *habeas corpus* to the U.S. Court of Appeals, Fifth Circuit.[30]

The appellate court, in a majority ruling handed down by Judge Emilio Garza, held that it was not unconstitutional to surrender Ntakirutimana to the ICTR even in the absence of a treaty, so long as extradition was authorized by statute; the district court's finding of probable cause was supported by sufficient preliminary evidence; and issues involving the legal validity of the creation of international tribunals by the Security Council, and whether the tribunal would guarantee the petitioner's rights under the U.S. Constitution and international law, were beyond the scope of *habeas* review.[31] The Fifth Circuit affirmed the denial of Ntakirutimana's petition for a unit of *habeas corpus* and lifted the stay of extradition.[32]

In a separate, specially concurring opinion in which he expressed his doubts about Ntakirutimana's probable guilt, Judge Robert Parker acknowledged the role of high politics in the Ntakirutimana saga. Speculating on the final decision of the secretary of state (whose prerogative it is to approve extradition) on the extradition of the Rwandan clergyman, he stated: "I fully understand that the ultimate decision in this case may well be a political one that it is driven by important considerations of state that transcend the question of guilt or innocence of any single individual. I respect the political process that is necessarily implicated in this case, just as I respect the fact that adherence to precedent compels my concurrence."[33]

Meanwhile Judge DeMoss, dissenting from the majority, acknowledged an opposing political factor—sovereignty.

Notwithstanding our nation's moral duty to assist the cause of international justice, our nation's actions taken in that regard must comport with the Constitution's procedures and with respect for its allocation of powers . . .

    The Attorney General . . . stakes her case on the validity and enforceability of a warrant issued by the United Nations International Criminal Tribunal for Rwanda, which is a non sovereign entity created by the United Nations Security Council, purporting to "Direct" the officials of our sovereign nation to surrender the accused. In defense of this, the Attorney-General relies exclusively on what my colleagues have termed a "Congressional Executive Agreement"—the coincidence of an "executive agreement" with the Tribunal, entered on behalf of the United States by an ambassador appointed by the President in the course of his duties to conduct foreign affairs, and a purported enabling act passed by simple majorities of both houses of Congress and signed into law by the President . . .[34]

In a last ditch effort, Ntakirutimana applied to the U.S. Supreme Court for a review and setting aside of the Fifth Circuit Court's decision. The Supreme Court denied his request. For the beleaguered pastor, all roads now led back to East Africa. In late March 2000, his extradition having been authorized by Secretary of State Madeleine Albright, a U.S. airplane carrying Ntakirutimana, accompanied by U.S. marshals, landed at Kilimanjaro International Airport at Arusha. Diplomats from the American Embassy in Rwanda and officials of the tribunal registrar's office made up the welcoming party. Procedural formalities quickly executed, the U.S. authorities handed him over to tribunal officials. Thus did the Ntakirutimana saga end. And with this demonstration of dogged commitment in the face of a political embarrassment, the United States, in the words of one commentator, "with little public notice . . . dipped its toe into the waters of international justice. It remains to be seen whether Uncle Sam will ever wade in deep enough to get his trunks wet. But he has crossed the water's edge."[35] Ntakirutimana was subsequently tried by the tribunal, found guilty, and sentenced to 10 years in prison. He appealed, but the conviction was upheld by the tribunal's appellate chamber.

## THE POLITICS

The level of direct political support that states have given the Arusha tribunal depends on a number of factors. These include the connection between particular states on the one hand and Rwanda (and the genocide) on the other. Another factor was the general foreign policy of particular states toward human rights questions (of which violations of international humanitarian law were at the top of the scale, whether or not those states were linked to Rwanda before or during the genocide). And third there was the practical question of the presence of fugitives from justice, sought by the international tribunal or the Rwandan government, on the territories of particular countries. In all three contexts, African, European, and North American (United States and Canada) states were the theaters for the politics and diplomacy of the capture of Rwandans (and in one case a non-Rwandan[36]) accused of perpetrating the 1994 genocide.

We have seen the basis of state cooperation with the tribunal and how questions of law played out in a case where a fugitive's surrender to the international tribunal encountered a robust challenge in the domestic legal sphere. What is clear, including from *Barayagwiza*, is that in all cases, political attitudes to accountability for genocide, crimes against humanity, and war crimes affect the level and depth of cooperation and support.

The United States, the prime mover of the Arusha tribunal among the great powers, supported the tribunal for a number of reasons. First it has sought to expiate its political guilt for inaction during the genocide by subsequently lending its political weight on the global stage to the charge for accountability. Closely allied to this reason was its historical leadership of the earlier effort at the Nuremberg trials. To be sure, the circumstances were different in 1994 from 1945, when U.S. troops fought in World War II, but the opportunity presented for latter-day moral leadership was essentially similar.

It is uncertain whether U.S. Secretary of State Madeleine Albright's Jewish origins as a genocide survivor in Europe played any role in her support for the creation of the tribunal. Either by this reason or independently of it, she had championed military intervention in the Balkans—the modern day European theater of mass atrocities—as the U.S. ambassador to the UN from 1992. Thus although she opposed similar intervention in Rwanda after Somalia in line with her government's policy at the time, she may have been psychologically primed to throw her weight behind a war crimes accountability effort. Third from a strategic point of view, American support for the tribunal was support in effect for Paul Kagame and a number of other anglophone leaders—Yoweri Museveni of Uganda, Meles Zenawi of Ethiopia, and Isiais Aferworki of Eritrea—in central and eastern Africa and the Horn of Africa, who were seen as representing a "new breed" of African leaders "worthy" of America's support. It should be noted that this factor is applicable far more directly to Kagame, and to the others more by extrapolation. Museveni, no conformist with conventional wisdoms, was no great fan of the Arusha tribunal. He believed it was a huge waste of time and money and, like Britain's Winston Churchill and the Soviet Union's Josef Stalin after World War II, that the perpetrators of genocide should simply be rounded up and shot for their crimes.

European countries have also been firmly supportive of the ICTR. Most have "ethical" foreign policies that place strong emphasis on the moral dimensions of international affairs, and are consistently in the lead in terms of humanitarian responses to global crisis—to the extent that there are such responses. European countries have also been favorite hiding places for Rwandan *genocidaires*. These countries, such as Belgium, Switzerland, and the Netherlands, have been quick to apprehend genocide suspects and indictees at the tribunal's request.

The growing support for institutionalized international criminal accountability in Europe in the 1990s was also a major contributory factor to European support for the ICTR. Thus although the United States has remained the largest financial backer of the tribunal through "assessed contributions" (compulsory levies on UN member states, which differs from country to country based on their economic strength) to the UN budgets of the Hague and Arusha tribunals, Europe was by far the leader in shoring up a voluntary contributions trust fund for the ICTR set up by the UN General Assembly in 1995. Moreover anglophone countries like Britain also saw support for the Arusha tribunal as an extension of support for the Anglophone Rwandan Patriotic Front (RPF) that was now wresting Rwanda from its francophone colonial roots.[37]

African support for the Arusha tribunal has been far more ambivalent, especially in the tribunal's early years. With the conspicuous exceptions of leaders like Alpha Omar Konare, the former president of Mali and the current chairman of the Commission of the African Union, Benjamin Mkapa (president of Tanzania, the tribunal's host country), President Mathieu Kerekou of Benin, and King Mswati III of Swaziland,[38] African leaders were initially unsure of just how to respond to the idea of an intrusive international tribunal in the creation of which they played little or no political role. Some were suspicious, some apprehensive, and the majority noncommittal, adopting a wait-and-see posture.[39]

Thus, although African states have largely cooperated in the apprehension of the war criminals from Rwanda, a certain reticence in public and political engagement with the Arusha tribunal has remained constant. Discussions on the tribunal in the UN have been dominated by non-African states.[40] Indeed to watch or participate in these discussions is to become aware of how marginal issues of international war crimes justice are to the foreign policies of most African states. This trend can be compared with the clear political support that European states have provided to the Hague tribunal for the former Yugoslavia—an attitude based on conscious foreign policy in several Western capitals and recognition of a linkage between the political evolution and enlargement of the European Union and resolving the question of war crimes in the former Yugoslavia.

Moreover, with one exception, no African state has contributed to the voluntary contributions trust fund of the Arusha tribunal, which has received contributions in excess of $8 million.[41] It is fair to say that were it left to African states, the Arusha tribunal would not exist, let alone operate, and this would not be simply for the reason of the oft-claimed "poverty" of these countries. It is clearly far more a question of a very limited commitment to legalism—liberal or not—as a dimension of conflict resolution and a means to the construction of political order. And yet, political discourse in many African countries is suffused with references to the Rwandan genocide and the need to avoid its repetition in any other African country. It is precisely this sentiment that led to the inclusion in the Charter of the African Union of a right to military intervention in cases of genocide, crimes against humanity, and war crimes. Of course the Rwandan genocide and the African response to it cannot be discussed in isolation from the politics of exclusion and ethnic domination that are still prevalent in the continent despite the gradual progress of democratization.[42] This kind of politics has often produced violence.[43]

To what, then, can we ascribe the general political apathy of African states toward, the Arusha tribunal? Three factors are clearly at play. First, a conceptual resistance to legal justice and a preference for amnesties and truth and reconciliations commission are major factors. This argument has several strands: war crimes trials could further destabilize fragile societies in transition from a period of conflict by trapping old hatreds within the quest for "vindictive" legal accountability; the new fad of war crimes trials is self-serving because the Western nations that are its chief advocates invariably provided support to despotic African regimes during the Cold War; Africa has more immediate needs for justice of a different kind—access to basic necessities like clean water and health care; and dialogue and reconciliation are seen as more reflective of societal/cultural norms than imported notions of legalism.[44]

But a second and self-interested reason is that of a fear of the possible unintended consequences of being too supportive of war crimes trials. There are few countries in sub-Saharan Africa where politically or ethnically inspired mass killings or war crimes have not occurred in the past four decades. These events necessarily implicate the responsibility of the political and military leadership, past or present, in these countries. Consequently there is little appetite for a normative approach that could return to haunt its supporters.

Third, the manner of the tribunal's creation—as an ad hoc and interventionist institution created not in the form Rwanda wished, but in the image of its Western sponsors—is one reason why several African political leaders look askance at it and provide it with cautious support. This is the question of ownership, of the tension between international and domestic justice. Many an African leader would be quick to condemn violations of international humanitarian law, but would simultaneously assert that the proper persons to judge war criminals are the courts of their own countries—if there is no better alternative than a legal trial. Lost in this response is any confrontation of the question of what happens where (as is frequently the case) domestic courts have no capacity or political will to bring highly placed individuals to justice for war crimes. (Ethiopia, where national courts have tried past officials for violations of international humanitarian law, is a striking exception.) Truth and reconciliation commissions thus became an easy halfway house that offers a path out of the dilemma. Rwanda is a rare exception to a continental political aversion to war crimes justice.

This third factor offers some insight into the apparent contradiction by which Africa's leaders are decidedly cool toward ad hoc international criminal tribunals, but several have led their countries to ratify the Rome Statute of the ICC. They can point to its consensual nature as a treaty-based international court. But here as well, there are, in a few cases, significant elements of strategic self-interest at play. For others, signing up to the Rome Statute may be a commitment that looks good on a foreign policy resume, but the consistency of which is yet to be tested. And even in the case of the ICC, the African states "missed the boat" by their general failure to engage more actively and politically with the Arusha tribunal.[45] That failure has placed them in a relatively weak position in the politics of the ICC.[46]

## OPERATION NAKI

After the genocide, members of the previous government and former military commanders fled to numerous countries. The Arusha tribunal's defendants have been apprehended in three continents—Africa, Europe, and North America. This is quite unlike the Hague tribunal where the arrest of accused war criminals has unfailingly happened within the former Yugoslavia. Here the alleged war criminals felt they had sympathetic and nationalistic governments that were unwilling to hand them over to an international tribunal. And they were right. It has taken great amounts of political pressure—and displays of force by NATO forces—to obtain arrests in the Balkans. For the Arusha tribunal, arresting war criminals has been no less easy, and the challenge was multiplied by the dispersal of the suspects and accused persons in numerous countries, with Rwanda ruled by genocide survivors and obviously not the place to seek refuge from justice. It is against the background of these factors that we can now turn to Kenya, a country with a pivotal place in any assessment of the cooperation of African states with the ICTR, and the role of U.S. war crimes diplomacy in that country and the Great Lakes Region in general. Under the leadership of then president Arap Moi, Kenya enjoyed close relations with the Habyarimana regime in Rwanda. It was thus understandably lukewarm to the idea of an international tribunal, especially as it had sought without success to link accountability for the genocide with the shooting down of Habyarimana's plane[47] (in obvious sympathy with Hutu extremist claims that the Rwandan Patriotic Army (RPA) bore responsibility for the plane downing). In the same period that the tribunal was beginning its work in 1995, several members of the defeated former Rwandan government and other leaders of the genocide had begun to move from Zaire to Kenya, where the capital, Nairobi, offered better lifestyles and more modern amenities. In these circumstances, Kenya soon acquired a reputation as the leading host to high-ranking fugitives from justice for the genocide. It thus became the main target area for the special investigators of the office of the Arusha tribunal's chief prosecutor, known as the "tracking team."

The tracking team's reports led the then chief prosecutor Arbour and her deputy, Muna, to plan a major arrest operation that was to apprehend a number of the tribunal's indictees and suspects in Kenya, to be executed by Kenyan law enforcement authorities. But it was clear to the international prosecutors that the exiled Rwandan *genocidaires* were living in Kenya with the blessing of Moi's government. How were they to proceed then? A major arrest operation could not be planned, let alone successfully executed, without the political approval of the Kenyan leader. Arbour and Muna decided to solicit the assistance of the great powers and a number of other influential states in applying political pressure on Moi.[48] A situation where Kenya had become the regional hub for the exiled Rwandan regime was becoming politically unsustainable for Kenya, a country that is largely dependent on donor aid.[49] At the same time, the Rwandan leader Kagame, whose relations with Moi were understandably frosty, was coming to the realization that he had to deal with Moi's government—unpalatable as the prospect was—in order to advance his country's strategic interests. At the top of those interests was that of the apprehension of the Rwandan *genocidaires* in Kenya, as well as economic ones.[50]

Meanwhile Arbour and Muna had obtained the support of Canada, which, through its ambassador in Nairobi, took the lead in the application of diplomatic pressure on Moi to break with his government policy of sheltering war criminals. Canada was supported in this effort by the United States, Britain, and South Africa. Arbour ultimately met with Moi, who assented to the planned swoop and asked the international prosecutors to meet with the Kenyan attorney general Amos Wako. Arbour and Muna met with Wako, with whom they prepared a strategy for the arrest operations. Muna then reported their plans and progress to tribunal registrar Okali, who subsequently undertook the wrap-up political and legal liaison for the operation in meetings with the Kenyan attorney general and Minister of Foreign Affairs.

On July 18, 1997, Kenyan authorities arrested seven persons in Nairobi at the international tribunal's request in a stunning raid code-named "Operation NAKI" (Nairobi–Kigali), and transferred them to the tribunal's detention center at Arusha.[51] At the top of the list of fugitives captured in the NAKI operation was former Rwandan prime minister Jean Kambanda. Others apprehended in the raid were Pauline Nyiramasuhuko, former Minister of Family Welfare and Women Affairs (the first woman ever to be indicted by an international criminal tribunal), her son Arsene Shalom Ntahobali, the journalist Hassan Ngeze, and erstwhile senior military commanders Gratien Kabiligi and Aloys Ntabakuze. The NAKI operation was the most successful such operation in the tribunal's history, and provided the ICTR with a much needed spike in legitimacy at a time when it was still a fledgling international judicial institution. But this success could not have been achieved without the political agreement of a reluctant sovereign state, and the political pressure applied by influential external parties in the nature of influential Western states and South Africa.

There are two ironies here. The first is that the execution of NAKI was delayed by a day because Kagame, returning from a trip to South Africa, visited Nairobi during that period and met with Moi, following the intercession of South African leader Nelson Mandela.[52] Six high-level Rwandan suspects escaped the dragnet of the operation as a result of a leak that occurred by reason of the delay.[53] The second irony is that although other accused persons or suspects were subsequently arrested in Kenya at the tribunal's request, none of those captured in Kenya included the wealthy persons that were close to Habyarimana and also had actual links with the Kenyan leadership.[54]

A number of other arrests of accused *genocidaires* have taken place in Kenya, some with their own drama as well. When members of the Kenyan Criminal Investigation Department (CID) showed up at former Rwandan Anglican bishop Samuel Musabyimana's refuge in Nairobi in 2001 with a warrant of arrest issued by the international tribunal, the clergyman was shocked. With little time to recover from his nervous state he was put in a vehicle and taken across the Namanga Kenya–Tanzania border to Arusha and placed in detention awaiting trial, availed of his right to defense counsel. As the vehicle in which he was transported sped from Nairobi to Arusha, Musabyimana kept opening and closing his Bible nervously, muttering repeatedly to no one in particular: "This is just like the movies; just like in the movies." It was as if, despite himself, he could not help but admire the swift and efficient execution of the arrest operation that had been negotiated by tribunal registrar Adama Dieng with senior Kenyan law enforcement officials. Meanwhile, in Nairobi, his lawyers, who were present during the arrest, issued statements on Kenyan radio claiming that their client had been "kidnapped" and taken to Arusha for trial on genocide charges. The Anglican Church at its global headquarters in England distanced itself from Musabyimana, who later died in detention of illness before his case came to trial.

## REWARDS FOR JUSTICE: THE BOUNTY HUNTERS

Of the few fugitives who escaped the dragnet of Operation NAKI, none has been more elusive than Felicien Kabuga, the millionaire Rwandan businessman who was a major shareholder in the hate radio station *Radio Television Libre des Milles Collines* (RTLM) and allegedly financed the murder squads and the importation of machetes and other weapons that were used to execute the genocide. He is wanted by the tribunal on charges of genocide. In 1994, Kabuga fled to Switzerland, from where he was expelled in 1995. He then settled in Nairobi, where he had strong relationships with powerful members of Moi's government, including mutually beneficial business deals. In 1995, Kabuga's daughter wed Habyarimana's son in Nairobi.

Kabuga is on the U.S. Federal Bureau of Investigation's (FBI) "most wanted list," together with Osama bin Laden, and the U.S. government has offered up to $5 million for information leading to Kabuga's capture. But the fugitive, deploying his considerable wealth, international connections, and multiple aliases and passports, has remained several steps ahead of international law. He was one of the "big fish" that escaped from the NAKI operation in 1997. A handwritten note found in the house where he was believed to be hiding revealed that he was tipped off by a Kenyan police informant.[55] In the words of a genocide survivor, "Kabuga is our Osama bin Laden."[56] Although Kenya, under international pressure, had revoked Kabuga's Kenyan residence permit in 1997, he is believed to have continued receiving protection from senior officials of the Moi-era government on his payroll.[57] The Arusha tribunal subsequently went after his financial assets, and $2.5 million in Kabuga's bank accounts in France, Belgium, and Switzerland were frozen at the tribunal chief prosecutor's request in 1999.[58]

It was around this period that the U.S. government began to take an active interest in bringing Kabuga to justice through its "Rewards for Justice" program. The total budget of that program is uncertain, but it is a global initiative that encompasses the Rwanda and Yugoslavia war crimes tribunals, and the $25 million reward for information leading to the capture of Bin Laden. Under the program, the full bounty of, say, $5 million in the Kabuga case could be given as reward to an informant, or a lesser sum could be disbursed. How much an informant is paid is determined by an internal committee, and the highest actual payment appears to have been $500,000.[59] A reward is paid in cash, unless otherwise indicated by an informant. In one case, the U.S. authorities brought three suitcases stuffed with cash to a payment meeting with an informant, who then indicated that he wanted half of his payment in cash and the other half in a bank account.[60] Such are the resources and pragmatic tactics that the U.S. authorities have deployed in their hunt for Kabuga, so far without success. Should he ever be captured, the impact of his arrest in Rwanda would be akin to that in America of nabbing Osama bin Laden, and he remains without question the most important outstanding fugitive from international justice at the Arusha tribunal. His arrest is one of the few with a potential to bring that process to a certain closure. It would give great satisfaction to Rwandans, serve as a reminder of the long arm of internationally sanctioned justice, and provide the Arusha tribunal an opportunity to close its doors on a high note. While Rewards for Justice Program brought the FBI close to locating Kabuga on a number of occasions, the scent of near success has frequently proved a mirage, on one occasion tragically.

In 2002, two Kenyan sources came forward, claiming to possess information that would lead to Kabuga's arrest.[61] One of the informants was William Munuhe, who contacted the U.S. embassy in Nairobi, the locus of the U.S. hunt for Kabuga in the region under the local direction of the U.S. ambassador to Kenya Johnny Carson and the overall guidance of war crimes ambassador Prosper.

The Kenyan sources told the American authorities that Kabuga was receiving protection from the high echelons of the Moi government. Washington obtained information on the vehicles in which Kabuga traveled—vehicles of a government security team.[62] The Americans tried to establish with Kenyan authorities a discrete plan to arrest Kabuga, but, as Prosper recalls, the informants became compromised.[63] One of the two informants was kidnapped for a weekend, threatened, released, and subsequently kidnapped a second time. The second informant (Munuhe) had by now become very scared. Realizing that the hunt for Kabuga was no ordinary criminal investigation, as the information the Americans were receiving appeared to point all the way to the then president Moi and a permanent secretary in his government, Prosper brought in the FBI to administer polygraph tests, first on the two informers (to ascertain the veracity of their claims), and then on the senior Kenyan official (the latter almost certainly with Moi's knowledge and acquiescence). For Prosper, this was a necessary precaution before the U.S. government could apply stronger political pressure on Moi to surrender Kabuga to the Arusha tribunal. While the two informants passed the lie-detector test, the Kenyan permanent secretary failed it—"miserably," in Prosper's recollection.[64]

With this outcome, the American authorities reverted to Moi. The septuagenarian politician's rule was coming to an end after 20 years, under pressure from opposition politicians to relinquish power. The Americans were now anxious to step up the momentum in the manhunt for Kabuga and apprehend him before Moi left office. A stakeout was set up to snare Kabuga at a house in the affluent Nairobi neighborhood of Karen.[65] Munuhe was to lure the Rwandan there. U.S. and Kenyan security agents waited outside in hiding, ready to pounce on Kabuga as soon as he appeared. Kabuga never showed up, and Munuhe was later murdered with a shot to the back of his head.[66] Thus ended—temporarily at least—the trail to Kabuga; the U.S. authorities relocated their second informant outside Kenya to assure his safety.[67]

In January 2003, a new Kenyan government headed by President Mwai Kibaki was elected. Kibaki pledged his support to the hunt for Kabuga. But first he needed to clean up Kenya's security and intelligence services, which at every turn had been shown to have been compromised by Kabuga or interests loyal to him.[68] Nearly two years later in late 2004, Prosper acknowledged that the search for Kabuga had lost momentum, but asserted that it would resume in earnest. Kabuga's pursuers in Washington believe that he has remained in

Kenya but entered and left the country frequently after the manhunt for him became intense in 2002.[69] The United States has publicly charged as much, with Prosper stating in the media: "All information points to Kenya as the country where Mr. Kabuga is hiding. We believe he is under some sort of protection, either from a civilian population or influential people."[70] The Kenyan authorities, however, have consistently discounted the possibility of Kabuga's presence on Kenyan territory. And the investigators of the Arusha tribunal admit they simply do not know Kabuga's whereabouts. "Sometimes we can be very close. Sometimes we can be very far," Richard Renaud, the tribunal's chief of investigations commented. "This guy is very smart. He has a lot of money. He has a lot of contacts. And he travels a lot."[71]

Meanwhile in the wider Great Lakes Region, the U.S. Rewards for Justice Program has made some progress, but ultimately not as much as had been hoped. The international conflict in the Democratic Republic of Congo (DRC) has served as the political context for the handover of some Rwandans sought by the international tribunal to stand trial. The historical slaughters of Tutsi in Rwanda over the past 45 years have contributed to a significant Tutsi minority in the DRC, who are resented by indigenous Congolese. And the 1994 genocide provided the immediate context for further conflict in the region when the defeated *genocidaires* blended into a million ordinary Hutu civilians and crossed the border into DRC in one of the swiftest and largest movement of refugees in history. There the war criminals regrouped, planned, and executed military incursions into Rwanda. Perceiving its national security to be under threat, Rwanda's new Tutsi-dominated army invaded DRC in 1996, defeated the Congolese despot Mobutu Sese Seko's army with little resistance (Mobutu fled into exile in Morocco and France and later died of illness), and installed Laurent Kabila, a flamboyant Congolese dissident business-man who had spent many years in exile in Tanzania, as the new head of state of DRC.[72]

Ultimately, however, Kabila fell out with his Rwandan godfathers and asserted his authority by aligning himself with the pro-genocide Hutu forces in the region and reportedly orchestrated mass killings of Tutsis, publicly supported by his political adviser Yerodia Ndombasi.[73] Rwanda responded in 1998 with a second invasion of DRC in order to oust Kabila. The Congolese ruler invited the military intervention of Angola, Zimbabwe, which ultimately saved him from certain defeat. The conflict, which involved up to seven African countries and was described as "Africa's first World War," lasted five years. Strategic commercial interests were also part of the fog of war, with interventionist countries on both sides profiting from Congo's vast mineral wealth.[74]

Kabila, who was reputed to have been fond of the good life and to have had a habit of sleeping with "conflict" diamonds under his pillow (and chuckling in his sleep at the thought of the material assurance the stones provided),[75] was assassinated in 2001 and was succeeded by his son Joseph Kabila. Several troops of the genocidal former Rwandan Government Forces fought on Kabila's side during the war. In their various incursions into the Congo since 1994, the Rwandan army is alleged to have massacred more then 200,000 Hutus, including both genocidal killers and innocents in the Congo.[76] International guilt over the "original sin" of the 1994 genocide while the world essentially stood by and watched it happen has stifled the prospect of any effective international investigation into these atrocities.

The Lusaka Peace Accords in 1999 (ultimately not respected by the warring parties) called for the handover to the Arusha tribunal of persons accused of the 1994 genocide who fought on Kabila's side. And it was in the context of subsequent negotiations that ultimately led to a peace deal between the parties in South Africa that the United States launched the Rewards for Justice Program in the Great Lakes Region, seizing what it saw as an evolving political window of opportunity.

From the beginning of the African part of the rewards program, Prosper adopted a partnership approach that sought to secure the buy-in of the political leadership of the three main countries that harbored Rwandan war criminals in the region—Kenya, DRC, and the Republic of Congo (Congo-Brazaville)—in cooperation with the Arusha tribunal, in particular its registrar Adama Dieng. Prosper was anxious to demonstrate to the region, through meetings and joint press conferences with these officials, that the American program had local political support, in clear contrast with the Balkans, where the governments of the states of the former Yugoslavia resisted endorsing the U.S. rewards program and thus robbed it of any political legitimacy in the region.[77]

In this context, two political factors influenced the generally moderate Congolese president Joseph Kabila. First he recognized that the strong presence of the ex-RGF forces, the *interhamwe* militia, and the Alliance for the Liberation of Rwanda (ALIR) in his military and governmental structures presented him with a major foreign relations problem. He had inherited this situation from his father. This topic was discussed during Kabila's meeting with President Bush in Washington, DC in 2002.[78] Second, it posed an internal security problem as well.

Some of the Rwandan exiles had aligned themselves with hardline elements in Kabilia's government, creating further political complications. Moving against them too precipitately might affect the internal political order in unpredictable ways.

Thus, although Kabila wanted to get rid of these wanted men, including approving their being brought to justice at Arusha, in doing so he would be making a significant gesture to Rwanda, and was reluctant to do so without a reciprocal action of equal significance by Rwanda.[79] The peace talks in South Africa's Sun City, which included Rwandan negotiators, provided an enabling environment for a quid pro quo. As Rwandan and other foreign forces began their withdrawal from the Congo under intense international pressure, Kabila made the political decision to support the apprehension of Rwandan war criminals in his country and their handover to the ICTR under the U.S. rewards program.

Nevertheless the results, although a remarkable achievement as against the situation prevailing before the rewards program, have been modest in comparison with the significant numbers of ringleaders of the Rwandan genocide believed to be hiding in the DRC. But without American support and diplomatic intervention, apprehending these fugitives would almost certainly not have happened. As of this writing, five persons have been captured and handed over to the Arusha tribunal. The biggest catch among them was Augustine Bizimungu, former chief of staff of the Rwandan Government Forces, who fought actively in the DRC army—and had been one of the tribunal's highest priorities for arrest. Bizimungu, whose alleged role in the genocide was prominently portrayed in the movie *Hotel Rwanda*, was arrested in Angola in August 2002 after American authorities confirmed his presence in that country. Others captured under the aegis of the American program are Tharcisse Renzaho, former governor of Kigali (arrested in DRC, 2002), Yusuf Munyakazi, a militia leader during the genocide (DRC, 2004), Jean-Baptiste Gatete, a senior civil administrator (Congo, 2002), and Idelphonse Hatagekimana (Congo, 2003).

As the Arusha tribunal works its way toward completing its trials by 2008, the DRC's cooperation has not lived up to initial expectations. The tribunal has vented its frustration that at least 14 important genocide suspects thought to be in DRC remain beyond its reach.[80] The extremist forces that slaughtered Rwanda's Tutsis in 1994 are still active in the Congo. Their agenda of finishing off what they see as the uncompleted business of the 1994 genocide continues to fester, though it is doubtful that they represent a credible military threat to their home country of Rwanda. DRC, meanwhile, is undergoing a political transition that is expected to result in a democratically elected government. In a large and unstable country in which Kabila's central government has little practical control over large swathes of its territory, that process is a delicate one. Considering the influence of Hutus in his country's domestic politics, Kabila has little political incentive to rock the boat. Not surprisingly, then, relations between Rwanda and DRC have been uncomfortable—and will likely remain so for as long as the Rwandan extremist Hutu refugees in the Congo are not disarmed to the Rwandan government's satisfaction.

In late 2004, Rwanda threatened to invade DRC yet again, this time preemptively, to forestall the threat from the Hutu militias, arguing against the UN's approach, which encouraged voluntary disarmament. On the question of disarmament, Kigali's position enjoys South Africa's support.[81] But there are those who question the degree of real threat the extremist Hutu forces pose, and argue that "Rwanda is more interested in maintaining military influence over the resource-rich region" of Eastern Congo, which produces more than half of the world's supply of coltan, a mineral that is essential for the manufacture of mobile telephones.[82] In this light, the 1994 genocide has become a convenient bogeyman for the maintenance of Rwandan economic interests in the region: "[The African Union] must see through the Rwandan discourse of 'genocide' and 'national security' to the network of economic interests acquired in the last two wars it has fought in eastern Congo. Rwanda's principal fear is that its influence and interests—which have been independently documented by a UN panel—are threatened by Congo's checkered progress toward elections and stability."[83]

On the whole it is clear that the genocide of 1994—mixed with other strategic interests—will continue to cast a shadow over the stability of Africa's Great Lakes Region. Meanwhile the moment of opportunity that U.S. diplomacy seized in 2002 to trigger Kabila's modest cooperation with the Arusha tribunal has passed. And the U.S. invasion of Iraq and its aftermath, preparations for the trial of Saddam Hussein, as well as the atrocities in the Sudan and the politics of the ICC, appear to have sapped the force from the great-power component of the hunt for Rwanda's genocidal killers.

# CHAPTER 8

# IMAGE AND REALITY:
# PERCEPTIONS OF WAR CRIMES
# JUSTICE

It was the purest genocide since 1945, and perhaps the greatest act of evil since Pol Pot turned Cambodia into a killing field. But how many people can name any of the perpetrators of the Rwandan genocide of 1994?

—*The Economist*

In April 2004, the tenth anniversary of Rwanda's genocide was widely covered by media around the world, especially in the United States, where the Public Broadcasting System (PBS) and Cable News Network (CNN) ran days-long footage of some of the most incisive post mortems of the genocide, the absence of an effective international response, and Rwanda today. It was an important and unprecedented spotlight on Rwanda in the Western media. The quest for justice, national (Rwandan local and traditional courts called "gacaca") and international (the Arusha tribunal), was part of the coverage. It was saturation coverage, and by the time it ebbed the Rwandan genocide was firmly in the consciousness of national and international publics. And it was a rare exception—and an indication of what difference policy choices by powerful media editors can make when they decide to train their cameras on particular issues in world politics. Was this carpet coverage of a huge crime committed a decade ago in a poor, landlocked Central African country an act of atonement?

## IMAGE MATTERS

By mid-2005, the Arusha tribunal had completed trials of 25 defendants, with 22 convictions and 3 acquittals. As of this writing, 25 defendants are on trial while 18 are waiting for their day in court. Of the 81 persons indicted by the international court since it began its work at the end of 1995, 69 are in the tribunal's custody.[1]

For anyone who knows how complex the work of international war crimes tribunals are, this would be a decent scorecard. But it all depends on *who* is measuring international justice, and *what* is being measured, and the *context* in which such assessments take place. A criminal attorney in a well-developed national judicial system would have a different perspective from, say, a poor victim/survivor of the Rwandan genocide who has lost all his or her family and is understandably impatient for justice, quite unconcerned with the niceties of Western-style justice or "judicial romanticism" that is geared more toward *process* than *substance*—"fair trials" and the rights of the defense; what about *his* or *her* right to justice that is not delayed? The image problem that international war crimes justice faces, including that of the Arusha tribunal, is a fundamental one: "How can we reduce the magnitude of the crimes of genocide and crimes against humanity to accommodate them within the lens of present-day international criminal law?"[2]

Small surprise, then, that the Arusha tribunal's achievements notwithstanding, it has had image problems. Perceptions of the tribunal have been mixed, with ebbs and flows over the decade of its lifespan. In the early years of the tribunal's work, its image was largely negative, harmed by criticism by the media, nongovernmental organizations (NGOs), and other interest groups. Some of that criticism was justified. Much of it, however, was tendentious, exaggerated, lacking in context, and can validly be subject to charges of double standards. From 1998 onward the tide began to turn for the better, with occasional reversals arising mostly from the politics of the tribunal's relations with Rwanda.

Why should the image of the Arusha tribunal matter? After all, it could be argued that the tribunal is a court of law and justice, not a political institution that needs to pander to public opinion. Seen from this narrow perspective, the tribunal's exclusive goal should be to complete the trials and render judgments on persons accused of responsibility for the Rwanda massacres of 1994. This is no doubt its principal objective, but the image of the Arusha tribunal—the perception of the tribunal both as a court and as an organization—is important for several reasons. In a world in which imagery is having an increasingly important influence in international relations, perceptions—whether created by the media or other actors—determine to a large extent the importance or relevance of global issues and activities. New dimensions of international relations such as war crimes justice are no exception to this reality.

Against this backdrop, the most profound reason why perceptions of the international war crimes tribunals matter is also the reason for their creation: the nature of the crimes over which they have jurisdiction, and their limitations as judicial institutions. These tribunals were created to address mass murders inspired and directed by powerful political, military, and other figures—genocide, crimes against humanity, and war crimes. Partly because these crimes are politically inspired, war crimes justice is, as I have explained earlier, "political" justice. It is justice at the interface of law and politics, and for that reason, it must have political impact in order to be effective. And in our contemporary world, media is a powerful tool in politics. A large part of whether or not institutions such as war crimes tribunals impact on domestic or international society thus depends on awareness that is created by media, reporting substantive developments in the otherwise cloistered world of war crimes tribunals.

In the preamble to United Nations (UN) Security Council resolution 955 that created the Arusha tribunal, for instance, the Council made clear that it established the tribunal to bring to justice the persons responsible for these violations of international humanitarian law, deter the recurrence of such crimes, and contribute to the restoration and maintenance of peace and reconciliation. The impact of the war crimes tribunals beyond the forensic combat of the courtroom, the perception of whether their trials and related activities can or will bring about these results, is thus just as important as what happens in their courtrooms. The deterrence and reconciliation that are the stated aims of the tribunals rely on the public's awareness and perception of their work. And, as we shall see shortly, media attention—or the lack thereof—is a political variable, not something that exists in a vacuum.

Furthermore, the effectiveness of war crimes tribunals as judicial institutions depends largely on the cooperation of states because they do not possess the automatic enforcement mechanisms of justice that are available to national jurisdictions. That the ad hoc international criminal tribunals created by the UN in recent years are quite different from national courts is easily apparent to a close observer. Such tribunals, especially those at Arusha and The Hague, differ fundamentally from national courts on many substantive and practical grounds. Although established to address crimes committed in specific geographical regions, these courts are essentially international. They are funded by member states of the UN. Their rules of procedure and evidence are a custom-made hybrid. Their operations are global—witnesses who testify at these tribunals travel from various countries including those under the courts' jurisdiction. In the case of the Arusha tribunal, individuals on trial have been arrested in a wide range of countries in three continents (Africa, Europe, and North America). Sentences imposed on persons convicted by the two tribunals are served in various countries that have entered into formal agreements with the UN for that purpose. The judges and staff members of the Arusha tribunal, for instance, come from over 90 countries. It is easy to see already how the interests of the public and the governments of various countries can become engaged in the work of the tribunals. This is yet another reason why public and political support for these international courts is essential for their success.

This chapter assesses and analyzes the image of the International Criminal Tribunal for Rwanda (ICTR). It demonstrates that the visibility of the tribunal is relatively low and assessments of the tribunal are frequently critical, although this negativity has declined substantially. This situation owes itself to a combination of factors, the most important of which is that it is the product of a firmly entrenched political worldview in international relations. We should also bear in mind that while the media largely shapes the image of the tribunal, there are other important constituencies that are factors in the question of the Arusha tribunal's image. These include governments and NGOs, professional associations, and academia. This chapter examines the frequency and nature of coverage of the tribunal in the media, the image of the institution in the eyes of its stakeholders, and the reasons for the extent and nature of the coverage it receives.

## Coverage

In assessing coverage of the Arusha tribunal, one important question is whether the tribunal gets the level of publicity its work deserves relative to its sister tribunal dealing with war crimes in the former Yugoslavia. For the purposes of analyzing coverage of the tribunal by the media, it is important to distinguish between what one might term "global media," which is dominated by television, radio, and newspapers in North America and Europe and which has a truly global audience, and African media. Let us begin with a look at global media coverage.

Media coverage of the Arusha tribunal has improved in recent years. The tribunal's activities are reported far more frequently and widely, especially in the print media, than most realize. Since 1998, concrete results of the tribunal's judicial work in terms of judgments have become apparent, and thus there was much more substance to be reported by the media. The trials at the tribunal are broadly interesting and have both news and educative value in addition to the substantive matter of meting out justice for a crime of such huge proportions as genocide. As in all criminal trials, however the daily courtroom tedium that follows some interesting moments is absorbing only to true believers in justice, or victims. Because of the prosecution's strategy, individuals from several thematic sectors of Rwandan society implicated in the genocide are on trial at Arusha, quite unlike the case at The Hague where the focus is on war crimes in the former Yugoslavia and thus on military personnel and politicians. At Arusha, it is not just soldiers and politicians who are on trial or have been tried, but journalists, clergy whose calling was to serve as spiritual shepherds of their flock, senior civilian administrators such as regional governors, and even a popular pop singer alleged to have provided morale-boosting tunes that accompanied the "work" of the *genocidaires*.

Relatively increased media coverage—for that is what we are discussing here, not, say, the gavel to gavel coverage of the O.J. Simpson or Scott Petersen trials in the United States—was also no accident, for it is quite possible that important judgments may have been ignored or simply not reported by the media. Thus it is also largely as a result of the tribunal's progressively increased media savvy, aided by the infusion of qualified staff members and a policy priority accorded this area of the tribunal's operations as from 1998. Reporting by the news media permanently based at the Arusha tribunal has also played some part, although these reports have tended to serve specialized and interested audiences rather than the general public. These factors and a number of strategic initiatives by the tribunal, including its Outreach Program to Rwanda,[3] brought about a new level of awareness of its work. But does the tribunal receive *adequate* coverage, enough to make a *sustained* political impact in Rwanda, the African continent, and beyond? The answer, clearly, is no. Many reports on the tribunal, because they are wire agency reports, are "spot news" reports that lack depth, content, and context that would truly enlighten readers. Thus while the Arusha tribunal may be widely reported, it is not reported in an in-depth manner except on an occasional basis.

Moreover, while radio reporting on the tribunal by global media such as the British Broadcasting Corporation (BBC) World Service Radio and Radio France Internationale is relatively frequent, the same cannot be said of television. With the exception of the episodic coverage of the tribunal's most important judgments and a few other news items on influential television media such as Cable News Network (CNN) and BBC, news of the ICTR is largely absent from the world's television screens. Because most of the world gets its news from television as opposed to newspapers, which now tend to be a news source for the elite, this lack of television coverage has a profound—and negative—impact on the global visibility of the tribunal.

A notable reason for the paucity of television coverage is the tribunal's distance from global media centers. Nairobi, Kenya, the largest city in the East African region and home to a substantial number of global media correspondents, is a four-hour drive from Arusha. The cost and logistical requirements of traveling to the court make it difficult for television crews to travel to Arusha to cover the trials, resulting in reporting that is less frequent than it would be had the court been located in a global media center. In this light, the matter of the tribunal's location assumes an importance of even wider political dimensions, comparable with the real estate business mantra: "location, location, location!" Whether this is a good enough reason for the near absence of television coverage is, of course, quite another matter. While location is important, war correspondents travel to and cover with greater frequency war zones that are more difficult to access than Arusha. And this distance did not stop many journalists from penning reports and opinions about the tribunal without visiting it, perhaps an indication that the location of the tribunal may not be as a large a factor in its coverage as might be assumed.

The Arusha tribunal's media deficit is starkly contrasted by the far more frequent, substantive and *sustained* global media coverage of the Hague tribunal. More than 500 journalists from various countries were present at The Hague to cover the opening of the trial of Slobodan Milosevic on February 12, 2002. In contrast, approximately 100 journalists were physically present at the ICTR at Arusha to cover the tribunal's verdict in the first-ever judgment by an international court for the crime of genocide on September 2, 1998.[4] This was the largest number of journalists to have covered a trial live at the tribunal. Despite significant improvements in the public awareness of the Arusha tribunal, it is far less visible than the Hague tribunal.[5] Ironically the Arusha tribunal's groundbreaking decisions have established legal guideposts for national courts and other international war crimes tribunals, including the permanent International Criminal Court. It is these decisions, then, especially as they concern the crime of genocide, that have done the early "heavy lifting" in the development of international justice at the close of the twentieth century.

## Political Priority and Visibility

The reasons for the comparatively inadequate publicity of the ICTR appear, at first sight, to be largely political. The governments in the capitals of North America and Europe, where the global media are mainly based, are actively involved in the pursuit of justice in the Balkans from a geographical, political, and military perspective. Their troops are involved in the North Atlantic Treaty Organization (NATO) peacekeeping and peace enforcement operations in the Balkans, and also are directly involved in the hunt for war criminals. To be sure, this situation was not "present at the creation" of the tribunal, but evolved in line with the geopolitics of Europe and the Western alliance in general. Writing about the Yugoslavia war crimes trials at The Hague, and specifically about how the tide turned for that tribunal after its early years in which it suffered a deficit of attention and political support, Chris Stephen writes: "In May 1997 everything changed and the fortunes of the Hague tribunal were revived by a single, apparently unrelated, event, which was the election in Britain of a Labor government. The Labour party of Blair arrived in office promising an 'ethical foreign policy.' The new Foreign Secretary, Robin Cook, was aware of [Louis] Arbour's bold stance . . . Now he won cabinet approval to use the SAS to go after war crimes suspects. With Cook backing the idea, Albright pushed America to give its support."[6]

With the politicians and the armed forces of the governments so directly involved in issues relating to the Hague tribunal, the media and public opinion in these countries naturally follow. Perceptions of national interest have heavily influenced the comparatively heavy coverage of the Hague court as opposed to the low coverage of the Arusha tribunal. This dichotomy in the global attention paid to the work of the two tribunals has been highlighted in the global media.[7] It was also partially the subject of a CNN television interview program that noted the vastly greater publicity and support given to the Hague tribunal's work in comparison to the Arusha tribunal's.[8] The responsibility of the global media needs to be emphasized: the imbalance in the publicity given to the two tribunals is more the fault of the media than that of governments. The Arusha tribunal has received significant material support from governments, but not enough from the perspective of some observers.[9]

The Arusha tribunal has on the whole not been a compelling subject for the powerful editors of the Western media outlets.[10] The war crimes author Peter Maguire has argued that Eurocentrism is a dominant reason for this reality: "The Eurocentric attitude of the world's major media groups combined with journalists' preference for the comforts of Europe (to the perceived hardship of a Tanzania posting) mean [the Arusha tribunal] has been neglected."[11] Thus, Maguire has noted, "consider the attention paid by the world's press to small-fish defendants like Dusko Tadic at the ICTY in the Hague, while the Arusha court was trying much more significant former leaders, yet they still could not get much attention."[12]

And yet, on a number of occasions when Western journalists have turned their serious attention to the question of justice for the Rwandan genocide, the Arusha tribunal, the crimes in its docket, and its defendants have come powerfully, evocatively, and hauntingly alive in their pages. One need only read the award-winning writings of Philip Gourevitch and the masterpieces penned by Peter Landesman and Bill Berkeley on the work of the Arusha tribunal to know that the problem is not one of absence of a compelling story.[13]

This question of imbalance in the global media coverage of the international war crimes tribunals is an important one. It is important not because the two tribunals are in competition—they are not—but because the two tribunals established to achieve positive, longer term political outcomes. These desired outcomes require the effective creation of public awareness if their "norm entrepreneurship" is to ultimately have any impact. Who would care about the judgments of genocide and crimes against humanity if no one knows about them in the first place? It is important that the global media adopt a balanced, evenhanded, and global approach to covering the subject. A highly disproportionate focus on the Balkans that fails to give significant, in-depth coverage to the work of the Arusha tribunal could be construed as an indication that the process taking place there is not as vitally important as it is. As journalism professor Todd Gitlin has noted, the media define reality through "principles of selection, emphasis, and presentation composed of little tacit theories about what exists, what happens, and what matters."[14]

The upshot of the media's unbalanced coverage of the two tribunals is the creation of a perception that the ideal of obtaining universal justice is more important in some places than in others. At a press conference after a visit to the Arusha tribunal, U.S. senator Russ Feingold expressed his concern about the lopsided focus on the Hague thus: "I've been concerned about what sometimes looks like a double standard in terms of our international policy, that we're more likely to act in terms of tragedies in Europe, but less likely to act when it comes to Africa." The U.S. senator opined that the Arusha tribunal was "an important test of whether the world will consider an African life as important as a life of somebody from somewhere else."[15] A perception—intended or not— that some victims are more important than others, even in death, has been created at the Arusha tribunal's expense. "Such cynicism," one writer has noted, "undercut the rule of law."[16]

The visibility of the Arusha tribunal within the African continent, in terms of its coverage by African media, is also low. This is tragic for reasons that will be presented in a moment. With the exception of media in Tanzania and Rwanda, the host countries of the tribunal, and to a more limited extent South African media, there is no original coverage of the Arusha tribunal by African media. The lack of original coverage exists here at two levels. The first is conceptual, while the second is practical. The conceptual problem is that of relative apathy on the part of many African journalists, some of who do not appear to fully appreciate the relevance of the work of the tribunal. Many do not see that the Arusha court is exacting accountability for heinous crimes from erstwhile powerful individuals and that this process is essential to the social and political evolution of the continent.

For all the critiques of international war crimes tribunals—that they represent a form of Western hegemony and "judicial imperialism," for example—accountability of national leaderships is not a bad thing for any society even after balancing the well-known tensions between peace and justice. The linkage between judicial accountability and Africa's progress has not been recognized in the African media to an extent where trials at the ICTR are accorded priority on a scale similar to European media reports on trials at the International Criminal Tribunal for the Former Yugoslavia (ICTY). Conflicts such as the Rwandan civil war in the early 1990s have occurred in several African countries, caused by—and resulting in—widespread violations of human rights and humanitarian law and perpetuating the relative poverty of the continent.

It ought to be obvious, but apparently is not, that the Arusha tribunal's example in meting out justice for mass crimes points to the need to institutionalize accountability at the national level. This is, in fact, the key to Africa's development above all else: accountability is at the heart of Africa's development conundrum—whether it be the responsible stewardship of national resources or abstinence from human rights violations and crimes against humanity that trigger civil wars. Contrary to the conventional wisdom, Africa is not "poor"—at least not on the scale it is portrayed to be. It is *impoverished* by corruption and conflicts bred by crimes such as genocide and crimes against humanity on trial at Arusha. Establishing a culture of the rule of law creates beneficial conditions for democracy and economic development. African media lag far behind the continent's civil society in advocating judicial accountability for mass crimes. One reason for this lag, as I mentioned earlier, is a tension felt throughout the continent between the need for criminal trials for such crimes and a belief that such trials may at the same time destabilize countries undergoing delicate transitions in the wake of conflict or repression. The result is a tendency to favor amnesties and truth commissions over criminal trials. In this context, the sheer scale of the Rwandan genocide is thus seen as an exception, one that clearly calls for criminal sanction—an example that must not necessarily be replicated in every instance of human rights crimes. This attitude is evident in the frequent sigh: "The Rwanda situation. How awful. But what's it got to do with us?"

A practical and just as pervasive problem is that few African media organizations have the financial resources to send their reporters and correspondents to Arusha to cover the tribunal and publish original accounts of its work. None of the three main news organizations that have correspondents and cover the tribunal on a permanent basis, Internews (USA), Hirondelle (Switzerland), and Intermedia (France), is African-owned. African media, therefore, rely exclusively on the often-cursory newswire reports from Associated Press, Reuters, and Agence France Presse. As will be shown later, this situation has important consequences for the image of the tribunal.

## A TILTED MIRROR: THE IMAGE OF THE ARUSHA TRIBUNAL

What, then, is the image of the ICTR? The image of the tribunal is much better than it used to be. Among those who follow its work, the tribunal is now generally respected although there are several important nuances in the way it is perceived, which must be explored.[17] In this context, the tribunal should be assessed from the perspective of two sets of important constituencies or stakeholders of its work: the geographical and the thematic. The geographical stakeholders are Rwanda, the wider African continent, and the wider international society. The thematic stakeholders consist mainly of governments, NGOs, and the media.

Another reason it is helpful to have a more careful assessment of external perceptions of the Arusha tribunal is that it is frequently the subject of criticisms from some of these constituencies. As informed observers have noted, most of these criticisms are unwarranted,[18] especially when the complexity of the task of the tribunal is considered. Much of this criticism stems from a lack of a full understanding of the tribunal or from subjective, self-serving motives. In such cases, the tribunal is criticized not because it has done or is doing anything wrong, but because, by its very nature, its work is bound to be seen differently by different interests at different times.[19] There is also a difference between dismissive criticism based on outright cynicism toward an institution and criticism that is motivated by disagreement with specific aspects of the institution amid a general acceptance of its relevance. While the former genre was more common in the tribunal's early years, the latter increasingly became the case in recent years.

## The View from Rwanda

The tribunal's image in Rwanda gyrates between high and low ebbs that depend largely on the political/strategic considerations of the moment for Rwanda, but as of 2005, can be described as marginally positive. The relationship improved in 2004 after the diplomatic battle to split the chief prosecutor post of the Arusha and Hague tribunals in 2003. While the relationship has been good and bad at different times, it is one that has some inherent frictions imbued in it.

Relations between the international tribunal and Rwanda were rocky in the tribunal's early years. This was largely because the tribunal cannot impose the death penalty, and its framework precluded explicit Rwandan control or influence. It thus suited Rwanda's political interests to highlight the Arusha court's deficiencies. Here a distinction should also be made among the Rwandan interests assessing the tribunal, for there is no monolithic view. Kagame, for example, has always been benign and strategic in his attitude to the tribunal, indeed generally positive. This may be because the Rwandan leader is not wont to be emotional and prefers to take a longer term view. The same cannot be said of several key officials with a responsibility for dealing with the tribunal over the decade of its existence. There exist among this group several "hardliners" and survivors of the genocide with little reason, from their perspective, to be excited about a court that is essentially foreign to them.

There was also an initial perception—based on understandable impatience for justice on the part of victims and a lack of appreciation of the tribunal's procedures and characteristics as an international court that respects the highest human rights standards—that the tribunal was ineffective. Here again things have changed significantly. One major reason for this shift was the tribunal's successes in apprehending the big fish, accused persons who most Rwandans knew were effectively beyond the reach of the domestic judicial system. Judgments in several cases, including the 1998 conviction of former prime minister Kambanda, based on his confession to the crimes of genocide and crimes against humanity, changed the perception that the tribunal was ineffective. That the tribunal will close its doors at the end of this decade and its chief prosecutor will transfer 45 case files to Rwanda (and presumably several of its detainees whose cases would not have been tried by 2008) has brought on a somewhat mellower approach to the international tribunal by Rwandan authorities: their strategic interest of holding trials of several middle-ranking individuals accused of genocide in Rwandan courts will be served by this scenario.

The problem the Arusha tribunal has not been able to overcome is that of its physical and psychological distance from Rwanda, despite the tribunal's Outreach Program, which had an important initial impact. But that impact has not been sustained, blunted as it is by the program's essentially limited reach. It has been beneficial for the urban elite in Kigali but has not been extended into the country's rural areas. Thus the initiative has remained essentially where it was when the international tribunal's *Umusanzu* Center was launched in Kigali in 2000. Part of the reason for this gap is the absence of resources. The tribunal's budget from the UN in New York does not include funds for an outreach program to Rwanda, which is separate from the court's traditional press functions for which resources are allocated. Scrounging up voluntary donations from countries for outreach activities has not been easy for the tribunal. A similar outreach program at the Hague tribunal, despite having received far more voluntary donor resources than its counterpart in Arusha, has similarly failed to make much impact on the regional population of the former Yugoslavia. Writing about the Hague tribunal's Outreach Program, David Tolbert complained: "The Outreach Program has never received funding from the UN, which illustrates the view that the tribunal's impact on the region is of marginal interest to UN policymakers."[20]

The use of radio broadcasts emanating not from Arusha, but from inside Rwanda to spread the word of the tribunal's work inside

Rwanda was considered, but has not come to fruition. The tribunal broadcasts its judgments on Rwanda radio via satellite link, but not the daily trials that would have made them part of everyday life for Rwanda, even if from a distance. Radio is the most important medium of communication in Rwanda. As we have seen in chapter 4, it was an important medium of hate propaganda during the genocide. Thus, just like the global media, control of the medium of communication here has political implications. Establishing an independent radio station for the tribunal in Rwanda, as some UN peacekeeping operations in failed states have done, would have to surmount political obstacles. Rwanda is not a failed state, and has firm control over its territory including its airwaves. Whether it would want to give the international tribunal free reign on those airwaves is an open question. A fully independent radio station operated by the tribunal would have to address questions about the non-indictment and trial of crimes committed by the Rwandan Patriotic Front (RPF) in 1994, and this will undoubtedly create fresh tensions between the tribunal and the current Rwandan government.

Broadly speaking, Rwandans remain skeptical about the Arusha tribunal. This is due only partly to the performance of the tribunal. More important are the wider policy and popular debates about the contextual relevance of international criminal justice to the societies in which the crimes they are adjudicating occurred. In this context, skepticism about the Arusha tribunal is based on a view that its seat should have been located in Rwanda itself. Furthermore Rwandans believe that trials at the tribunal place an excessive emphasis on respect for the rights of the accused persons and not enough on those of the victims and survivors. The prevalent viewpoint in Rwanda is that the rights of victims to direct representation in the proceedings and to restitution from resources of the international community (in addition to the retributive justice of the tribunal that focuses on alleged perpetrators of the crimes within its jurisdiction) should have been part of the definition of "justice" for the genocide.[21]

## The Global Viewpoint

In other African countries, with few exceptions, not much is known about the activities of the Arusha tribunal and much of what is known is not positive because most of the media outlets there are not able or willing to make independent, original assessments of the court. The exceptions are African countries with special links to the tribunal: Benin, Mali, Swaziland, for example, have agreements on the enforcement of the tribunal's sentences in those countries. Cameroon and Kenya, meanwhile, have links to the court because major arrests of ICTR suspects have been made there. Thus the best that can be said of the Arusha tribunal's image in Africa is that it is ambiguous. The image of the tribunal in the wider international community is generally positive. However that image is variable among thematic constituencies such as the media (some positive, others less so), NGOs (mostly negative), and governments (mixed, but has evolved in a more positive direction than was previously the case). The tribunal's image in academia and among professional associations is mostly positive—not surprising when it is considered that this group of stakeholders is more interested in what has in fact been the tribunal's greatest strength, its normative impact. The reason for the tribunal's now essentially positive image, despite the absence of strong enthusiasm for it in some global media institutions and NGOs, is the sheer weight of its achievements. Its precedent-setting judgments for the crime of genocide and its success rate in apprehending high-ranking suspects are facts that cannot be overlooked by any serious observer.

Nevertheless there remains a wide gulf between the reality of the achievement and potential of the tribunal, on the one hand, and its perception in some constituencies, on the other. There appears to be in some quarters a reflexive tendency to view the Arusha tribunal from a critical standpoint that emphasizes its institutional shortcomings even when evidence of the tribunal's achievements abound. Moreover it is doubtful that the fault for most of its imperfections can be laid at the feet of tribunal officials. In this context, the perfect became the enemy of the good. Conversely a close observer cannot help but notice a tendency among these critics not to see the Hague tribunal through a critical lens, even when, objectively speaking, problems common to both tribunals exist. Comparatively speaking, although the Hague tribunal is the subject of the occasional criticism, the portrayal of that tribunal in the global media tends to be hagiographic, emphasizing its significance and the substance of its judicial work.[22] Thus it was that the *Tadic* trial, involving a lowly camp guard who was that tribunal's first defendant (and which, as that tribunal's first trial, doubtless was important), was breathlessly billed by some Western media commentators as "the trial of the century," about five years before Milosevic appeared in the dock as a defendant. The Milosevic trial has, however, exposed the difficulties of international and political justice and attracted much criticism as he seemed to be getting the better of the tribunal with his theatrical showmanship.

## LIFTING THE VEIL

There are a number of important reasons why the Arusha tribunal has frequently been the subject of negative reporting and calculated attacks by the media, NGOs, and even by some public officials. The most important is outdated perceptions, though these have progressively receded into the background of distant memory. First some criticisms of the tribunal were accurate and valid. Like any other institution, the Arusha tribunal surely has its share of shortcomings, some of them significant, others less so. If this is true, as it surely is, it should be factored into any assessment of its external perceptions. The emphasis has thus been on reforming areas of weakness and communicating such changes to its stakeholders. Second, as noted in chapter 3, the tribunal suffered from a serious management crisis in 1996 and early 1997.

The early management crisis no longer is a major point of current criticism of the Arusha court. Other aspects of its work are fairer game at this point. Nevertheless the wide media coverage of these teething management problems of the tribunal left a lingering negative impression in the minds of some people, and has fed into other, more fundamental reasons for frequently critical coverage. As late as 2001, for example, a critical report on the tribunal published by a leading Japanese newspaper was still centered on the audit report of 1997.[23] And yet, as Pascal Besnier, one of the most respected defense lawyers at the tribunal at the time, commented: "History will retain the analytical work done by magistrates and not the administrative headaches of this tribunal."[24]


### A "Slow" Pace: Justice Denied?

A third point of criticism of the Arusha tribunal is a strong perception of its judicial work as slow and unproductive relative to the resources expended on it. At this point, the gripe of its critics is that the tribunal has completed the trials of "only" 25 persons after nearly 10 years of existence. The criticism of the rate of its judicial productivity in terms of the number of completed cases has been a constant one, especially since management-focused criticism has waned. In the past two years, trials at the Arusha tribunal have moved at a very brisk pace. While the infusion of additional judges by the Security Council has helped, it also shows that trials can move briskly with determination on the part of the judges, the prosecution, and the defense. It does not hurt that the ad hoc tribunals for Rwanda and the former Yugoslavia have been focused by the exit strategy they were pressured to come up with by the Security Council and the great powers.

This criticism that the pace of justice at the tribunal is too slow, one of the most important critiques of the Arusha tribunal, reflects a crisis of expectations that international criminal justice faces in general. There is a wide gulf between what the victims and the global public expect of the Arusha and Hague tribunals and the reality of what they can accomplish when their complex operational imperatives and difficulties are considered. In the case of the Arusha tribunal, the management and institutional difficulties in its early years, problems that were principally attributable to its location and, more importantly, to a lack of an adequate infrastructure at the headquarters of the tribunal when it was established, exacerbated this crisis of expectations. It is not clearly understood by the victims of the Rwandan atrocities and other observers that the Arusha tribunal was not established to prosecute the more than 100,000 individuals suspected of involvement in the genocide and who are detained in Rwandan prisons. That task is the responsibility of the Rwandan domestic judicial system. Rather the tribunal was set up to apprehend and bring to justice the high-ranking individuals suspected of masterminding and directing the massacres. Thus the tribunal will not try more than 70 or so persons on the whole. Against this backdrop, the tribunal has been quite successful given its commendable track record of successfully apprehending and detaining several such figures and bringing them to trial.[25] These individuals were all arrested in various countries, where they were beyond the reach of the Rwandan government as many foreign governments were reluctant to surrender the suspects because of the application of the death penalty in the Rwandan judicial system. As James Meernik and Kimi King have perceptively observed: "The ICTR's record is quite impressive, but it is all the more remarkable given that so much work had to be done in the Tanzanian city of Arusha whose infrastructure is challenging at best. Courtrooms had to be built, communications systems devised, judges, prosecutors and staff had to be found and provided for and judicial and administrative procedures had to be worked out all from scratch. Too often outsiders, who spend little time at the tribunal before writing about it, do not take these challenges into consideration."[26] Another important contextual fact is that the Arusha tribunal is a pioneering institution that had no precedents to go by. Its imperfections in the last few years can therefore be seen as the price that was paid for the decision to address the Rwanda massacres through the mechanism of an international tribunal.

There are those who believe that price has been high when the resources expended and the results obtained are compared. There is very little merit to this point of view. It lacks the nuance that a deeper understanding of international war crimes tribunals would confer. It is one thing to say that the trials at the Arusha tribunal have been slower than they should have been. After all, 22 defendants were tried at Nuremberg within a one-year period. Even considering the differences in context between Nuremberg and Arusha, that is an appropriate comparison. But it is quite another—and somewhat simplistic—to say, as several critics have, that the resources spent on the trials at Arusha would have been better spent as direct compensation to victims of genocide. Without retributive justice, reparations would address only one element of the fundamental questions of justice.

For the biennial financial year 2004–2005, the budget of the Arusha tribunal was $251 million with a total staff strength of 1,042. For the Hague tribunal, $271 million was budgeted for the same period, with 1,238 staff members. The matter of the cost of justice is an interesting one. Critics, however, rarely take account of the fact that international war crimes tribunals have an almost completely different context from national trials, and even in many developed countries, for example, is still a lot cheaper than comparable national trials. International tribunals must spend significant resources on the construction of detention facilities for defendants awaiting trial or on trial, legal aid systems, and translation of documents and interpretation of proceedings into two or three languages. The cost of contributing to the establishment of the rule of law in war-torn societies is worth it, and the only valid criticism arises when resources are expended on international trials and domestic judicial capacity is not simultaneously strengthened. Whatever may be said of the Nuremberg trials, for example, few can argue today that those trials—and their subsequent impact on German society—were not worth the cost.

Moreover, the lives of the victims of mass atrocities are worth the resources spent on trials for their killers, provided, as we have seen, that it is advantageous to provide, in addition, material restitution to victims. And in the scheme of things in world politics, the resources spent on international war crimes tribunals are miniscule compared to other expenditures that many may consider of questionable utility. The fact, then, is that whatever shortcomings may be laid at the door of international justice—and there are several—that they are expensive is not a sustainable critique. Responding in the *Financial Times* to a sharply worded critique by a Rwandan genocide survivor of the "extraordinary expense" of international justice with "only 20 people convicted in nine years",[27] a former official of the tribunal had this perspective:

> As for the "extraordinary expense" of the ICTR, a better comparison would be with other exceptional judicial processes. For example, the Lockerbie trial (270 victims, two accused) cost 75 million pounds and this week it was announced that the Bloody Sunday inquiry in Londonderry (14 victims) has so far cost about 130 million pounds and that the final cost will exceed 150 million pounds. It is hardly surprising that the prosecution of those responsible for about 1 million deaths in Rwanda should cost a comparable amount. The deaths of so many Africans deserve at least equal efforts to bring the perpetrators to justice as do those of Europeans.[28]

It is worth recalling that the international tribunal was established at the request of the government of Rwanda. That request arose from that government's recognition of its own lack of capacity to take on the totality of the task.

There have been many avoidable delays in the judicial work of the tribunal in the past. The initially glacial pace of the work was due in part to many unavoidable factors that are built into its very complex nature as an international judicial institution, making it very different from anything to which its observers are accustomed.[29] Trial proceedings are conducted in three languages (English, French, and Kinyarwanda). While there is simultaneous interpretation from French into English and vice versa, interpretation into and from Kinyarwanda vis-à-vis English and French was for several years largely consecutive. This situation often triples the amount of time witness testimony takes because a significant number of witnesses testify in the Kinyarwanda language. The tribunal's administration has successfully trained Kinyarwanda interpreters in simultaneous interpretation from and into French. This innovation has cut trial delays by at least 25 percent. Also witnesses have to be brought to the tribunal from various countries. National courts do not have these complications.[30] All court documents must be translated into English and French, the official working languages of the tribunal. Add all these complexities and more to the fact that the tribunal's procedural rules, though a hybrid, rely heavily on the time-consuming common law adversarial system, and the result is a process that has in-built delays.[31]

In my view, the institutional attempts at perfection in judicial trials resulted in several actions or failures to act—by the judges, the prosecution, and the defense—that prolonged trials. Absent these acts and omissions, the trials would still have stood the test of time, an understandable concern of the judges and staff of the tribunal. This was no doubt, as well, part of a steep learning curve in what was essentially a voyage in uncharted waters, coupled with inadequate numbers of judges in the early years at the Arusha and Hague tribunals that led to crowded dockets and bottlenecks—too many cases were coming in as new arrests of suspected criminals were made, but not enough cases were going out of the bottle.

But for too many years as well, the Arusha tribunal was scared stiff by the bogeyman of "victor's justice" and allowed the defense in several cases to waste enormous amounts of time, leading to "justice delayed" and, it could be said, justice denied. This is not advocacy for a kangaroo court. But there was much that could have been done differently without sacrificing the principles of a fair trial. The problem arises when a "fair trial" is exclusively about the rights of the defendant, who, by the way, is also entitled to an expeditious trial under international human rights law, but for political reasons may seek to discredit the international tribunal by making it impossible for the tribunal to try his case in good time. The tribunal's prosecution, for its part, was frequently not "trial-ready" before obtaining arrest warrants, which contributed to delays.[32] But in the early years of the tribunal, this must be weighed against the prospect of letting alleged *genocidaires* roam the world at large.

As we have discussed and will return to in a moment, the tribunal's image is at this point arguably that of a "victor's court" anyway. So what was the point? If the tribunal does not indict and prosecute any Tutsis, it would have arrived at precisely the scenario it was trying to avoid in the first place by placing emphasis on the wrong area, a fixation with procedural justice. This striving for perfection and consequent loss of momentum—in a tribunal that has ultimately a political context and purpose—is one of the most valid indictments of the Arusha tribunal. Small surprise, then, that the tribunal squandered some of its political capital, with many victims and observers giving up any hope for expeditious justice.

By 2000, there was a growing recognition within the tribunal of an urgent need to dispose off cases more quickly. A more aggressive process of amending the tribunal's procedural rules to eliminate delays and achieve this outcome began. The judges began to exert a greater degree of control over judicial proceedings, reducing the numbers of witnesses called by the parties and denying with sanctions "frivolous motions" deemed to be an abuse of the court's process. Most important, the tribunal asked the UN Security Council for additional judges, a request that was granted in 2002.

## Pride and Prejudice: Worldviews and
## Double Standards

One of the most important reasons why the Arusha tribunal received a steady stream of criticism and critical reporting is the stereotypical image and neglect of the African continent in the global media. There have been strong indications, judging from the admissions of some journalists in the international press, that there is more to their reporting of Africa than meets the ordinary eye. The general lack of adequate coverage outside of the negative is attributable to a mixture of ignorance, misunderstanding, and calculated editorial decision making by the editors of some global media.[33] The tribunal's highly publicized problems in its start-up phase simply reinforced this more fundamental disadvantage.

Thus the Rwandan genocide, portrayed as "tribal chaos and anarchy" in order to locate it within the prevailing stereotype of the African continent as one in perpetual crisis, was given wider global media coverage than the search for justice for the genocide by an international court sitting in Africa.[34] This perpetuates the worldview that Africa does not matter. According to this view, the continent, signified in microcosm by the work of an international tribunal seeking justice for mass crimes in an African country, was frequently portrayed not from a nuanced perspective of an institution succeeding against many odds, but as one that is dysfunctional. Positive facts and analysis about the tribunal have often been given inadequate emphasis or acknowledged in only a cursory fashion when such facts are simply so significant that they cannot be ignored.[35]

These portrayals send a subliminal message: this is Africa, where nothing (supposedly) works—what else is to be expected? Conversely the frequently hagiographic portrayal of the Hague as a properly functioning international court sends a subconscious or calculated message: this is Europe, where things work; the massacres in the former Yugoslavia were a reprehensible aberration and their perpetrators can only be brought to efficient justice at The Hague. In the perception of the powerful Western media and punditocracy, the glass at Arusha was always nearly empty; at the Hague it was always almost full.[36] This is also part of the politics of international justice: the global (Western) media deciding, in effect, to rank the status of victims of mass atrocities—and the efficacy of the efforts to render justice on their behalf—in our subconscious.

This double standard in the reporting and assessments of the Arusha tribunal vis-à-vis its counterpart at The Hague has been evident not

only in the media but also in other important stakeholders of international criminal justice such as some private international organizations,[37]
NGOs, and other circles. But what informs these double standards?
Both tribunals face certain common challenges inherent in the nature
of international criminal justice and their dual pioneering roles. The
best example is that of the slow pace of trials, a problem faced by both
tribunals for several years, for which media, governments, and NGOs
have exclusively criticized the ICTR. Normal institutional and organi-
zational difficulties common to both tribunals have been magnified
out of proportion in relation to the Arusha tribunal as earthshaking
catastrophes. There is palpable excitement and well-deserved extended
coverage in the global media when the Hague tribunal records a significant achievement, less so (although equally deserved) in the case of
the Arusha tribunal. In some cases, possibly inadvertently, precedents
in international criminal justice established by the Arusha tribunal
have been attributed to the Hague tribunal.[38]

In an example of the jaundiced "criticism" the Arusha tribunal has
received in the past (and which the uninformed general reader would
doubtless have assumed to be accurate), some Canadian defense
lawyers and would-be defense lawyers made several allegations in the
*National Post*, a Canadian newspaper, in 2001.[39] Their complaints
ranged from exaggerated and false statements about working conditions in the tribunal to their longstanding campaign for indigent
accused persons whose defense counsel are assigned and paid by the
tribunal to have absolute freedom to choose the lawyers to be
assigned to them. The preferred "choice" is that of lawyers of a particular nationality. This campaign ignored the prevailing international
and human rights law, affirmed by the tribunal's Appeals Chamber in
its judgment in the *Akayesu* case, that indigent accused persons on
legal aid do not have a right to choose the lawyer assigned to them.
While the practice of the registrar's office at the Arusha tribunal has
been to take the detainee's preference into consideration, the registrar
is not bound by the wishes of an indigent accused and has wide
discretion that he exercises in the interests of justice.[40]

The news report in the *National Post* declaimed:

> Some Canadian lawyers who, since the tribunal was set up in 1994, have
> regularly made the 20 hour trek to Arusha, a malaria-infested town of
> 200,000 in the northeastern part of Tanzania, to defend their clients,
> say it is often difficult to find a working photocopier or even a glass of
> clean water. The computers, as one lawyer put it, are "steam driven," and
> transcripts of court proceedings are sometimes difficult to obtain . . . [41]

UN officials wanted to try accused Rwandan war criminals in Africa, rather than at The Hague because they did not want to be accused of colonialism and felt it would be "culturally and socially" relevant to try Africans in an African context, even though many of those accused of genocide are Western-educated and have spent little time in Africa, their defense lawyers say.[42] "It is difficult to communicate with your client because only one in 10 telephones work. There is no running water and malaria is rampant," said one Canadian defense lawyer who did not want to be identified for fear that his criticisms might prejudice his case.[43]

What the *National Post* described as a 20-hour "trek" to a "malaria-infested" town to defend Rwandans accused of genocide was hardly motivated by altruism, any more than the colonial "scramble for Africa" in the late nineteenth century was motivated by self-sacrifice rather than the economic exploitation of the colonies. The lawyers who inspired this article were not engaged in pro bono work: defense lawyers paid by the tribunal for defending indigent accused persons under its legal aid scheme earn up to $120 per hour and could bill up to a maximum of 175 hours per month. [The findings of a report of the Office of Internal Oversight Services (OIOS) on allegations of fee-splitting between defense lawyers and accused persons at the ICTR and the ICTY[44] referred to "counsel from one particular group" (nationality not specified) in relation to the ICTR in the context of the possibility of fee-splitting.] A separate article that reflected the tribunal's perspective[45] was published simultaneously with the article containing their criticisms of the tribunal.

Against this backdrop, it becomes clear how the virtually exclusive reliance of the African media on the global media for information about the work of the Arusha is a disservice to the tribunal. The victims of the crimes the tribunal is adjudicating, the continent in which it is located, and the political and social evolution that it is expected to affect, as well as its global impact, also suffer. The lack of original, direct coverage of the tribunal by African media allows the domination of distorted perspectives that do not relate its work to the overall development and promotion of the rule of law in Africa. It has robbed the Arusha tribunal of the sort of profile it should have in the continent in which the crimes it is addressing occurred.

The problem is compounded by the dearth of strong, public political support for the tribunal among African governments. In the absence of such visible political support, the tribunal was often fair game for jaundiced journalism and other interest groups of questionable objectivity that have written highly critical reports on it, heralded by press statements and press conferences.[46] The situation is in stark contrast, as has been demonstrated, with the frequent and strong public statements by leaders of European and North American countries in support of the Hague tribunal. It is easy for any observer to conclude that there is little agreement among African leaders that a tribunal trying high-ranking individuals who have committed massive human rights abuses is a welcome idea. Surely, though, such a dim view of international criminal justice, were it indeed the case, is not unique to African leadership.

## Victors' Justice?

Yet another contributing factor to the image of the ICTR is the criticism that its prosecutions are one-sided, directed against the Hutu extremists who perpetrated the genocide of the Tutsis. Impartiality is supposedly a core dimension of international criminal justice, yet one in which international war crimes tribunals have been, and will continue to be, sorely tested. It is not just that these tribunals must be impartial. They must be seen as impartial.[47] Guilt for violations of international humanitarian law in times of conflict is rarely equal, and so indictments need not be equally distributed to various sides to the conflict in order to demonstrate impartiality. It is nevertheless important to manage the perception of the work of the tribunals in this context, provided the actions of the tribunals are supported by facts.

In its early years, the Hague tribunal also faced a similar challenge stemming from a perception in some quarters that its work was biased against the Serbs. But the tribunal has overcome this perception with indictments of top Croatian military commanders and Bosnian Muslim leaders. It is important that the war crimes tribunals established by the UN avoid a future judgment of history that criticizes them—as several critics have done to the international military tribunals established at Nuremberg and Tokyo after World War II—as victors' or partial tribunals. Should such criticisms be well founded, they could damage the historical legacy of these tribunals and reduce their actual contribution to the resolution of the conflicts that gave rise to them.

The reality, however, is that in fractured societies, attempts will be made to deflect efforts to exact individual accountability with propaganda that seeks to undermine the perception of the impartiality of justice. It is, as noted above, sometimes the case that crimes within the mandate of an international tribunal may have been committed preponderantly, even if not exclusively, by individuals from specific groups, against those of another. In Rwanda, for example, the genocide, by definition, sought to exterminate the Tutsi group who were its main victims. But the Arusha tribunal also has a mandate that includes crimes against humanity and war crimes.

We have discussed this issue at length in chapter 6. The point here is that perceptions that the Arusha tribunal is—or is likely to be—an instrument of victor's justice have been harmful to the tribunal. Such an outcome would also not be inconsistent with the nature of political justice. The Hague tribunal presents a rare case because none of the protagonists of the Balkan wars—the Serbs, the Croats, or the Bosnian Muslims—"won" the war like the Tutsis clearly did in Rwanda. The war was stopped by the military intervention of an outside power, hence none of its protagonists has the high moral ground that Rwanda's Tutsis have tried to occupy because they are victims *and* victors. And the strategic imperatives in the Balkans are arguably more compelling for the great powers than in Central Africa; thus the willingness to expend political and military capital to enforce an evenhanded justice.

## CONCLUSION

Given the countdown before the Arusha tribunal completes its trials in 2008, the opportunity to take a number of steps to improve its image in Rwanda, continentally and globally, may be lost as the tribunal must focus on the complex business of executing its exit strategy than on image-making. Its image will depend largely on its ultimate impact in Rwanda, and that will depend on a number of factors that will be discussed in the following chapter.

The fundamental questions to ask regarding the Arusha tribunal are: why was the tribunal established? If it had not been created, would the domestic courts of Rwanda have been able to bring the high-ranking perpetrators of the violations of humanitarian law in that country to justice? The obvious answer to the latter question is in the negative. The international tribunal is in the process of accomplishing this goal for which Rwandan courts were ill equipped due to a lack of capacity, while the courts of other states were also ill equipped due to lack of jurisdiction or political will.[48] Its ultimate success will be hard-won, but the expected completion of its trials later this decade would be a better point in time at which to look back and reflect on the achievements of the tribunal and attempt a historical judgment on the institution.[49] Fifty years after the Holocaust, the impact, achievements, and weaknesses of the Nuremberg trials are still being assessed.

Criticism is easy, but too many pundits are prematurely writing history's judgment with a presumption of conclusiveness while the tribunal is still making history.

As I will argue in the next chapter, its architecture was flawed from the beginning for the mission it was meant to accomplish. Thus exaggerated expectations on the part of all the players involved is an important element of its image. Some of the tribunal's image problems were also self-made. But it remains a pioneering judicial institution that has recorded landmark achievements and become an effectively functioning institution, overcoming many obstacles. Should what the musician Michael Franks termed in another context "the eloquent gloom of the prophets of doom" obscure the reality of the tribunal's success? We can now turn to those factors that will influence the judgment of history on the tribunal.

# Conclusion: The Impact of the Arusha Tribunal

> What have we better than a blind guess to show that criminal law in its present form does more good than harm?
> —Oliver Wendell Holmes

In the preceding chapter, I noted that all that can be attempted at this stage is a tentative assessment of the impact of the International Criminal Tribunal for Rwanda (ICTR) (figure 9.1). Thus a more definitive judgment of history must await the work of historians in future years. The experience of the Nuremberg trials, where the impact of the International Military Tribunal established by the Allied Powers after World War I was not immediately apparent at the time but underwent a steady metamorphosis, is instructive.

**Figure 9.1** The judges, prosecutor (far left) and registrar (far right) of the International Criminal Tribunal for Rwanda.

Even with that caveat, and considering the necessarily limited ambition that must accompany this brief analysis, it is essential to be clear-eyed. Again, as observed earlier, inflated expectations are attached to the Arusha tribunal by reason of it being the sole form of international intervention in Rwanda, thus distorting some assessments. And even at that the tribunal was not configured by the states that established it to meet the expectations its creation generated. It could not render the restitutive justice for which victims yearned. And, as will become clear in a moment, despite its many accomplishments, the tribunal's impact on reconciliation across Rwanda's Hutu–Tutsi divide is tenuous at best.[1] Much of this is really not the fault of the Arusha tribunal in and of itself, rather the explanation can be found in the political architecture of its framework. Yet much commentary proceeds as if the tribunal was self-constituting and had much of a choice in the factors that have affected it.[2]

Against this backdrop, I will briefly assess the Arusha tribunal against the three-point narrative and interpretative paradigm established at the outset of this work, namely, normative impact, contextual relevance, and the question of victor's justice. Without question, the Arusha tribunal has had major impact in creating norms of international law and even political behavior. In prosecuting and punishing genocide for the first time in an international forum, it made clear that genocide, the "crime of crimes," can and should be punished—and set the standards for doing so. Thus the tribunal gave life to the Genocide Convention for the very first time since that treaty was adopted. This impact is apparent from the political debates that occurred over whether genocide occurred in the Darfur region of Western Sudan and the type of forum where those responsible may be put on trial. The Arusha tribunal's work has been consistently cited in this context and is seen as providing clear normative guidelines for meeting the challenge of evil.

This normative impact is limited by the problem of the arguably deterrent effect of international war crimes trials and tribunals. Deterrence is a problematic but nonetheless fundamental purpose of criminal law. The Security Council identified it as one of the philosophical and practical aims of the tribunal in the preamble to the statute of the ICTR. The question must be asked, then: has the Arusha tribunal deterred genocide, crimes against humanity, and war crimes in the African region or globally? We cannot pretend that there are easy answers to this question. Clearly the tribunal's work has not deterred the commission of atrocities, including rapes, in Darfur or in the Democratic Republic of Congo (DRC), any more than the prosecutions for war crimes in the former Yugoslavia at the Hague tribunal in the mid-1990s were able to prevent ethnic cleansing in Kosovo in 1999 (it took NATO's bombs to put an end to that criminal activity). Criminal prosecutions in national settings have not made crime history.

The reality is that criminal law is a necessary but reactive response and does not eradicate the root causes of deviant behavior. Those causes are sociological, spiritual, and, in the case of violations of international humanitarian law, political as well. We cannot wish evil away, and crimes must still be punished even if punishment does not wipe out crime. The alternative, which is to say non-punishment, would be worse. But it is clear that criminal law does serve *some* deterrent function: in national societies, individuals frequently weigh the consequences of committing crimes from shoplifting to murder. At the international level, we may never know where else genocide or crimes against humanity might have erupted but for the knowledge that the possibility exists of facing a war crimes trial, however inconsistently applied and political that kind of justice may be.

Relating this to the Arusha tribunal, it is important, therefore, to define and differentiate its core and wider mandates. Its main task is to prosecute the persons responsible for the atrocities committed in Rwanda in 1994. By this logic, Hannah Arendt has noted: "Justice demands that the accused be prosecuted, . . . and that all the other questions of seemingly greater import—of 'How could it happen?' and 'Why did it happen?,' of 'Why the Jews' and 'Why the Germans?,' of 'What was the role of other nations?' . . . be left in abeyance."[3] Without necessarily excluding these "other questions," it is important not to confuse the Arusha tribunal's wider possibilities—or inflated expectations of those possibilities—for its core mandate. Thus stripped bare, we can see the tree from the forest, and it becomes clear that in successfully apprehending in several countries, prosecuting, and punishing the architects of the genocide, the tribunal is succeeding in its main task.

Indeed were it not for two important limitations, the Arusha tribunal's normative impact would have been nearly complete. The first factor that limited the tribunal's impact was its extremely limited, selective, and focused temporal remit. In restricting the tribunal to crimes committed in Rwanda and neighboring countries in the calendar year 1994, thus excluding crimes allegedly committed in some of those states after the genocide as an extension of the conflict of 1990–1994, an important opportunity to achieve the aims of political justice in the Great Lakes Region as a whole was lost. For this reason, the Hague tribunal, which has a temporal mandate to prosecute violations of international humanitarian law committed in the territory of the former Yugoslavia from 1991 but no further temporal limits (except those imposed by the recently established sunset clause for it and the Arusha tribunal), will probably have a greater political impact in the region of its jurisdiction than the Arusha tribunal might have in its own. Because the Hague court's mandate was essentially open-ended, it was able to assert jurisdiction over crimes in Kosovo and widen its engagement with the politics of the region.

Similarly the media publicity deficit suffered by the Arusha tribunal again weakened its potential normative impact. This is true especially in the African continent. It could be argued, for example, that the *janjaweed* militia in Sudan's Darfur region, who killed, maimed, and raped their victims with impunity, had never heard about the Arusha tribunal's *Akayesu* judgment, despite the publicity the verdict received in the Western media. Had Africa been differently configured in the context of international information flows, the question of a militia being aware that rape is a grave crime of war or genocide might have arisen and perhaps it would consciously have decided "and so what?"

As for the Arusha tribunal's contextual relevance—and thus impact—on Rwandan society, history's judgment might come as something of a surprise. The limitations imposed by its not being located in Rwanda notwithstanding, the tribunal's relevance to it will probably be established by a number of accomplishments and contemporary factors. First, the ICTR is an additional forum to national justice in Rwandan courts, but nevertheless an essential one. Not only did Rwanda's government request the creation of the tribunal, but it was clear—and remains clear—that the Rwandan judicial system had no capacity to undertake the kind of justice that was vested in the Arusha tribunal. By virtue of the international cooperation it commands relative to national jurisdictions, the Arusha tribunal has been able to apprehend and prosecute high-ranking individuals who played important, if negative, roles in Rwanda's contemporary history. These individuals, such as former prime minister Jean Kambanda, had taken refuge in other countries and were effectively beyond Rwanda's reach. It would surely have made a mockery of Rwanda's quest for justice if this category of individuals, accused as they were of masterminding the massacres, had not been brought to justice. Its political posturing in relation to the tribunal notwithstanding, this fact is not lost on Rwandans.

Second, the Arusha tribunal's work has established an indisputable record of the planning and direction of the genocide at the highest levels of the Rwandan state. This is exactly what the Rwandan government wanted to achieve through the internationalization of accountability. Whatever may be the motivations for this—and the political uses to which this record has been put—it is essential for the Rwandan society because genocide did indeed happen. The Arusha tribunal—a court independent of his former political adversaries—was probably the only forum where Kambanda could have made his confession to genocide, which triggered several confessions by accused persons in Rwandan jails. Third the Arusha tribunal has greatly contributed to the banning of extremists and extremist political philosophies from the Rwandan political space and has sidelined them to the periphery, where their potency is now highly questionable. This is important because it will facilitate the longer term development of a democratic culture in Rwanda and the region. These aspects of the Arusha's tribunal's relevance to Rwanda will become clearer with time.

But the tribunal itself cannot reconcile Hutus and Tutsis because it is not in the mainstream of Rwandan daily existence, and indeed it is doubtful that any court can achieve this outcome. It can only make a background contribution to a process that must be internal to Rwandan society and must be political and sociological, not legal. Reconciliation cannot be imposed from outside. Investing the possibility of such an outcome on a legal process—an international one, for that matter—might be asking for too much from a court of law. In 1994, the Czech diplomat Korel Kovanda, who as his country's representative on the United Nations (UN) Security Council actively participated in the negotiations that created the Arusha tribunal, observed somewhat presciently: "Justice is one thing; reconciliation, however, is another. The Tribunal might become a vehicle of justice, but it is hardly designed as a vehicle of reconciliation. Justice treats criminals whether or not they see the error of their ways; but reconciliation is much more complicated, and it is certainly impossible until and unless the criminals repent and show remorse. Only then can they even beg their victims for forgiveness, and only then can reconciliation possibly be attained."[4] As we will see in a moment, it can be argued that the tribunal would have had a greater impact in this area if it had been able to prosecute some Tutsis for war crimes. Neither Nuremberg nor Tokyo directly "reconciled" Nazis and Jews, if indeed such reconciliation has taken place, or World War II era Japanese military expansionists with their Allied conquerors. What both trials accomplished was to remove extremist philosophies from the political space by establishing for the historical record the crimes they spawned. This has facilitated the development of liberal democracy in both countries.

That outcome is the political justice that was engineered by the Nuremberg and Tokyo war crimes tribunals.

What did water down the Arusha tribunal's relevance to Rwandan society was its excessive emphasis on the rights of the defendants in its early years, which led to slow trials, combined with the very nature of the tribunal's proceedings and the absence of resources for a massive public information program targeted at Rwanda as part of the tribunal's original institutional framework. A civil law international tribunal would also have been better for Rwanda. A number of arrangements that the tribunal has recently negotiated with Rwanda could change this picture. First secure in the knowledge that several outstanding cases at the Arusha will end up in its domestic dockets, Rwanda is no longer vociferous in its condemnation of the pace of trials at Arusha. Also should a formal agreement for the enforcement of sentences be signed between the tribunal and Rwanda, this would have a major psychological impact that could ameliorate previous perceptions of the tribunal as remote from the Rwandan social process, and thus bolster its impact. Transferring cases from Arusha to Rwandan courts and sending some convicts to Rwandan jails would be a win–win situation for the two members of this inherently difficult partnership. However much work remains to be done on Rwanda's part before these scenarios can materialize, chief of which is expunging the death penalty from its statute books. This is a politically sensitive issue in Rwanda, but President Kagame appears willing to request Rwanda's Parliament to scrap these laws if doing so will help Rwanda achieve its strategic goals vis-á-vis the Arusha tribunal. Even if this were to happen, the wild card would still be the judges of the Arusha tribunal. Will they be able to see beyond an exaggerated sensitivity to portrayals of victimization by the defendants, to the need to render justice *for* Rwanda?

In conclusion, the question of whether or not the Arusha tribunal will indict any Tutsis will have an important impact on history's judgment of the tribunal and the search for political justice in Rwanda. At the Arusha tribunal, this issue has again come to the fore, with one of the defendants moving the tribunal to dismiss the case against him on the grounds of "selective prosecution."[5] In a letter to the international tribunal's chief prosecutor Hassan Bubacar Jallow, the Belgian scholar Professor Filip Reyntjens suspended his cooperation with the prosecutor's office as an expert witness unless and until the ICTR indicted Tutsi soldiers of the Rwandan Patriotic Front (RPF) against whom he asserted the tribunal had "compelling evidence" of massacres committed in 1994.[6]

Jallow has kept his cards close to his chest, maintaining that he has "no deadline" for investigations into alleged war crimes committed by the RPF in 1994.[7] As part of negotiations between Rwanda and the ICTR chief prosecutor, Rwanda is hoping that case files of investigations of alleged RPF crimes will be handed over to its courts for domestic prosecution as part of the tribunal's sunset arrangements. The implication of this scenario, should it unfold, would in effect be that the tribunal will end up not prosecuting alleged RPF atrocities. Many observers of the tribunal would undoubtedly judge this to constitute victor's justice, for it would mean that the two sides to Rwanda's war would not have been equal before the tribunal. The strategic factors behind this possibility have been examined in previous chapters. But this scenario would weaken the tribunal's impact tremendously, removing any trace of its possibilities of contributing to reconciliation. This does not mean that reconciliation will not be possible in Rwanda; just that the Arusha tribunal's role would not have been particularly influential in that particular process.

The question is often asked: in light of the trials at the Arusha tribunal, could genocide recur in Rwanda? Almost certainly the answer is no. While the Arusha tribunal cannot claim greater credit than the Rwandan state itself for this answer, the tribunal's work has indeed much to do with it. If that is the case, as I argue it is, the Arusha tribunal would have significantly accomplished its historical mission.

# Notes

## Introduction: Political Justice

1. I use this phrase in a general sense in this book to represent violations of international humanitarian law, and would like to remind the reader that the ICTR is far more concerned with genocide and crimes against humanity, although war crimes, in the technical sense (in this case, violations of Article 3 common to the Geneva Conventions), also come within the tribunal's remit.
2. David Scheffer, "International Judicial Intervention," *Foreign Policy*, spring 1996, 34–51.
3. Ibid.
4. See John Hagan, *Justice in the Balkans: Prosecuting War Crimes in the Hague Tribunal* (Chicago and London: University of Chicago Press, 2003), 106. See also Christopher Rudolph, "Constructing an Atrocities Regime: The Politics of War Crimes Tribunals," *International Organization* 55, 3, summer 2001, 681.
5. Shane Brighton, "Milosevic on Trial: The Dilemmas of Political Justice," www.bbc.co.uk/history/war/milosevic_trial.
6. This phrase was used by Martti Koskenniemi, quoted in George J. Andreopoulos, "Violations of Human Rights and Humanitarian Law and Threats to International Peace and Security," in Ramesh Thakur and Peter Malcontent, eds., *From Sovereign Impunity to International Accountability: The Search for Justice in a World of States* (Tokyo, New York and Paris: United Nations University Press, 2004), 80.
7. Andreopoulos, "Violations of Human Rights and Humanitarian Law," 80.
8. Kingsley Chiedu Moghalu, *Justice and High Politics: War Crimes and World Order in the 21st Century* (2006).
9. Rachel Kerr, *The International Criminal Tribunal for the Former Yugoslavia: An Exercise in Law, Politics, and Diplomacy* (Oxford and New York: Oxford University Press, 2004), 2.
10. Ibid., 3.
11. Final Report to the Prosecutor by the Committee Established to Review the NATO Bombing Campaign Against the Federal Republic of Yugoslavia, June 13, 2000, www.un.org/icty/pressreal/nato061300.htm, September 5, 2000.
12. Kerr, *The International Criminal Tribunal*, 203.

13. BBC World TV Interview with the author on *HardTalk with Tim Sebastian*, January 16, 2002.
14. See Bob Braun, "Rwandans Face a Reckoning in UN Trials," Newhouse News Service, September 17, 2002.
15. Scheffer, "International Judicial Intervention," 38–39.
16. Interview with Pierre-Richard Prosper, Washington, DC, June 16, 2004 (on file with the author).

## 1 THE "FINAL SOLUTION" TO THE "TUTSI PROBLEM"

1. Philip Gourevitch, *We Wish to Inform You that Tomorrow We Will be Killed With Our Families* (New York: Picador USA, 1998).
2. Emmanuel Gasana Jean-Bosco, Byanafashe Deo, and Alice Kareikezi, "Rwanda," in Adebayo Adedeji, ed., *Comprehending and Mastering African Conflicts* (London and New York: Zed Books, 1999), 141–142.
3. Ibid., 143.
4. Amy Chua, *World on Fire* (New York: Anchor Books, 2004).
5. Gasana et al., "Rwanda," 145.
6. See Adam Hochschild, *King Leopold's Ghost: A Story of Greed, Terror and Heroism in Central Africa* (Boston: Houghton Mifflin, 1998), 225–234.
7. Chua, *World on Fire*.
8. Gourevitch, *We Wish to Inform You*, 47–49, 55–56.
9. Bill Berkeley, *The Graves Are Not Yet Full: Race, Tribe and Power in the Heart of Africa* (New York: Basic Books, 2001), 258.
10. Alan Kuperman, *The Limits of Humanitarian Intervention: Genocide in Rwanda* (Washington, DC: Brookings Institution Press, 2001), 6.
11. Gasana et al., "Rwanda," 151.
12. Kuperman, *Humanitarian Intervention*, 6.
13. Chua, *World on Fire*, 167.
14. Ibid.
15. Kuperman, *Humanitarian Intervention*, 7.
16. Gasana et al., "Rwanda," 159.
17. Kuperman, *Humanitarian Intervention*, 9.
18. For a legal discussion of the right to one's homeland, see Alfred de Zayas, "The Right to One's Homeland, Ethnic Cleansing and the International Criminal Tribunal for the Former Yugoslavia," *Criminal Law Forum* 6, 2, 1995, 257–314. Rwanda is one of the world's most densely populated countries. The struggle for access to land, with its origins in the *ibikingi*, may have been a contributing factor to the genocide.
19. Romeo Dallaire, *Shake Hands With the Devil: The Failure of Humanity in Rwanda* (Canada: Random House, 2003), 62.

20. Kuperman, *Humanitarian Intervention*, 9.
21. Ibid., 10.
22. Dallaire, *Shake Hands With the Devil*, 55.
23. Gasana et al., "Rwanda," 162.
24. See report of the independent inquiry into the actions of the UN during the 1994 genocide in Rwanda, UN Doc S/1999/1257,15.
25. Dallaire, *Shake Hands With the Devil*, 254–257.
26. Gourevitch, *We Wish to Inform You*, 133.
27. See Jackson Nyamuya Maogoto, *War Crimes and Realpolitik: International Justice from World War I to the 21st Century* (Boulder and London: Lynne Rienner, 2004), 179.
28. *Prosecutor v Jean Kambanda*, Plea agreement.
29. See Kuperman, *Humanitarian Intervention*, Nicholas Wheeler, Saving Strangers: Humanitarian Intervention in International Society (Oxford: Oxford University Press, 2000); and UN Doc S/1999/1257, 15.
30. Samantha Power, *"A Problem from Hell": America and the Age of Genocide* (London: Flamingo, 2003), xv (preface).
31. "The Clinton Administration's Policy on Reforming Multilateral Peace Operations," Presidential Decision Directive, 25, May 3, 1994.
32. See comments by Michael Sheehan in an interview with the U.S. Public Broadcasting System (PBS) program Frontline: "Ghosts of Rwanda," www.pbs.org, April 1, 2004.
33. Linda Melvern, *A People Betrayed: The Role of the West in Rwanda's Genocide* (London: Zed Books, 2000), 180. See also Dallaire, *Shake Hands With the Devil*, 374.
34. "Statement by the President of the Security Council," UN Doc S/PRST/1994/21, April 30, 1994.
35. S/1999/1257, 68.
36. See comments by Ibrahim Gambari in "Ghosts of Rwanda," www.pbs.org, April 1, 2004.
37. Dallaire, *Shake Hands With the Devil*, 375. See also Kuperman, *Humanitarian Intervention*, 92.
38. Ibid.
39. Kuperman, *Humanitarian Intervention*, 35.
40. *Prosecutor v Ferdinand Nahimana, Jean-Bosco Barayagwiza, and Hassan Ngeze*, Judgment, December 2003.
41. Kuperman, *Humanitarian Intervention*, 92.
42. See Sharon LaFranière, "Court Convicts 3 in 1994 Genocide Across Rwanda," *New York Times*, December 4, 2003.
43. Dallaire, *Shake Hands With the Devil*.
44. S/Res/1994/929, June 22, 1994.
45. Dallaire, *Shake Hands With the Devil*, 425–426.
46. Gambari, "Ghosts of Rwanda."
47. See "UN Chief's Rwanda Genocide Regret," BBC News, March 26, 2004.

48. Kuperman, *Humanitarian Intervention*, 87–91.
49. S/1999/1257, 68.
50. Ibid.
51. See Gambari, "Ghosts of Rwanda."
52. See "Rwanda, Remembered," *The Economist*, March 27, 2004, 11.
53. Wheeler, *Saving Strangers*, 285–310.
54. "Annan Calls for Urgent Action, Even Military Intervention, to Prevent Genocide," UN News Service, January 26, 2004, www.un.org.

## 2  SEND IN THE LAWYERS: THE POLITICAL ARCHITECTURE OF JUSTICE

1. Letter dated October 1, 1994 from the secretary general addressed to the president of the Security Council, UN Doc S/1994/1125, October 4, 1994, Annex [Preliminary report of the Independent Commission of Experts established in accordance with Security Council resolution 935 (1994), 9].
2. Ibid.
3. UN Doc E/CN.4/1995/7 of June 28, 1994.
4. E/CN.4/1995/12 of August 12, 1994.
5. S/1994/1125, 13.
6. Ibid., 15.
7. Ibid., 39.
8. Ibid., 26.
9. Ibid., 27.
10. Ibid., 37.
11. Ibid.
12. UN Doc S/1994/115.
13. David Scheffer, "International Judicial Intervention," *Foreign Policy*, spring 1996, 39.
14. Jackson Nyamuya Maogoto, *War Crimes and Realpolitik: International Justice from World War I to the 21st Century* (Boulder and London: Lynne Rienner, 2004), 187.
15. S/Res/1994/955, November 8, 1994.
16. UN Doc S/PV 3453 (1994), containing the text of speeches delivered in the Security Council by its members following the adoption of resolution 955.
17. Ibid., 3.
18. Ibid., 15.
19. Statute of the ICTR, S/Res/1994, Annex, Article 8.
20. Ibid., Article 9.
21. *Prosecutor v Joseph Kanyabashi; Prosecutor v Alfred Musema.*
22. S/PV 3453, 5.
23. Ibid.

24. Statement by Mr. Yáñez-Barmevo, permanent representative of Spain, ibid., 12.
25. S/PV 3453.
26. Ibid., 11.
27. Ibid., 13.
28. Letter dated October 31, 1994 from the charge d'affaires a.i. of the Permanent Mission of Uganda to the UN addressed to the president of the Security Council, UN Doc S/1994/1230, October 31, 1994.
29. Ibid.
30. Jose Alvarez, "Crimes of States/Crimes of Hate: Lessons from Rwanda," *Yale Journal of International Law*, summer 1999, 5.
31. Ibid., 4.
32. Ibid., 5.
33. S/PV 3453.
34. Ibid., 16.
35. Ibid., 17.
36. UN Doc S/RES/1995/977, February 22, 1995.
37. Interview with Bernard Muna, former deputy prosecutor of the ICTR, London, United Kingdom (July 17, 2004; on file with the author).
38. Madeline H. Morris, "The Trials of Concurrent Jurisdiction: The Case of Rwanda," 7 *Duke Journal of Comparative and International Law* 349, spring 1997.
39. S/PV 3453, 5.
40. "Rwanda Executes Genocide Convicts," BBC News, April 24, 1998, http://news.bbc.co.uk.
41. Ibid., 17.
42. S/PV 3453, 4, 12.
43. Ibid., 8.
44. *Prosecutor v Jean-Paul Akayesu*, Judgment.
45. Statement of Brazilian ambassador Sardenberg, S/PV 3453, 9.
46. Ibid., 10.
47. Ibid., 11.
48. Rana Mitter, "An Uneasy Engagement: Chinese Ideas of Global Order and Justice in Historical Perspective," in Rosemary Foot et al., eds., *Order and Justice in International Relations* (Oxford: Oxford University Press, 2003), 207–235.
49. Ibid.,
50. Wu Hui, "Understanding International Responsibilities," GGXX.4 (1999), 8, quoted in Mitter, "An Uneasy Engagement."
51. Case No. ICTR-96-15-T, Decision on the defence motion on jurisdiction, June 18, 1997.
52. Ibid.
53. Ibid., 5.
54. *Prosecutor v Dusko Tadic*, Case No. IT-94-1-T, August 10, 1995, and the decision by the Appeals Chamber, Case No. IT-94-1-AR72, October 2, 1995.

55. *Prosecutor v Dusko Tadic*, Case No. IT-94-1-T, August 10, 1995, and the decision by the Appeals Chamber, Case No. IT-94-1-AR72, October 2, 1995. See also Jose E. Alvarez, "Nuremberg Revisited: The Tadic Trial," *European Journal of International Law 7*, 2.

56. Decision on defence motion on jurisdiction.

57. For an analysis of the origins of UN peacekeeping, see Kingsley Chiedu Moghalu, "The Legacy of Ralph Bunche," *The Fletcher Forum of World Affairs* 21, 2, summer/fall 1997, 165–177.

58. Ibid.

59. Ibid.

60. Ibid.

61. See Ralph Zacklin, "The Failings of Ad Hoc International Tribunals," *Journal of International Criminal Justice* 2 (2004), 541–545.

62. See the preamble to the Statute of the ICTR, S/Rs 955 (1994), Annex.

63. For a thorough discussion of this point, see Alvarez, "Nuremberg Revisited."

64. Samantha Power, *"A Problem from Hell": America and the Age of Genocide* (Flamingo, 2003), 484.

65. Michael Hourigan, a former investigator in the tribunal's prosecution office has claimed that he was investigating the plane crash and was later instructed by Chief Prosecutor Louise Arbour to close the investigation as it was not within the tribunal's remit. Hourigan claims this was the result of political interference in the work of the tribunal. See "Questions Unanswered 10 years After Rwandan Genocide," interview of Hourigan by the Australian Broadcasting Corporation, March 30, 2004, www.abc.net.au/pm.

66. See "Chambers Order Release of Hourigan's Memorandum to Parties," ICTR Press Release, Arusha, June 8, 2000, www.ictr.org.

67. Agwu Okali, e-mail interview. July 22, 2004.

68. "Who Shot the President's Plane?" *The Economist*, March 27, 2004, 26.

69. Betty Pisck, "Long-Lost Rwandan Black Box at UN," *Washington Times*, March 12, 2004.

70. Prunier, The Rwanda Crisis: History of A Genocide (London: Hurst & Co., 1995), 213–229.

71. Ibid., 223.

72. Bernard Muna, interview. London, July 17, 2004.

73. See "French Judge Interviews Genocide Suspects," United Nations Integrated Region Information Network Central and Eastern Africa Weekly Round-up 20, May 13–19, 2000, www.cidi.org.

74. Muna, interview. See also Prunier, The Rwanda Crisis.

75. Muna, interview.

76. "Who Shot the President's Plane?"

## 3   THE ARUSHA TRIBUNAL

1. Yves Beigbedger, *Judging War Criminals: The Politics of International Justice* (Basingstoke and New York: Macmillan, 1999), 177.

2. See Barbara Crossette, "UN Told a Tribunal Needs Help," *New York Times*, May 24, 1998.

3. "Secretary-General Expresses Profound Sadness at Death of Judge Laity Kama, First President of Rwanda Criminal Tribunal," UN Doc SG/SM/7794, May 8, 2001.

4. See David P. Forsythe, "Politics and the International Tribunal for the Former Yugoslavia," in Roger S. Clark and Madeleine Sann, eds., *The Prosecution of International Crimes* (New Brunswick and London: Transaction Publishers, 1996), 192–193.

5. "Judge Goldstone Retires from Concourt," www.iafrica.com/news/sa, September 26, 2003.

6. See "Tribunal Lays Goundwork to Expedite Trials," ICTR Press Release, August 13, 1999, www.ictr.org.

7. Of the three defendants in this trial, only one, Lt. Samuel Imanishimwe, was convicted. He was sentenced to 27 years in prison following his conviction on six counts of genocide, crimes against humanity, and war crimes (serious violations of Article 3 common to the Geneva Conventions and of Additional Protocol II). The other two, André Ntagerura, former Minister of Transport and Communications, and Emmanuel Bagambiki, former Prefect of Cyangugu, were acquitted of similar charges. See "Trial Chamber Convicts Imanishimwe. But Acquits Ntagenura and Bagambiki," ICTR Press Release, February 25, 2004.

8. See Sukhdev Chhatbar, "New Head Justice Determined to Complete ICTR by 2008," *The East African*, October 25, 2004. This decision was taken by the current prosecutor of the tribunal, Hassan Bubacar Jallow, after a review of the policies of his office related to trials.

9. See Peter Landesman, "A Woman's Work," *The New York Times Magazine*, September 15, 2002.

10. See "Mrs. Hilary Rodham Clinton Visits the International Criminal Tribunal for Rwanda," ICTR Press Release, March 26, 1997, www.ictr.org.

11. See Binaifer Nowrojee and Regan Ralph, "Justice for Women Victims of Violence: Rwanda after the 1994 Genocide," in Ifi Amadiume and Abdullahi An-Na'im, eds., *The Politics of Memory: Truth, Healing and Social Justice* (London and New York: Zed Books, 2000), 162–175.

12. See John Hagan, *Justice in the Balkans: Prosecuting War Crimes in the Hague Tribunal* (Chicago and London: University of Chicago Press, 2003).

13. "Profile: Carla Del Ponte," BBC News, August 14, 1999, www.news.bbc.co.uk.

14. See Rachel Kerr, *The International Criminal Tribunal for The Former Yugoslavia: An Exercise in Law, Politics, and Diplomacy* (Oxford and New York: Oxford University Press, 2004), 205.

15. Ibid.

16. Report of the Office of Internal Oversight Services on the audit and investigation of the ICTR, UN Doc A/51/789, February 6, 1997.

17. Barbara Crossette, "UN Told A Tribunal Needs Help," *New York Times,* May 24, 1998.

18. See "Rwandan Anger At Slow Justice," BBC News, August 28, 2003, www.news.bbc.co.uk.

19. See "The International Criminal Tribunal for Rwanda and Women Victims and Witnesses of the Rwandan Genocide—The Facts," ICTR Press Release, February 18, 1998, www.ictr.org.

20. This provision partly inspired a similar one in the Rome Statute of the permanent International Criminal Court. Article 43(6) of the ICC Statute provides that a Victims and Witnesses Unit shall "provide . . . counselling and other appropriate assistance for witnesses, victims who appear before the court, and others who are at risk on account of testimony given by such witnesses."

21. For an excellent empirical study of restorative justice, in particular medical assistance for women victims of rape during the Rwandan genocide, see Françoise Nduwimana, *The Right to Survive: Sexual Violence, Women and HIV/AIDS* (Montreal: Rights & Democracy, International Center for Human Rights and Democratic Development, 2004), 30–37.

22. Agwu Ukiwe Okali, "Rwanda Genocide: Towards a Victim-Oriented Justice—The Case for an ICTR Assistance to Victims Program," June 22, 1998, unpublished and nonconfidential paper circulated to the judges, prosecutor, and staff of the ICTR (on file with the author).

23. See Rules 105 (restitution of property) and 106 (compensation of victims) of the ICTR Rules of Procedure and Evidence, www.ictr.org. These provisions address circumstances where restitution could be ordered again if an accused was found guilty by the tribunal where unlawful taking of property was done in the course of committing genocide, crimes against humanity, or war crimes, and where compensation could be paid to a victim in a case before the tribunal by the government of Rwanda if the tribunal made such a ruling. Okali was making this point not to say that these rules provides direct support for the kind of program he was proposing, but rather to demonstrate to skeptics and critics that the notion of restitutive justice was not totally beyond the purview of the tribunal.

24. Okali, "Rwanda Genocide," 6.

25. Ibid., note 7.

26. Ibid., 11.

27. The costs included lost wages for workers and farmers, who often had to spend weeks in Arusha during their testimony. Some witnesses also lost earnings in the process of relocations occasioned by the tribunal's witness protection program.

28. Okali, "Rwanda Genocide," 1.

29. See "Address by Judge Erik Mose, President of the International Criminal Tribunal for Rwanda to the United Nations General Assembly," October 9, 2003, www.ictr.org.

30. See International Crisis Group, "International Criminal Tribunal for Rwanda: Justice Delayed," *Africa Report*, no. 30, June 7, 2001.

31. "The Rule of Law and Transitional Justice in Conflict and Post-Conflict Societies," Report of the secretary general to the Security Council, UN Doc S/2004/616, 19, paragraph 55.

32. Report of the International Commission of Inquiry on Darfur to the UN secretary general (pursuant to Security Council resolution 1564 of September 18, 2004), January 25, 2005, 152, paragraph 601.

33. "The Rule of Law and Transitional Justice," 18–19, paragraph 54.

34. See "ICTR Launches Victim Support Initiative in Rwanda," ICTR Press Release, September 26, 2000, www.ictr.org.

35. Letter from defense counsel for Jean-Paul Akayesu to Dr. Agwu Okali, registrar of the ICTR, October 2, 1990, see press briefing by the spokesman of the ICTR, October 9, 2000, www.ictr.org.

36. Registrar's reply to Philpot's letter, October 5, 2000. See press briefing by the spokesman of the ICTR, October 9, 2000.

37. Agwu Ukiwe Okali, registrar of the ICTR, Statement to the preparatory committee on the establishment of an international criminal court, March 16–April 3, 1998.

38. Rome Statute of the International Criminal Court, Article 75.

39. Ibid., Article 79.

40. Wendy Kaminer, "Victims Versus Suspects," *The American Prospect*, March 13, 2000, 18–19.

41. See United Nations Economic and Social Council, The right to a remedy and reparation for victims of violations of international human rights and humanitarian law, Note by the high commissioner for human rights, UN Doc E/CN.4/2003/63, December 27, 2002, paragraph 57.

42. See ICTR, briefing note on the ICTR challenges and achievements, www.ictr.org.

## 4   UNCHARTED WATERS: JUDGING GENOCIDE

1. Nicholas D. Kristof, "The Man Who Didn't Abandon Rwanda," *International Herald Tribune*, July 22, 2004.

2. See Ralph Zacklin, "The Failings of Ad Hoc International Tribunals," *Journal of International Criminal Justice* 2, 2004, 541–545.

3. Bill Berkeley, *The Graves are Not Yet Full: Race, Tribe and Power in the Heart of Africa* (New York: Basic Books, 2001), 254.

4. See Samantha Power, *"A Problem from Hell": America and the Age of Genocide* (London: Flamingo, 2003), 42.

5. Ibid.

6. UN Doc S/Res/1994, Annex.

7. *Prosecutor v Jean-Paul Akayesu*, ICTR-96-4-T, Judgment by Trial Chamber I, September 2, 1998, paragraph 497.

8. *Akayesu* Judgment, paragraph 498.
9. *Akayesu* Judgment, paragraph 511.
10. *Akayesu* Judgment, paragraphs 512–515.
11. See Paul J. Magnarella, *Justice in Africa: Rwanda's Genocide, Its Courts, and the UN Criminal Tribunal* (Ashgate Publishing Ltd., 2000), 98.
12. *Akayesu* Judgment, paragraph. 516.
13. Magnarella, *Justice in Africa*, 99.
14. Power, "*A Problem from Hell.*"
15. Summary of the judgment of the ICTY in the Kirstic case, quoted in Marlise Simons, "General Guilty in Srebrenica Genocide," *The New York Times*, August 3, 2001, 1.
16. No accused person in the ICTR has yet been convicted of rape as a violation of Article 3 common to the Geneva Conventions, or even of any other aspect of that crime itself, although some accused persons and convicts have been charged with rape under this rubric.
17. *Amicus curiae* brief submitted under Rule 74 of the Rules of Procedure and Evidence of the ICTR in May 1997 by the Coalition for Women's Human Rights in Conflict Situations.
18. David Scheffer (former U.S. ambassador at large for War Crimes Issues), *Rape as a War Crime*, Remarks at Fordham University, New York, October 29, 1999, www.converge.org.nz.11z/pma.rape.htm.
19. *Akayesu* Judgment, paragraphs 596–598.
20. *Prosecutor v Anto Furundzija*, Case No. IT-95-17/I-T, Judgment, December 10, 1998.
21. *Prosecutor v Delalic et al.*, Case No. IT-96-21-T, Judgment, November 16, 1998.
22. *Prosecutor v Kunarac et al.*, Case No. IT-96-23/2, Judgment, February 22, 2001.
23. Ibid.
24. See also Joe Lauria, "Rape Added to Rwandan Women's UN Charges," *The Boston Globe*, August 13, 1999. For an excellent, comprehensive sociological and psychological analysis of Pauline Nyiramasuhuko's trial, see Peter Landesman, "A Woman's Work," *The New York Times Magazine*, September 15, 2002.
25. See comments by human rights activist Betty Murungi in Simon Robinson, "War Criminal Behavior," *Times*, September 14, 1998.
26. See Marlise Simons, "Trial Centers on Role of Press During Rwanda Massacre," *The New York Times*, March 3, 2002, discussing the crucial precedents legal specialists believe will be established by the outcome of the joint "media trial" at the ICTR of *Prosecutor v Jean-Bosco Barayagwiza, Ferdinand Nahimana, and Hassan Ngeze*.
27. These former officials are among several cabinet ministers in Mr. Kambanda's government who have been tried, are currently on trial, or detained by the ICTR. Mr. Ntagerura was acquitted after his trial, but the chief prosecutor appealed the verdict.

28. *Prosecutor v Jean Kambanda*, plea agreement between Jean Kambanda and the Office of the Prosecutor, Annexure A to the joint motion for consideration of plea agreement between Jean Kambanda and the Office of the Prosecutor, April 29, 1998.

29. Ibid.

30. Article 6, which provides for individual criminal responsibility for crimes within the tribunal's competence, states in subpara (2): "The official position of any accused person, whether as Head of state or government or as a responsible government official, shall not relieve such person of criminal responsibility nor mitigate punishment." An identical provision is contained in the Statute of the ICTY, and the Nuremberg Charter contained a similar provision. However the ICTR judgment in *Kambanda* was the first ever application of the provision in practice to an individual of such senior rank in a government.

31. *Prosecutor Jean Kambanda*, paragraphs 42, 44.

32. *Jean Kambanda v Prosecutor*, Case No. ICTR-97-23-A, Judgment of the Appeals Chamber, October 19, 2000.

33. Magnarella, *Justice in Africa*, 85, 93.

34. See Kingsley Chiedu Moghalu, "Rwanda Panel's Legacy: They Can Run But Not Hide," *International Herald Tribune*, October 31–November 1, 1998, 6.

35. *Regina v Bartle and the Commissioner of Police and Others (Appellants) Ex Parte Pinochet (Respondent); Evans and Another and the Commissioner of Police and Others (Appellants) Ex Parte Pinochet (Respondent)*, Decision of the House of Lords on appeal from a divisional court of the Queen's bench division, November 25, 1998.

36. Case No. ICTR-99-52-T. Summary of the Judgment of Trial Chamber I.

37. See "Accused Online," *The Economist*, February 10, 2001, 45. Barayagwiza also had an external website.

38. Ibid., 18.

39. Ibid., 7.

40. Ibid., 23.

41. Ibid., 4.

42. *The Judgment at Nuremberg* (London: The Stationery Office, 1999), 214.

43. *Prosecutor v Nahimana, Barayagwiza, and Ngeze*, Summary of the Judgment, 21–22.

44. Ibid., 27.

45. Ibid.

46 Ibid., 3, 29.

47. "Justice in Rwanda," *The New York Times*, December 6, 2003.

48. See, e.g., John Philpot I, "The International Criminal Tribunal for Rwanda: Justice Betrayed," at www.udayton.edu/rwanda/articles/philpot.html, where the author uses the phrase: "The history of

Rwanda has been punctuated by *mutual* killings in particular in 1959, 1963, 1964 and 1973" (emphasis mine). While Philpot makes some valid points about the limitations of the framework of the ICTR, limitations that only confirm the political dimensions of war crimes justice, he clearly seeks to deny or at least minimize the 1994 genocide by attempting to drown it in the phrase "mutual killings." This is the false theory of the "double genocide."

49. Andre Ntagerura, former Minister of Transport, and Emmanuel Bagambiki, former Prefect (Governor) of Cyangugu region. The prosecution has appealed the verdicts of the trial chamber. Ignace Bagilishema has been unconditionally released.

50. *Prosecutor v Clément Kayishema and Obed Ruzindana*, Case No. ICTR-95-1-A, Judgment of the Appeals Chamber, June 1, 2001, paragraph 69.

51. Rules 44–46, Rules of Procedure and Evidence; ICTR directive on the assignment of defense counsel, see www.ictr.org. See also Article 20(d) of the statute of the ICTR, which stipulates the right of the accused person to "defend himself or herself in person or through legal assistance of his own choosing; to be informed, if he or she does not have legal assistance of this right; and to have legal assistance assigned to him or her, in any case where the interests of justice so require, and without payment by him or her in any such case if he or she does not have sufficient means to pay for it."

52. A new post of finance investigator for defense-counsel-related matters was approved in the tribunal's budget in its 2002–2003 financial year and was recruited. Given the scale of the complex issues involved in tracing the finances of detainees, however, the impact of this post in the overall scheme of the legal aid program will be limited.

53. See "Defense Lawyers Association at the ICTR—No Official Recognition," *Hirondelle News Agency*, November 19, 2004.

54. *Prosecutor v Akayesu*, Judgment, September 2, 1998, paragraph 69.

55. See "The Six Lawyers of Akayesu," ICTR Press Release, February 25, 1999, www.ictr.org.

56. *Prosecutor v Akayesu*, ICTR-96-4-A, Judgment of the Appeals Chamber, June 1, 2001.

57. Ibid.

58. See *Slobodan Milosevic v Prosecutor*, Decision on Interlocutory Appeal of the Trial Chamber's Decision on the Assignment of Defense Counsel, Case No. IT-02-54-AR73.7, November 1, 2004.

59. See Marlise Simons, "Wily Milosevic Keeps Hague Judges Guessing," *International Herald Tribune*, September 22, 2004.

60. Rule 45 *quarter*, Rules of Procedure and Evidence.

61. *Prosecutor v Barayagwiza*, Case No. ICTR-97-19-AR72, Decision on the request for withdrawal of defense counsel, January 31, 2000.

62. See Nina H.B. Jørgensen, "The Right of the Accused to Self-Representation Before International Criminal Tribunals," *American Journal of International Law*, October 2004, 711–726.

63. See Judith Armatta, "Justice, Not a Political Platform," *International Herald Tribune*, October 8, 2004.

64. Nina H.B. Jørgensen, "The Right of the Accused," 711.

65. Ibid.

66. Article 26, Statute of the ICTR.

67. See "International Criminal Tribunal for Rwanda: General Information," www.ictr.org.

68. Martin Ngoga, deputy prosecutor-general of Rwanda, telephonic interview with the author, December 28, 2004.

## 5  A BAPTISM OF FIRE: THE BARAYAGWIZA AFFAIR

1. *Jean-Bosco Barayagwiza v The Prosecutor*, AR72. Decision of the Appeals Chamber, Case No. ICTR-97–19, November 3, 1999.

2. *Prosecutor v Barayagwiza*. Decision on the extremely urgent motion by the defense for orders to review and/or nullify the arrrest and provisional detention of the suspect. Case No. ICTR-97-19-1, undated but filed on November 17, 1998.

3. Article 9(1) of the Statute of the ICTR provides that a person cannot be tried before a national court for a violation of international humanitarian law under the tribunal's statute who has been tried before the tribunal for the same offence. See Statute of the ICTR, www.ictr.org. Although Ntuyahaga had not yet been "tried" at the ICTR, in the sense of establishing his guilt or innocence, he had been formally indicted by the tribunal, the case against him was on the court's docket, and he had already entered a plea of not guilty. This provision was thus a jurisdictional one-way street, as persons tried before a national court could be tried again by the international tribunal if the acts they were previously tried for were ordinary crimes, or if the national prosecution was a kangaroo proceeding designed to shield the person from international criminal responsibility. See Article 9(2) of the Statute. A similar provision in the tribunal's Rules of Procedure and Evidence was later amended, inspired by the Ntuyahaga debacle, allowing the transfer to a national court of an accused person before the international tribunal, but without giving up the tribunal's primacy. See Rule 11*bis*, Rules of Procedure and Evidence, ICTR, www.ictr.org.

4. "Extradition Call for Rwanda Suspect," BBC News, March 20, 1999, http://news.bbc.co.uk.

5. See Decision by the registrar in execution of the decision by Trial Chamber I ordering the release of Bernard Ntuyahaga, ICTR-98-40-T, March 29, 1999.

6. See "Ntuyahaga Released: Trial Chamber Finds His Motion for Stay of Execution Inadmissible," ICTR Press Release, Arusha, March 29, 1999, www.ictr.org.

7. Following five years of tangled legal wrangling, the legal proceedings in Tanzania involving Ntuyahaga were terminated due to a "procedural

error," and Ntuyahaga was transferred to Belgium in 2004, reportedly of his own free will, to face a likely trial. See "Rwanda Killings Suspect Detained in Belgium," *Reuters*, March 27, 2004.

8. See Rule 40*bis*, Rules of Procedure and Evidence of the ICTR. Under the rule, the prosecutor has a 90-day period from the accused's transfer to the tribunal to bring a formal indictment or else release the accused.

9. Appeals Chamber decision of November 3, 1999, 3.

10. Ibid., 4–6.

11. Ibid., 11–12.

12. Ibid., 37–38.

13. Ibid., 38–39.

14. ICCPR, Article 9(3), quoted in Decision of the Appeals Chamber, November 3, 1999, 37–41.

15. See Elizabeth A. Martin, ed., *A Dictionary of Law* (Oxford and New York: Oxford University Press, 1994), 181.

16. Decision of the Appeals Chamber, 43.

17. *R v Horseferry Road Magistrates Court, exparte Bennett* [1994] 1 AC 42, 95 1.L.R. 380 (House of Lords, 1993), quoted in Decision of Appeals Chamber, November 3, 1999.

18. Decision of the Appeals Chamber, November 3, 1999, 45.

19. Ibid., 51.

20. Ibid., 59.

21. Interview with Bernard Muna, London, July 17, 2004.

22. This apt phrase was ascribed to the situation by Agwu Okali, the tribunal's then registrar. E-mail interview with Agwu Okali, July 22, 2004 (on file with the author).

23. "Rwanda Bars Top UN War Crimes Prosecutor," www.cnn.com, November 22, 1999.

24. See "Ms. Del Ponte Welcomes Cooperation of Rwanda Government," ICTR Press Release, Arusha, October 20, 1999, www.ictr.org.

25. Ibid.

26. Interview with Pierre-Richard Prosper, U.S. ambassador at large for War Crimes Issues, held in Washington, DC, on June 18, 2000 (on file with the author).

27. See "Del Ponte Welcomes Cooperation."

28. Ibid.

29. Okali, interview. It is noteworthy that this memorandum regulating the relationship between Rwanda as a host country and the tribunal was signed only in 1999, four years after the tribunal was established on the ground. That time lag is indicative of the continuing grievance Rwandan authorities nursed over the framework of the ICTR.

30. Okali, interview.

31. Decision of the Appeals Chamber, November 3, 1999, separate opinion of Judge Shahabuddeen.

32. Interview with Agwu Okali.

33. Ibid.

34. Ibid.

35. Ibid.

36. See "Press Conference by Permanent Representative of Rwanda at the United Nations," November 11, 1999, www.globalsecurity.org.

37. Okali, interview.

38. *The Prosecutor v Jean-Bosco Barayagwiza*. Notice of intention to file request for review of decision of the appeals chamber of November 3, 1999 (Rule 120 of the Rules of Procedure and Evidence of the ICTR).

39. Article 25, Statute of the ICTR; Rules 120 and 121, Rules of Procedure and Evidence.

40. See, e.g., Testimony of Larry A. Hammond Before the [U.S.] House of Representatives International Relations Committee, February 28, 2002, "Markup and Hearing Before the Committee on International Relations, House of Representatives One Hundred Seventh Congress, Second Session, Markup of H. Res 339," February 28, 2002 Serial No.107–71. www.house.gov/international-relations.

41. *The Prosecutor v Jean-Bosco Barayagwiza*: Extremely urgent appellant's response to the prosecutor's notice of intention to file review of decision of the Appeals Chamber of November 3, 1999.

42. Ibid.

43. Ibid.

44. *The Prosecutor v Jean-Bosco Barayagwiza*. Prosecutor's motion for review or reconsideration of the Appeals Chamber decision rendered on November 3 in *Jean-Bosco Barayagwiza v The Prosecutor* and request for stay of execution.

45. Ibid., 20.

46. Ibid.

47. *Prosecutor v Jean Bosco Barayagwiza*. Memorial *amicus curiae* of the government of the Republic of Rwanda pursuant to Rule 74 of the Rules of Procedure and Evidence.

48. Ibid., 2–7.

49. Ibid., 21–22.

50. That this was Del Ponte's expectation is clear from an interview she granted to *Internews*. See J. Coll Metcalf, "An Interview with United Nations Chief War Crimes Prosecutor, Carla Del Ponte," *Internews*, February 15, 2000, www.internews.org.

51. *Jean-Bosco Barayagwiza v The Prosecutor*. Decision (prosecutor's request for review or reconsideration), March 31, 2000.

52. Ibid.

53. Ibid.

54. Ibid.

55. Ibid.

56. *The Prosecutor v Jean-Bosco Barayagwiza*. Decision on defense counsel motion to withdraw, November 2, 2000.

57. Okali, interview.

58. Okali, interview.
59. Ibid.
60. Amnesty International, "International Criminal Tribunal for Rwanda: Jean-Bosco Barayagwiza Must Not Escape Justice," Press Release AFR 47/20/99, November 24, 1999.
61. Muna, interview.
62. *Mushikwabo v Barayagwiza*, 94 Civ. 3627 (JSM) (Southern District of New York 1996), in which five plaintiffs suing on behalf of Tutsi relatives murdered in genocidal campaign orchestrated by Barayagwiza were awarded over $104 million in a suit brought under the Alien Tort Claims Act.
63. Muna, interview.
64. Okali, interview.
65. Ibid.
66. Ibid.
67. *Jean-Bosco v Barayagwiza v The Prosecutor*. Decision of March 31, 2000, declaration of Judge Rafael Nieto-Navia.

## 6 CARLA DEL PONTE "AXED"

1. Article 15(3), Statute of the ICTR.
2. Security Council Resolution 1503 (2003).
3. See Jackson Nyamuya Maogoto, *War Crimes and Realpolitik: International Justice from World War I to the 21st Century* (Boulder and London: Lynne Rienner, 2004), 188.
4. See Richard Goldstone's interview with Radio Netherlands, "Del Ponte Axed from Rwanda Tribunal," www.rnw.nl, August 29, 2003.
5. M. Cherif Bassiouni, "From Versailles to Rwanda in Seventy-Five Years: The Need to Establish a Permanent International Criminal Court," *Harvard International Human Rights Journal* 10, 1997, 11, 49.
6. Ibid.
7. Report of the OIOS on the review of the Office of the Prosecutor at the ICTR and ICTY, January 7, 2004, UN Doc A/58/677, 6–7. The conclusions of the report, which was issued after a separate chief prosecutor had been appointed for the ICTR, appear to have been in an investigation conducted prior to the Security Council decision.
8. Statement after the Security Council vote on resolution 955, UN Doc S/PV 3453.
9. Ibid.
10. See Goldstone's interview with Radio Netherlands.
11. UN Doc A/58/677.
12. Martin Ngoga, deputy prosecutor-general of Rwanda, telephone interview with the author, December 28, 2004.
13. Report of the Expert Group to conduct a review of the effective operation and functioning of the ICTY and the ICTR, UN Doc A/54/634, November 22, 1999, recommendation # 46, 108.

14. UN Doc S/Res/2003/1503.

15. UN Doc S/Res/2003/1504.

16. Ibid.

17. As of November 2004, more than 100 countries were in arrears of their annual contributions to the budgets of the Hague and Arusha tribunals. See "UN Budget Committee Told Unpaid Contributions to Former Yugoslavia, Rwanda Tribunals, Resulting Recruitment Freeze, Could Affect Completion Dates," M2 Presswire, November 25, 2004.

18. Between 1993 and 2004, a total of $966 million has been spent on the ICTY, and the total expenditure on the ICTR since 1995 is approximately $800 million. See www.icty.org (the figure for the ICTR is a rough estimate from the author's personal knowledge, since there are no official figures available on its public documents). In comparison, annual global military spending for 2004 is projected at nearly $1,000 billion, i.e. $1 trillion. Moreover the Lockerbie trial at Camp Zeist, Netherlands, which lasted for about nine months and ended in early 2001, cost an estimated $80 million. See Peter Ford, "Lockerbie Success As New Model," *The Christian Science Monitor*, February 1, 2001.

19. S/PV 3453.

20. See S/Res/1503.

21. See Statement by U.S. ambassador for War Crimes before the International Relations Committee, U.S. House of Representatives, February 28, 2002. See also Jess Bravin, "U.S. Seeks Timetable to Close UN War-Crimes Tribunal," *Wall Street Journal*, March 1–3, 2002.

22. Ibid.

23. Ibid.

24. See Andrew F. Tully, "U.S. Defends Diplomat's Criticism of War Crimes Courts," Radio Free Europe, March 4, 2002, http://truthnews.com.

25. Prosecutor's address to the Security Council, November 2001 (on file with the author).

26. Ibid.

27. Interview with a staff member of the ICTR, Arusha December 2004. Identity with held upon request.

28. Report of the OIOS, A/58/677, 8.

29. Ibid.

30. Interview with Pierre-Richard Prosper, Washington, D.C., June 16, 2004.

31. See Aryeh Neier, "Effort to Oust Prosecutor is Misguided," *International Herald Tribune*, August 8, 2003, where the author identifies Britain's strong support for Rwanda's campaign, and the "somewhat more ambivalen[t]" support of the United States.

32. Carla Del Ponte, interview with the author, The Hague, September 13, 2004 (on file with the author).

33. Prosper, interview.
34. Ibid.
35. Ibid.
36. Ibid.
37. See the secretary general's comments as reported in transcript of press conference by Secretary General Kofi Annan at UN Headquarters, July 30, 2003, UN Press Release SG/SM/8803, www.un.org, at 9.
38. Felicity Barringer, "Annan is Said to Want a New Prosecutor for Rwanda War Crimes," *New York Times*, July 29, 2003.
39. Prosper, interview.
40. John Hooper, "I was Sacked as Rwanda Genocide Prosecutor for Challenging President, Says Del Ponte," *The Guardian*, September 13, 2003.
41. Ibid.
42. Ibid.
43. Ibid.
44. See "Rwandan Anger at Slow Justice," BBC News, August 28, 2003, http://news.bbc.co.uk.
45. Del Ponte, interview.
46. Ibid. The African member states of the Security Council in 2003 were Angola, Cameroon, and Guinea.
47. Yifat Susskind Madre, on the CNN program "Diplomatic License," August 8, 2003. See transcripts, "Diplomatic License," aired August 8, 2003, www.cnnstudentnews.cnn.com/Transcripts/0308/08/i_dl.00.html.
48. See "UN Tribunal Registrar Meets Rwandan Vice-President Paul Kagame," ICTR Press Release, Arusha, July 24, 1998.
49. See Miki Tasseni, "Rwanda Genocide Tribunal: We are Not Prosecuting the Vanquished, Says Legal Adviser," *The Tanzania Guardian* (interview with the author), December 31, 1997.
50. Catherine Cisse, former policy advisor to the prosecutor, ICTY/ICTR, telephone interview with the author, June 4, 2004.
51. Bernard Muna, interview, London, July 17, 2004.
52. Ibid.
53. Ibid.
54. Ibid.
55. Rodrique Ngowi, "Rwandan Army Ready to Cooperate with Investigation into Alleged Abuses," Associated Press, April 9, 2001.
56. See Chris McGreal, "Genocide Tribunal Ready to Indict First Tutsis," *The Guardian*, April 5, 2002.
57. Ibid.
58. Ibid.
59. Bob Braun, "Rwandans Face a Reckoning in UN Trials," Newhouse News Service, September 17, 2002.
60. News Release by the government of Rwanda, November 21, 2002, www.gov.rw.

61. Ibid.
62. Presentation by Ms. Carla Del Ponte, prosecutor of the ICTR to the All Party Parliamentary Group on the Great Lakes Region and Genocide Prevention, London, November 25, 2002 (on file with the author).
63. Ibid.
64. Ibid.
65. Jim Lobe, "Rights: Groups Urge UN to Ensure Impartiality of Rwanda Tribunal," Inter Press Service, August 12, 2003.
66. Ibid.
67. Ibid.
68. Quoted in Kevin Kelley, "War Crime Prosecutor: Is She Ineffective or Unfairly Targeted?" *The East African*, August 4, 2003.
69. Prosper, interview.
70. Ngoga was later appointed deputy attorney general of Rwanda.
71. Del Ponte, interview.
72. Ibid.
73. Ibid.
74. Prosper, interview. It is unclear if the suspects were to have been identified by the tribunal or by Rwanda itself, but it appears they would more likely have been identified by the Rwandan authorities.
75. Ibid.
76. Ibid.
77. Ibid.
78. Ibid.
79. Ibid.
80. "Del Ponte Loses Rwanda Mandate," Swissinfo, August 28, 2003, www.swissinfo.org.
81. Marlise Simons, "Rwanda is Said to Seek New Prosecutor for War Crimes Court," *New York Times*, July 28, 2003.
82. Felicity Barringer, "Annan is Said to Want a New Prosecutor for Rwanda War Crimes," *New York Times*, July 29, 2003.
83. "Security Council Members Support Annan's Proposal on Rwanda and Yugoslav Tribunals," www.english.peoplesdaily.com.cn, August 9, 2003.
84. Prosper, interview.
85. Ibid.
86. Ibid. See also S/Res/1503.
87. See Ms. Carla Del Ponte—Press Conference, The Hague, September 12, 2003, Press release by the Office of the Prosecutor, www.icty.org.
88. See John Hooper, "I was sacked as Rwanda Genocide Prosecutor for Challenging President, says Del Ponte," *The Guardian*, September 12, 2003.
89. Ibid.
90. Del Ponte, interview.
91. Ibid.
92. Ibid.

93. "Civil Society Groups Deeply Concerned About Renewal of Carla Del Ponte as ICTR Prosecutor: A Petition from Civil Society Groups to the UN Security Council," July 2003 (on file with the author).
94. Ibid.
95. Shinoda, "Peace-Building by the Rule of Law: An Examination of Intervention in the Form of International Tribunals," *International Journal of Peace Studies*, Volume 7:1, spring/summer 2002, 46.
96. Catherine Cisse, interview deputy prosecutor-general of Rwanda, telephone interview with the author.
97. Agwu Ngoga, interview deputy prosecutor-general of Rwanda, telephone interview with the author.
98. Agwu Okali, interview. U.S. ambassador Prosper also admits to some concern about this situation, noting that the whole point of the agreement he tried to broker between Rwanda and the ICTR prosecutor in 2003 was to ensure substantial progress on this matter before the December 2004 end date for initiating investigations (Prosper, interview).
99. Muna, interview.

## 7   Hot Pursuit: Fugitives from Justice

1. The following discussion of the legal basis of state cooperation with the ICTR draws from an earlier publication by the author. See Kingsley Chiedu Moghalu, "International Humanitarian Law from Nuremberg to Rome: The Weighty Precedents of the International Criminal Tribunal for Rwanda," *Pace International Law Review* 14, fall 2002, 273–305.
2. Article 28 of the statute provides: (1) States shall cooperate with the ICTR in the investigation and prosecution of persons accused of committing serious violations of international humanitarian law. (2) States shall comply without undue delay with any request for assistance of an order issued by a Trial Chamber [of the Tribunal], including but not limited to (a) the identification and location of persons; (b) the taking of testimony and production of evidence; (c) the service of documents; (d) the arrest and detention of persons; (e) the surrender or the transfer of the accused to the ICTR.
3. As of December 31, 2004, individuals sought by the tribunal have been arrested in, and transferred to, the seat of the tribunal at Arusha from the following states: Angola, Belgium, Benin, Burkina Faso, Cameroon, Congo, Côte d'Ivoire, Democratic Republic of Congo, Denmark, France, Kenya, Mali, Namibia, the Netherlands, Senegal, South Africa, Switzerland, Tanzania, Togo, Uganda, United Kingdom, United States, and Zambia.
4. J.G. Starke, *Introduction to International Law* (London: Butterworths, 1984), 68–71.

5. The phrase municipal law is used in classic international law, which refers to public international law as "the law of nations," to describe the internal legal codes of sovereign states.

6. Starke, *Introduction to International Law*, 69.

7. See Dagmar Stroh, "State Cooperation with the International Criminal Tribunals for the Former Yugoslavia and for Rwanda," *Max Planck Yearbook of United Nations Law*, Volume 5 (The Hague, London, and New York: Kluwer Law International, 2001), 282.

8. Ibid., 271. Examples include Austria, Australia, Belgium, Denmark, Germany, France, New Zealand, the Netherlands, Norway, Sweden, Switzerland, the United Kingdom, and the United States.

9. Report of the secretary general pursuant to paragraph 2 of Security Council resolution 808, UN Doc S/25704/Add.1 (1993).

10. Starke, *Introduction to International Law*, 85.

11. *The Prosecutor v Elizaphan Ntakirutimana and Gerard Ntakirutimana*, Case No. ICTR-96-9.17.I, dated September 7, 1996.

12. Ibid.

13. Ibid.

14. *The Prosecutor v Elizaphan Ntakirutimana*, warrant of arrest and order for surrender, September 7, 1996.

15. National Defense Authorization Act, Public Law No. 104–106 (1996). This legislation validated the executive agreement between the U.S. government and the ICTY and ICTR.

16. Agreement on surrender of persons, U.S.–ICTY, October 5, 1994, and Agreement on surrender of persons, U.S.–ICTR, January 24, 1995. Both agreements entered into force on February 14, 1996. See Kenneth J. Harris and Robert Kushen, "Surrender of Fugitives to the War Crimes Tribunals for Yugoslavia and Rwanda: Squaring International Legal Obligations with the U.S. Constitution," *Criminal Law Forum*, 7, 3, 1996, 563.

17. Evan J. Wallach, "Extradition to the Rwandan War Crimes Tribunal: Is another Treaty Required?" *UCLA Journal of International Law and Foreign Affairs* 59, summer 1998. See also Sean D. Murphy, "Surrender of Indictee to International Criminal Tribunal for Rwanda," *American Journal of International Law* 131, January 2000. It should be noted that although the American courts discussed the Ntakirutimana case in the context of U.S. extradition law, surrender to the ICTR or the ICTY is technically different from an extradition. The tribunals, though supranational institutions, are not states, and extradition can only occur when a state releases an individual to another state to face judicial proceedings usually on the basis of a bilateral treaty.

18. Brief of the lawyers committee for human rights as *amicus curiae*, April 28, 1997.

19. Wallach, "Rwandan War Crimes Tribunal."

20. See Eric D. Bocherding, "Validating a Constitutional Shortcut— The 'Congressional–Executive Agreement': *Ntakirutimana v Reno*

(Fifth Circuit 199)," *University of Cincinnati Law Review* 1055, spring 2001.

21. This argument was amplified by the government and Amicus submissions to the Court. See Wallach, "Rwandan War Crimes Tribunal."

22. Louis Henkin, *Foreign Affairs and the Constitution* (1972), cited in Harris and Kushen, "Surrender of Fugitives," 564, at note 7.

23. Harris and Kushen, "Surrender of Fugitives," citing the *Restatement (Third) of the Foreign Relations Law of the United States* (1987).

24. See Barbara Crossette, "Judge in Texas Jars UN Effort on War Crimes," *New York Times*, December 30, 1997.

25. Quoted in Crossette, "Judge in Texas."

26. Ibid.

27. Ibid.

28. Bocherding, "Validating a Constitutional Shortcut."

29. Ibid.

30. *Elizaphan Ntakirutiman v Janet Reno, Attorney General of the United States; Madeleine Albright, Secretary of State of the United States; Juan Garza, Sheriff of Webb County, Texas*, United States Court of Appeals, Fifth Circuit, No. 98-41597, August 5, 1999.

31. Ibid.

32. Ibid., 10.

33. Ibid., 11.

34. Ibid.

35. Douglass Cassel, "U.S. Cooperation with International Justice: A First Step," commentary, April 12, 2000, www.law.northwestern.edu.

36. Georges Ruggiu, a social worker of Italian and Belgian nationality who became a broadcaster with the hate radio RTLM during the genocide. Ruggiu was arrested in Belgium at the Arusha tribunal's request, and later pleaded guilty at the international tribunal to genocide and was convicted and sentenced to a 12-year prison term. See *Prosecutor v Georges Ruggiu*, Case No. ICTR-97-32-1, Judgment and Sentence.

37. Agwu Okali, e-mail interview, July 22, 2004.

38. Benin, Mali, and Swaziland have signed agreements with the ICTR to enforce its sentences in their territories, and several persons convicted by the tribunal, including former Rwandan prime minister Jean Kambanda, are serving their prison sentences in Mali.

39. Okali, interview.

40. But South Africa and Nigeria have been active in their diplomatic support for the tribunal at the UN, although in the case of Nigeria, this is far more the result of the competence of particular diplomats at its Permanent Mission to the UN in New York than of a conscious foreign policy in Abuja on war crimes issues.

41. Egypt contributed $1,000 in 1995. See also "The European Commission to Fund Tribunal Projects," ICTR Press Release, Arusha, May 10, 2004.

42. Bernard Muna, interview, London, July 17, 2004.

43. Ibid.

44. See Ian Fisher, "War Crimes in Africa: Where Justice Takes a Back Seat to Just Ending a War," *New York Times*, July 15, 2001.

45. Muna, interview.

46. I discuss the politics of the ICC at length in Kingsley Chiedu Moghalu, *Justice and High Politics: War Crimes and the World Order in the 21st Century* (2006).

47. Okali, interview.

48. Muna, interview.

49. Okali, interview.

50. Rwanda is a landlocked country, and Kenya is the region's economic hub from which land-based commerce and the shipping port of Mombasa are indispensable to the Rwandan economy.

51. See "Rwanda: Top Figures of Former Regime Arrested," ICTR Press Release, Arusha, July 18, 1997, www.ictr.org.

52. Muna, interview.

53. Ibid.

54. Okali, interview.

55. See Sudarsan Raghavan, "Ten Years Later, Rwanda Still Seeking Justice " *Kansas City Star*, April 2, 2002, quoting a report by the International Crisis Group.

56. Ibid.

57. Ibid.

58. Ibid.

59. Prosper, interview, Washington DC, June 18, 2004.

60. Ibid.

61. Ibid.

62. Prosper, interview.

63. Ibid.

64. Ibid.

65. Raghavan, "Ten Years Later."

66. Ibid

67. Proper, interview.

68. Ibid.

69. Ibid.

70. Kevin J. Kelley, "Kenya Under Pressure from U.S. Over Kabuga?" *Daily Nation*, August 29, 2002.

71. See Raghavan, "Ten Years Later."

72. For a good account of the geopolitical circumstances of the Tutsis in Central Africa, see "The 'Jews' of Africa," *The Economist*, August 21, 2004.

73. Ibid.

74. See Adam Hochschild, "The Dark Heart of Mineral Exploitation," *International Herald Tribune*, December 24–26, 2004.

75. Ibid.

76. Ibid.

77. Prosper, interview.

78. Prosper, interview.
79. Ibid.
80. "Rwanda Tribunal Says DR Congo Not Cooperating in Arrest of Genocide Suspects," BBC, November 25, 2004.
81. See "Security Council Urges Rwanda Not to Invade DRC," South African Broadcasting Corporation News, November 25, 2004, www.sabcnews.com.
82. Ibid.
83. Omar McDoom, "Calling the UN and the African Union," *International Herald Tribune*, December 24–26, 2004. See also Hochschild, "The Dark Heart of Mineral Exploitation."

# 8   IMAGE AND REALITY: PERCEPTIONS OF WAR CRIMES JUSTICE

This chapter is a significantly revised and updated version of a previously published article: Kingsley Chiedu Moghalu, "Image and Reality of War Crimes Justice: External Perceptions of the International Criminal Tribunal for Rwanda," *The Fletcher Forum of World Affairs* 26, 2, summer/fall 2002.

1. These statistics are dynamic. For current statistics on the tribunal, see its website http://www.ictr.org.
2. Ramesh Thakur, "Dealing With Guilt Beyond Crime: The Strained Quality of Universal Justice," in Ramesh Thakur and Peter Malcontent, eds., *From Sovereign Impunity to International Accountability: The Search for Justice in a World of States* (Tokyo, New York, and Paris: United Nations University Press, 2004), 272.
3. The program commenced in 1998 and consists of a strategically tailored set of activities designed to enhance public awareness and support for the international tribunal inside Rwanda. These activities began with bringing Rwandan journalists, judges, political leaders, and representatives of civil society to the tribunal's seat at Arusha, Tanzania, at the tribunal's expense to observe and report on the trials and verdicts. In its second phase, an ICTR Information and Documentation Center, known as *Umusanzu mu Bwiyunge* (contribution to reconciliation) in Kinyarwanda language, was established in Kigali, the Rwandan capital, in September 2000. The Center provides written and audiovisual information on the work of the tribunal, as well as a research library service, to various strata of Rwandan society. The ICTR Information Center has made a significant impact, receiving 21,000 visitors in 2001, and the Outreach Program has been markedly successful. Nevertheless efforts to improve the program's reach and impact are continuing, and include advanced plans for increased dissemination of the work of the ICTR in all parts of Rwanda.
4. See *Prosecutor v Jean-Paul Akayesu*, Case No. ICTR-96-4-T, Judgment.

5. Since the establishment of the ICTY and the ICTR, there have been approximately 24,830 articles about the former and 16,156 regarding the latter in the print news media as of October 9, 2004. Source: Lexis-Nexis. See also James Meernik and Kimi Lynn King, "Bringing Justice," *Fort Worth Star Telegram*, September 10, 2001. The authors stated, inter alia: "With the hoopla over the criminal tribunal in the former Yugoslavia, much of the world has overlooked the important work done first in Rwanda."

6. Chris Stephen, *Judgment Day: The Trial of Slobodan Milosevic* (London: Atlantic Books, 2004), 128.

7. "Judging Genocide," *The Economist*, June 16, 2001.

8. CNN Q & A, interview with this author, August 2, 2001.

9. Contributions to the Voluntary Contributions Trust Fund of the ICTY have reached approximately $30 million. In contrast, contributions to the Voluntary Trust Fund of the ICTR have totaled approximately $8 million. See also "Feingold to Push for More Funding of Rwanda War Crimes Tribunal," *Associated Press* newswire report, February 25, 2002.

10. See Kingsley Chiedu Moghalu, "Let's Hear More About the Work in Arusha," *International Herald Tribune*, February 15, 2002.

11. See Robert Carmichael, "Avoiding Arusha—Lessons for Cambodia's Genocide Tribunal," *Phnom Penh Post*, October 24–November 6, 2003.

12. Ibid.

13. See, Philip Gourevitch, *We Wish to Inform You That Tomorrow We Will be Killed With Our Families* (New York: Picador USA, 1998); Peter Landesman, "A Woman's Work," *The New York Times Magazine* on Sunday, September 15, 2002 (cover story); and Bill Berekeley, "Aftermath: Genocide, The Pursuit of Justice and the Future of Africa," *The Washington Post Magazine*, October 11, 1998. See also Bill Berkeley, *The Graves Are Not Yet Full: Race, Tribe and Power in the Heart of Africa* (New York: Basic Books, 2001), 245–284.

14. Quoted in Daniel W. Drezner and Henty Farrell, "Web of Influence," Foreign Policy, November/December 2004, 34.

15. "Feingold to Push for More Funding of Rwanda War Crimes Tribunal," Associated Press newswire report, February 25, 2002.

16. Jackson Nyamuya Maogoto, *War Crimes and Realpolitik: International Justice from World War I to the 21st Century* (Boulder and London: Lynne Rienner, 2004), 188.

17. See "Rwanda: A Year of Controversies and Progress for ICTR, All Africa Global Media," December 31, 2004, www.allafrica.com.

18. See UN Department of Management, *Report of the Management Review of the International Criminal Tribunal for Rwanda* (United Nations: New York, July 2001), 46.

19. Statement by the ICTR registrar, Adama Dieng, on the International Crisis Group report regarding the ICTR, ICTR/INFO-903-01, June 11, 2001, http://www.ictr.org.

20. David Tolbert, "The International Criminal Tribunal for the Former Yugoslavia: Unforseen Successes and Foreseeable Shortcomings," *The Fletcher Forum of World Affairs*, summer/fall 2002, 15.

21. Mary Kayitesi-Blewitt, "Give More Help to Rwanda Casualties," *Financial Times*, November 20/21, 2004 (Letter to the Editor).

22. See Steven Edwards, "Rwanda Tribunal Coming Undone: 'Concern for Fairness': Night-and-Day Contrast with Balkan War-Crimes Inquiry," *National Post*, March 5, 2001. In contrast, see also Marlise Simons, "A Taboo-Breaking UN Jurist Adds Judgements of Her Own," *International Herald Tribune*, January 25, 2002. This article is based on interviews with Judge Patricia Wald, then judge of the ICTY, and is one of the very few in which some of the problems faced by that tribunal in its judicial functioning are appraised in a critical but objective manner.

23. "More Injustice Found in International Tribunals," *Mainichi Shimbun*, January 17, 2001. This was part of a series of negative articles by the newspaper on "mismanagement" in the UN Secretariat in general, written from the perspective of Japan as a major contributor to the organization's budget.

24. Lara Santaro, "One for the Law Books: In Africa, A UN Court Prosecutes Genocide," *Christian Science Monitor*, March 13, 1998.

25. See Meernik and King, "Bringing Justice."

26. Ibid.

27. Kayitesi-Blewitt, "Give More Help to Rwanda Casualties."

28. Tom Kennedy, "Do Not Dismiss Achievements of Rwanda Tribunal," *Financial Times*, November 27/28, 2004 (Letter to the Editor).

29. See Report of the expert group to conduct a review of the effective operation and functioning of the ICTY and the ICTR, UN Document A/54/634, November 22, 1999, 14–15.

30. See Adama Dieng "Africa and the Globalization of Justice: Contributions and Lessons from the International Criminal Tribunal for Rwanda," paper presented at an international conference on "Justice in Africa" held at Wilton Park in Sussex, United Kingdom, from July 30 to August 2, 2001.

31. See Statement by the registrar, Adama Dieng, on the International Crisis Group report regarding the ICTR.

32. See Premy Kibanga, "Rwanda Tribunal Slammed for Delays," *The East African*, February 9–15, 1998.

33. For an insightful report on this subject, see Michelle Hakata, "Home Truths by European Journalists," *New African*, July–August 2001, 36–37. The article is a report on the proceedings of a recent media seminar organized in London by the Conflict and Peace Forum's

"Reporting The World" project, under the theme: "*Is Coverage of Africa Racist?*"

34. Ibid.
35. See Mark Turner, "Giggling Judges Undermine Case for International Justice," *Financial Times*, February 14, 2002.
36. See "Paying for War Crimes," *The Economist*, January 31, 1998.
37. A very notable exception is the International Committee of the Red Cross (ICRC), which monitors and promotes the observance of international humanitarian law worldwide. The ICRC, an organization that is not "agenda-driven," has consistently rated the work of the ICTR, in the areas that are within the remit of the ICRC, in a positive light.
38. An example was the judgment of the ICTY in the *Kunarac* case (February 2001) in which the accused persons were convicted of rape. The international press widely and erroneously reported that this was the first conviction by an international criminal tribunal for rape as a crime against humanity—a precedent established by the ICTR in its judgment in the *Akayesu* case on September 2, 1998. The spokesman for the secretary general issued a clarification confirming the correct position in his daily press briefing of February 23, 2001. Following a subsequent intervention to *The New York Times* by the ICTR, that newspaper published a correction of its erroneous article on the ICTY judgment on March 17, 2001.
39. See Isabel Vincent, "Canadian Lawyers Say Hands Tied in Arusha," *National Post*, July 28, 2001.
40. *The Prosecutor v Jean-Paul Akayesu*, ICTR-96-4-A, Judgment of the Appeals Chamber, June 1, 2001.
41. Vincent, "Canadian Lawyers."
42. It should be noted that contrary to the impression these defense lawyers sought to create in this article, 98 percent of the persons indicted and detained by the ICTR as of this writing were born in Rwanda and spent most of their life in that country. Most important, they were believed to be present in Rwanda at the time of the crimes covered in their indictments.
43. Ibid.
44. See UN Doc A/55/759.
45. Isabel Vincent, "Lawyers Deny Splitting Fees at Rwanda Tribunal," *National Post*, July 28, 2001.
46. See "International Criminal Tribunal for Rwanda: Trials and Tribulations," *Amnesty International*, April 29, 1998. See also media statement by the International Crisis Group: "International Criminal Tribunal for Rwanda: Justice Delayed," June 7, 2001, heralding its report. These critical NGO reports are rarely, if ever, written about the Hague tribunal. In the event that NGO assessments are written about that tribunal, they have not been publicized in the media, let alone

with the fanfare that usually attends such exercises in relation to the Rwanda tribunal at Arusha.

47. See Aleksandar Fatic, *Reconciliation Via the War Crimes Tribunal?* (Aldershot, Hampshire: Ashgate Books, 2000), 81.

48. Belgium is the only country other than Rwanda to have tried individuals on crimes committed in the context of the Rwandan genocide, in the exercise of "universal jurisdiction" for heinous crimes such as genocide enacted under its domestic law.

49. The tribunal's "completion strategy" foresees the completion of trials at first instance by 2008–2009.

## CONCLUSION: THE IMPACT OF THE ARUSHA TRIBUNAL

1. This statement is a substantial revision of my numerous previous assessments of the tribunal's role in reconciliation in Rwanda. Those judgments, infused with the hope that many had in the 1990s, must necessarily be revised by events in the past few years, in particular, developments regarding the tribunal's failure thus far to indict any Tutsi for war crimes committed during the Rwandan conflict—a fact that makes the tribunal's work essentially one-sided, the preponderance of the genocide against Tutsis notwithstanding.

2. See Jackson Nyamuya Maogoto, "International Justice for Rwanda Missing the Point: Questioning the Relevance of Classical Law Theory," *Bond Law Review*, Volume 13:1, June 2001, 190–223.

3. Hannah Arendt, *Eichmann in Jerusalem: A Report on the Banality of Evil* (London: Faber & Faber, 1963), 5.

4. U.N. Doc. S/PV.3453, 7.

5. *Prosecutor v Joseph Nzirorera*, Case No. ICTR-98-44-T; Motion to dismiss for selective prosecution, March 24, 2004.

6. Letter from Professor Filip Reyntjens to Hassan B. Jallow, prosecutor, ICTR, dated January 11, 2005.

7. See "ICTR Prosecutor Has No Deadline for Investigations on RPF War Crimes," AllAfrica, Inc., January 19, 2005.

# INDEX